After Confession

After Confession

Poetry as Autobiography

Graywolf Press

SAINT PAUL, MINNESOTA

Publication of this volume is made possible in part by a grant provided by the Minnesota State Arts Board through an appropriation by the Minnesota State Legislature, and by a grant from the National Endowment for the Arts. Significant support has also been provided by the Bush Foundation; Dayton's Project Imagine with support from Target Foundation; the McKnight Foundation; a grant made on behalf of the Stargazer Foundation; and other generous contributions from foundations, corporations, and individuals. To these organizations and individuals we offer our heartfelt thanks.

Special funding for this volume has been provided by the College of Saint Benedict.

Published by Graywolf Press
2402 University Avenue, Suite 203
Saint Paul, Minnesota 55114
All rights reserved.

www.graywolfpress.org

Published in the United States of America
Printed in Canada

ISBN 1-55597-355-8

2   4   6   8   9   7   5   3   1
First Graywolf Printing, 2001

Library of Congress Control Number: 2001088671

Cover design and art: Jeanne Lee

Acknowledgments

We gratefully acknowledge the cooperation of editors, publishers, and authors for their permission to reprint the following works. All best efforts were made to secure permissions for material used in this book.

"Staying News: A Defense of the Lyric," copyright © 1988 by Joan Aleshire. Reprinted with permission by the author. This essay first appeared in *The Kenyon Review,* Volume X, Number 3, Summer 1988.

"My Grandfather's Tackle Box: The Limitations of Memory-Driven Poetry," copyright © 2001 by Billy Collins, was originally written for *After Confession* and first appeared in *Poetry,* August 2001.

In "Degrees of Fidelity," the poem "The Routine Things Around the House" from *New and Selected Poems: 1974–1994,* copyright © 1994 by Stephen Dunn, is used with permission of W. W. Norton & Company, Inc.

The first brief version of "Coherent Decentering" by Annie Finch was commissioned for a symposium on "Subjectivity and Style" in the November 2000 issue of *Fence.*

"Self-Pity" (Part 1) by Carol Frost is reprinted from *Prairie Schooner* by permission of the University of Nebraska Press. Copyright © 1998 by the University of Nebraska Press. The poems "Waking" (in Part 1) and "Thaw" and "Flicker" (in Part 3) from *Love and Scorn: New & Selected Poems,* copyright © 2000 by Carol Frost, are used with permission of TriQuarterly Books/Northwestern University Press, 2000.

"The Poet and the Natural World," copyright © 1993 by Brendan Galvin. Reprinted by permission of the author. This essay first appeared in *The Georgia Review,* Volume XLVII, Number 1, Spring 1993.

Contents

III ⌐ Degrees of Fidelity: Ethical & Aesthetic Considerations

IV ⌐ Codes of Silence: Women & Autobiography

Sharon Olds

Take the I Out

But I love the I, steel I-beam
that my father sold. They poured the pig iron
into the mold, and it fed out slowly,
a bending jelly in the bath, and it hardened,
Bessemer, blister, crucible, alloy, and he
marketed it, and bought bourbon, and Cream
of Wheat, its curl of butter right
in the middle of its forehead, he paid for our dresses
with his metal sweat, sweet in the morning
and sour in the evening. I love the *I,*
frail between its flitches, its hard ground
and hard sky, it soars between them
like the soul that rushes, back and forth,
between the mother and father. What if they had loved each other,
how would it have felt to be the strut
joining the floor and roof of the truss?
I have seen, on his shirt-cardboard, years
in her desk, the night they made me, the penciled
slope of her temperature rising, and on
the peak of the hill, first soldier to reach
the crest, the Roman numeral I—
I, I, I, I,
girders of identity, head on,
embedded in the poem. I love the *I*
for its premise of existence—our I—when I was
born, part gelid, I lay with you
on the cooling table, we were all there, a

forest of felled iron. The *I* is a pine,
resinous, flammable root to crown,
which throws its cones as far as it can in a fire.

from *Blood, Tin, Straw*

David Graham & Kate Sontag

Containing Multitudes

> *Do I contradict myself?*
> *Very well, then, I contradict myself.*
> *(I am large, I contain multitudes.)*
>
> —Walt Whitman, "Song of Myself"
>
> *Identity, the having and being an "I," is what separates me*
> *from all the others, and also what unites me with them. . . .*
> *Self is self-in-relation: no other kind exists.*
>
> —Alicia Ostriker, "I Am (Not) This: Erotic Discourse
> in Elizabeth Bishop and Sharon Olds"

For good or ill, we live in the age of memoir. As autobiographies, memoirs, fictionalized biographies, and works of creative nonfiction fill bookstores with ever-growing frequency, discussion of the nature and boundaries of autobiographical writing has grown both common and heated.

Much of this debate, however, centers around works of prose. *After Confession* began with our wondering where poetry might fit into the grand scheme of things. More than forty years after the poets and the poetry first tagged "confessional" ignited critical controversy, American poetry continues to display a notable confessional strain—some would say exhaustively and exhaustedly so. As the intense interest that greeted Ted Hughes's *Birthday Letters* demonstrated anew, readers remain fascinated by these issues, and both poets and critics divide profoundly on many key matters. *After Confession* addresses not only the legacy of confessional poetry but also the deeper concerns that have always underpinned such discussion. We asked ourselves: How do contemporary poets negotiate the often controversial historical, ethical, and critical considerations related to autobiographical poetry? What do today's poets have to say about the nature of truth-telling and authorial responsibility, and how do they reflect on their own places within the historical context of the lyric "I"?

It turns out that American poets have rather a lot to say on these topics. In essays personal and polemical, in autobiographical musings and critical arguments, in creative as well as analytical prose, in historical studies as well as reviews of new poetry, poets of every aesthetic stripe have weighed in on the nature of autobiographical poetics. Yet these essays have for the most part remained scattered in a variety of books and journals; to our knowledge, this anthology is the first to collect such a range of statements on this particular theme. *After Confession* gathers important treatments of autobiographical poetry by some of our most powerful poets, and adds to them new essays written especially for this volume.

As our contributors demonstrate, autobiographical poetry is an especially contested topic these days—for reasons ranging from ethics to politics. *After Confession* addresses the controversy in four interrelated and overlapping sections. Part I, *Staying News,* offers critical and historical perspectives. From William Matthews's pithy summary of the complexity of these issues to Billy Collins's skeptical gaze directed at a certain kind of contemporary lyric, this section introduces and argues many of the key terms of the larger discussion. It also presents, in Joseph Bruchac's "The Self within the Circle," a strong reminder of how culturally embedded these issues are; essays later in the book by Kimberly Blaeser, Marilyn Chin, Kimiko Hahn, and Carol Muske-Dukes carry forward this theme in their distinct ways.

Part II, *Our Better Halves,* collects essays and musings of a more explicitly autobiographical cast, shedding light on the poetics and the autobiographical context of poets as various as Yusef Komunyakaa, Annie Finch, Thylias Moss, Stanley Plumly, Claudia Rankine, and Colette Inez.

In Part III, *Degrees of Fidelity,* the essays address the complex ethical and aesthetic concerns raised by autobiographical poetry—particularly with respect to the implications of fictionalizing one's own experience in lyrics that are or appear to be autobiographical. In this section Ted Kooser, Carol Frost, and Andrew Hudgins conduct a mini-symposium on the subject of poetic "lying," while Stephen Dunn, Kimiko Hahn, and Brendan Galvin bring their diverse perspectives and aesthetics to the discussion.

Finally, Part IV, *Codes of Silence,* gathers an array of essays by and about women. In reading for this anthology, we were struck by how frequently discussions of confessional and post-confessional poetry centered—explicitly or not—around issues of gender, sexuality, and the explosive growth in recent decades of women's poetry. The essays here by Alicia Ostriker, Pamela Gemin, Marilyn Chin, Carol Muske-Dukes, and other women poet-critics thus comprise a small anthology of critical views on a vitally important development within American poetics.

✐ ✐ ✐

Rather than supporting any single perspective on autobiographical poetry, then, *After Confession* presents a range of views. Because we believe our theme requires such vigorous debate, our essayists frequently disagree with each other, sometimes quite directly. Just as Walt Whitman claimed for himself a shifting and expansive selfhood ("I am large, I contain multitudes"), current American poets of each distinct camp have seemed intent on proving Whitman right—even when agreeing on no other matter. Surely the present era in our poetry is the most pluralistic—or balkanized—ever. No matter what poetic flag one pledges allegiance to, at the heart of such pluralism, we believe, lie the issues of self and other, private and communal identity, confession and reticence, sincerity and artifice with which this book concerns itself. This may not be an exclusively *American* debate, but the legacy of Whitman certainly points to its centrality within our tradition.

Aesthetically speaking, personal poems can go wrong in many ways: they might indulge in the elevation of trivial or merely uninteresting domestic detail; they might simply whine, recounting, in Robert Frost's handy dichotomy, not "griefs" but "grievances"; they might ignore important aspects of the world beyond the poet's doorstep and thus remain

cloistered in the prison of self; they might mistake the tawdry or sensational for the boldly honest; and, in fact, they might fall anywhere along
the deadly spectrum that runs from cocktail-party bore to megalomaniac.

Attacks on current autobiographical lyrics that suffer from these
problems are therefore to be expected. In an interview, contributor
Marilyn Chin provides a particularly vigorous example:

> Poetry has moved to the suburbs. Current literary journals contain a lot
> of poems about the mythology of the self. I suppose this was first in-
> spired by the confessional poets. American poets have veered away
> from Whitman's idea of the democratic self as a representative or na-
> tional self. Their poems are self-centered, short-sighted; they don't ex-
> tend to larger concerns.

Such dismissals, interestingly, come from multiple aesthetic angles. We
are no more surprised to hear Chin dismiss the backyard epiphanies of
the average suburban lyricist than we are to hear a middle-aged male re-
viewer scorn the glut of poems that follow Sharon Olds's lead in exploring private experiences of sexuality, alcoholism, and abuse. Meanwhile,
the Language poets wish a plague on both houses for their presumed
shared sense of self-enclosure, their inability to see how fraught romantic individualism truly is. The Expansive poets, who otherwise share few
attitudes with Language poets, agree. A critical opinion this widespread,
we feel, deserves a probing look, especially given the excellent personal
poetry that many would argue *has* emerged in recent years. One virtue of
the debate conducted in these pages is the way it highlights many fine
autobiographical poems, by our contributors as well as other poets. And
one recurring motif is the notion that first-person lyrics can embrace a
larger social vision, achieving revelation over narcissism, universal resonance over self-referential anecdote.

But to what extent are these issues new, or particularly American;
and to what extent are they ancient and universal? Consider this typical
indictment of American poetic solipsism: "Each poet . . . usually spends
his time considering the interests of a very insignificant person, namely
himself. . . . There is a danger, that he may be shut up in the solitude of
his own heart." Granted, we have tampered with this quotation, substi-

tuting "poet" for "citizen in a democracy"; but otherwise, we did not need to alter the words Alexis de Tocqueville wrote in 1840, long before Whitman announced "I celebrate myself." English critic Richard Gray, from whose *American Poetry of the Twentieth Century* we take the Tocqueville quotation, maintains that "every major American poem could be called 'song of myself.'" He further points out:

> Solitude or isolation, self-reliance or egotism, freedom or loneliness, self-sufficiency or pride: the terms may vary—and, indeed, do so throughout American writing—but they can all be traced back to the structure of feeling that Tocqueville perceived, a structure that has as its keystone the idea of the individual, the simple, separate self.

Clearly, when poets today react against personal poetry as narcissistic, cut off from greater social, political, moral engagements—they join a long procession of such critics.

The same is true regarding sensational or indecorous subject matter. For instance, when reviewers turned up their noses at Anne Sexton's poems about menstruation or her uterus, they may not have been aware of participating in a rather long tradition of complaint about poets who challenge the proprieties: the Romantics were familiar with such criticism. Even earlier, in the eighteenth century, according to critic Susan Rosenbaum, Charlotte Smith's proto-confessional poems were accused of "exploiting personal experience. . . ." We suspect that Sappho may have faced similar charges.

In fact, lyric poets in many eras and many cultures have cultivated the illusion of a sincere voice revealing its intimate secrets, although poets and cultures have varied in the degree to which they expected readers to believe this fiction. And just as scholars and lay people alike cannot prevent themselves from gossiping about Shakespeare's Dark Lady or the precise nature of Tennyson's friendship with Arthur Hallam, we are not likely to see the end to sensations like Ted Hughes's *Birthday Letters,* whose critics trotted out all the well-worn arguments against autobiographical poetry, including the claim that it panders to low sensationalism. The truth is that, strictly speaking, both Hughes's and Plath's poetic versions of their marital problems are fictions. We really have no way of knowing, apart from always contestable biographical research, whether a given poem actually does confess personal intimacies, or simply wants to give that impression. Does it matter? Is Robert Frost's great poem "Home Burial" *about* the children he and Elinor Frost lost? What better answer will we ever have than *yes and no*?

Lyrics have always entangled artifice with confession. Our essayists recognize and reckon with the inevitable risks of narcissism, assuredly, but as a whole focus more on pondering the possibilities of this still-vital tradition. As Joan Aleshire writes in her essay "Staying News," included here, ". . . the poem of personal experience—the true lyric poem—can, through vision, craft, and objectivity toward the material, give a sense of commonality with unparalleled intimacy." The deepest value of auto-biographical poetry as we have seen it develop in the past forty years, then, may be that it refocuses attention on these fundamental aesthetic problems, not that it solves them.

I

Staying News:

Critical & Historical Perspectives

William Matthews

Personal and Impersonal

A comic strip called *Tips from the Top* used to run on the sports pages. In four panels an always smiling Jack Nicklaus would explain arcane golfing procedures, such as how to hit a 4-wood out of a fairway bunker from a sidehill lie. What he never described—perhaps the compression of the four-panel format made it impossible—was that the shot was easier to hit for someone who had practiced it 6,000 times than for someone who never worried about it until it came up in the course of play. In which case that poor soul was reduced to searching the watery files of memory for the comic strip in which Nicklaus (smiling because he had hit the shot for the 6,000th time long ago in fierce and lonely practice) explained what should be done. In competition, Nicklaus seldom smiles; what we see in his eyes is dry ice.

The practice of a craft suggests the anonymity of apprenticeship, the subjugation of ego to procedures proven valuable by collective and traditional experience.

An apprentice not only learns the tools and materials of a craft, but commits to memory and muscle memory the characteristic motions of an activity. Such repetition is not only a sort of calisthenics. We know that in human evolution greater brain capacity is linked to greater hand-to-eye coordination. Presumably the increasing complexity of physical chores stimulated more complex brain activity. Perhaps lifelong immersion in intricate processes such as writing poetry or playing the piano works similarly.

In any case, an apprentice begins by confronting those parts of a craft that are easiest to describe with words like *anonymous, collective,* and *traditional.* But a skillful apprentice moves toward a condition of mastery by which quite opposite words are invoked: *hallmark, signature, style.*

"You only have so many notes," said Dizzy Gillespie, "and what makes a style is how you get from one note to another."

So the "personal" and the "impersonal" are intricately braided, and thus both difficult and perhaps not even useful to separate, in the way a craft—let's say the craft of poetry—is practiced. But you'd hardly know this from reading and listening to discussions of poetry.

Probably what seems most personal to a poet is style, the study of which is, indeed, akin to ballistics.

But what many readers and critics often mean by personal is the relationship between poet and subject matter. Can the speaker of the poem be identified with the poet? Does the poem describe a biographically actual, as opposed to an imagined, experience? How much of the emotional temperature of the precipitating impulse of the poem has been retained or lost in the poem? And, to borrow an easy locution from workshop jargon, does the poem "take risks?"

Note that all these questions are 1) *ad hominem* or *ad feminam,* as the case may be; 2) impossible for the reader to answer without information only the poet knows, and thus closer to gossip than to thought; and 3) the equivalent of asking not if an object is useful or beautiful but how much it cost.

In fact we have a hard time thinking, questions of poetry aside, about what constitutes a self, what can be meaningfully termed personal, what constitutes personality.

One urge we have is to be consistent, coherent, predictable. We long for a nuclear ego. It's to this sense of self the miscreant party-goer refers when he says, apologizing for his behavior, "I wasn't myself." But who was he, then? "You know me," he might begin a hopeful sentence to a friend. He's "a regular guy."

Another urge is to be unpredictable, complex (as Zoot Sims once said of Stan Getz, "he's a great bunch of guys"), a microcosmic burble of human variety.

We're neither so various nor so consistent in our idea of ourselves as it might please us to think. We're an anthology of selves, and so, inconsistent; but the anthology is chosen by the same editor, and so, consistent. The word *anthology* comes from a Greek word that means bouquet. Perhaps the resolution of different scents into harmony is the most consistency we'll achieve or should strive for.

The narratives we compose (and revise continuously) of our lives are an attempt at such a harmony. But they're not documentaries. "History is what one age finds worthy of note in another," Jacob Burckhardt wrote. The history of an individual is probably similar.

The language we write in is anonymous, collective, and traditional, and likely it's with the language itself that we should strike a personal relationship, a style without which content is simply imposed upon us by the massive power of conventional rhetoric and cliché. Too little attention is paid to style as a prophylaxis against cant.

No surprise that we cleave to our autobiographies. At least they belong to us, whereas the language in which we tell such stories belongs—and this is one secret of its trustworthiness—to no one. The same impersonality is also a danger to us, of course: like social insects, we could diligently trace received patterns and find that work sufficient.

As Hebbel wrote, "If language had been the creation, not of poetry, but of logic, we should have only one."

"Originality does not consist of saying what no one has ever said before, but in saying exactly what you think yourself," James Stephen wrote. It turns out this is surprisingly difficult. Perhaps that's why the diction we use in workshops, where we try to help each other do it, is such a Calvinist diction. Does the poem *work?* Does it *earn* its last line? Does it *take risks?*

But all these questions betray an urge to locate the poem's authority in an attitude the poet took toward the poem, to allay the anxiety we feel when we remember that the poem on the page, neither personal nor impersonal but itself, is the only source of whatever authority it has.

Jack Nicklaus didn't hit that shot out of a fairway bunker from a sidehill lie with his personality; he hit it with a 4-wood.

Joan Aleshire

Staying News: A Defense of the Lyric

At a time when the world is threatened with nuclear annihilation—as well as regional wars and acts of repression that demand attention—many writers have criticized the self-absorption that has dominated poetry in the last twenty-five years, and have urged their poets to include greater historical awareness and social empathy in their work. The term "confessional," first used to describe the self-revealing poetry of Robert Lowell, W. D. Snodgrass, John Berryman, Sylvia Plath, and Anne Sexton has become—often with justification—pejorative. At the same time, however, all poems with a high emotional content in which the speaker can be identified as the poet are being labeled confessional, as if all were, willy-nilly, overly subjective.

Jonathan Holden, in an essay called "Postmodern Poetic Form: A Theory,"[1] describes Louise Glück and Carolyn Forché as confessional poets as a matter of course. Sandra Gilbert in "My Name Is Darkness: The Poetry of Self-Definition" calls Yeats a "male confessional poet,"[2] along with Berryman and Lowell, without trying to distinguish whether the intent of their poems is self-display, or an argument with the self or the world with which the reader may identify.

What has happened to "lyric" as a descriptive term? It is used most often in its meanings of "rhapsodic" or "spontaneous" or "songlike," but rarely in its original sense: as a poetry directly expressing the poet's thoughts and emotions. Such a poetry has often been, in itself, a political statement; Osip Mandelstam and Anna Akhmatova wrote insistently and subversively of the self in a period that demanded political and artistic conformity. As their work shows, the poem of personal experience— the true lyric poem—can, through vision, craft, and objectivity toward the material, give a sense of commonality with unparalleled intimacy. A poem from Russia in the 1930s or from fifth-century Greece becomes new in the reading.

When contemporary poets are praised for their objectivity, all too often this means that they have excluded emotion from their work; too often their poems are bits of filigree rather than true bridges from the poet's consciousness to the reader's, carrying essential information. Direct expressions of emotion are suspect, particularly in English. Poets who write out of their own lives have reason to be uncertain, even defensive— but they may be writing not confessionally but lyrically. The lyric tradition allows for the expression of direct emotion but imposes a degree of objectivity on the material by formal—but not always traditional— devices.

As a reader, I've always been drawn to poems where the first-person speaker is indistinguishable from the poet, because these poems give access, on an elemental level, to intimate experience. In the poems I admire, the personal details convey the essence of the poet's communication without drawing attention to themselves. The "I" of the poem is the fulcrum on which the action of the poem turns, the agent by which the reader can enter the experience, can—in that overused but apt word here—"share" experience with the speaker. The lyric "I" of the poem is the medium of communication, and in its partial quality, its singularity, there is a certain—because limited—reliability. The effectiveness of the speaker lies in his or her vulnerability, when the "I" makes no claims to knowledge outside its own experience. This clear limitation, this bias can convince the reader that the speaker is telling the truth—at least at the moment of composition. T. S. Eliot in "The Three Voices of Poetry" defines the lyric as the voice of the poet speaking to himself, oppressed by a burden that he must bring to relief.[3] But this conversation with oneself is not necessarily private, for as Eliot continues, the voice of the poet speaking to himself and the voice of the poet speaking for an audience of any size are often found together. "Even though . . . the author of a poem may have written it without thought of an audience, he will also want to know what the poem which has satisfied him will have to say to other people . . . the unseen audience."[4]

Shakespeare in the sonnets, Keats, and Yeats speak from the self's particular viewpoint, but for these poets, it's not only life's experience that interests, but how what has been thought and felt—the burden seeking release—can be made into the experience of a poem. The act of making the poem as a piece of work outside the self draws the poet's attention away from the self and into the work, which makes its own demands. True concentration on craft is an act of forgetting the self.

In the confessional poem, as I'd like to define it, the poet, overwhelmed or intoxicated by the facts of his or her life, lets the facts take over. To say that a poem is confessional is to signal a breakdown in judgement and craft. Confession shares with the lyric a degree of self-revelation but carries implications that the lyric resists. The *Oxford English Dictionary* defines confession as the declaration or disclosure of something that one has allowed to remain secret as being prejudicial, humiliating, or inconvenient to oneself; the disclosure of private feeling; a plea of guilty, an admission of what one has been charged with; a formal confession made in order to receive absolution. I see the confessional poem as a plea for special treatment, a poem where the poet's stance is one of particularity apart from common experience. Confession in art, as in life, can be self-serving—an attempt to shift the burden of knowledge from speaker-transgressor to listener.

Lowell's poetry shows the shifting borders of lyric tradition and confession. Stephen Yenser, in discussing *The Dolphin,* makes a useful distinction between "gossip (fact, data, raw material)" and "gospel (parable, pattern, truth)," emphasizing that where there is more gossip than gospel, "the pattern of experience cannot emerge."[5] The poems in *Life Studies* and *The Dolphin* are particularly full of the sort of factual detail that reveals the speaker's life and only intermittently conveys larger, impersonal truth. In "Unwanted," from his last book, Lowell writes:

> Alas, I can only tell my own story—
> talking to myself, or reading, or writing,
> or fearlessly holding back nothing from a friend,
> who believes me for a moment
> to keep up conversation.

The concern with himself and with truth—often in the literal sense, not the metaphoric—is the ground note of the poetry. In "Father's Bedroom," a short but not atypical example of the family poems in *Life Studies,* the sharp eye and ear can't compensate for the lack of communicating metaphor or myth or "gospel." The facts lie, separate and particular, on the page; though the father's precision and a bit of his history are suggested, the speaker/son makes no imaginative entry into his inner world:

Father's Bedroom

In my father's bedroom:
blue threads as thin
as pen-writing on the bedspread,
blue dots on the curtains,
a blue kimono,
Chinese sandals with blue plush straps.
The broad planked floor
had a sandpapered neatness.
The clear glass bed-lamp
with a white doily shade
was still raised a few
inches by resting on volume two
of Lafcadio Hearn's
Glimpses of Unfamiliar Japan.
Its warped olive cover
was punished like a rhinoceros hide.
In the flyleaf:
"Robbie from Mother."
Years later in the same hand:
"This book has had hard usage
on the Yangtze River, China.
It was left under an open
porthole in a storm."

It seems to me that this poem is interesting only if one is already interested in Lowell; it conveys little sense of the unseen connections, the emotion that draws a reader to identify and to participate in the experience of the poem. The poem places a demand on the reader's indulgence rather than helping the reader to see as the poet does. Even in poems at the end of *Life Studies* where the speaker's emotion is conveyed—"Waking in the Blue," "Home After Three Months Away," "Man and Wife"—Lowell's focus is on the self rather than on life as seen through the speaker's eyes. In "Waking in the Blue," the poet's evaluating and controlling intelligence dominates the emotional experience, and prevents the reader from reacting to the poem's experience without always being conscious of the poet himself. Even though Lowell acknowledges, "We are all old-timers here," after distinguishing himself from the other inmates at McLean's Hospital, the tight control and the encapsulated presentation work to keep the reader, like those "locked razors," at bay.

There are moments in the poems—notably in *History,* in "For the Union Dead," in "The Public Garden," in "Skunk Hour"—where Lowell loses himself in meditation on something other than himself. In "Skunk Hour," the sense of the poet watching the "love cars" and finally, the skunks—who are given a full and attentive description—allows the reader to share the poet's experience without the interference of the poet's mediating self-consciousness. Lowell learned from Elizabeth Bishop's objectivity, and through it actually became most truly lyric. The poems in *The Dolphin* war with detail, including verbatim quotes from Elizabeth Hardwick's letters, but clearly try to discern a larger meaning in the facts. "On the End of the Phone" conveys one couple's separation but also all ruptures, because ambivalence is so brilliantly shown:

> My sidestepping and obliquities, unable
> to take the obvious truth on any subject—
> why do I do what I do not want to say?
> When everything matters, ask and never know?
> Your rapier voice—I have had so much—
> hundred words a minute, piercing and thrilling . . .
> the invincible lifedrive of everything alive,
> ringing down silver dollars with each word. . . .
> Love wasn't what went wrong, we kept our daughter;
> what a good father is is no man's boast—
> to be still friends when we're no longer children. . . .
> Why am I talking from the top of my mouth?

I am talking to you transatlantic,
we're almost talking in one another's arms.

In *The Classical Tradition in Poetry* Gilbert Murray describes the first form of expressive ritual that preceded the lyric: the *molpê*, or dance-and-song. The song was "inspired," or breathed into by the gods; the dance mimicked the longing for what can't be expressed in words. The *molpê*'s chief subjects were Love and Death, and then Strife—about which Murray writes. ". . . [I]t is largely strife which gives to love or death its value. The world is not greatly interested in a marriage which has involved no difficulty and no opposition, or even in a natural and expected death. It is Love won in spite of obstacles and enemies; it is Death in the midst of strife and glory, especially Death averted or conquered."[6] In the thwarting of Death, some idea of transcendence arises, simply through the observation of the seasonal cycle; or through *mimesis* and *methexis*. Murray defines mimesis as the striving to be like something one longs to be, and methexis as participation and communion through ritual. Both mimesis and methexis, according to Murray, involve transcendence of the self: "some ecstasy or 'standing outside' of the prison of the bard's ordinary identity and experience."[7] The bard performed the *molpê* with the dancers, singing words the maker or poet has composed.

The epic, as recorded by Homer and other singers, grew out of the *molpê*; the lyric grew out of the epic but is informed by both traditions. In the earliest known epics, singers reported the old stories without reflection, as pure narratives of the exploits of heroes and gods. Precise detail made the narratives more vivid, and the use of simile stimulated the audience's imagination. The singers performed at feasts, where they were questioned by their listeners, who often asked the singers to repeat or to give more detail. The German scholar Hermann Fränkel describes these exchanges as "free conversations."[8] Someone would ask, "How did Agamemnon die?" and the singer would make that part of the story more vivid without, however, changing the basic plot. The epic singer, Fränkel says, was "poised, phrase by phrase, verse by verse, between enduring tradition and momentary improvisation."[9] Though the speaker didn't comment on the action, and appeared detached, he conveyed emotion through the details he chose. Sometimes, a singer would seem to the audience to *become* the character whose words he was speaking, giving the listeners a shock of surprise and the sense of intimacy.

Gradually, as people tired of the old stories, singers abandoned the epic masks and began to sing in their own words, often to the accompaniment of Apollo's instrument: the small harp or lyre. In reaction to the epic, the lyric can be seen as antiheroic, realistic, idiosyncratic; in short, it was subversive. Hesiod, writing about peasants' lives in *Works and Days* (eighth century B.C.) prepares the way for the individuality and specificity of the lyric:

> Take good note when you first hear the cranes flying over, coming each year without fail and crying high in the heavens. They will give you the sign for ploughing and tell when the winter's rains are at hand: at their call the man without oxen trembles. Then give your oxen plenty of fodder—if you have oxen. It is easy to say: "Please lend me your oxen and wagon," easy also to answer, "I'm sorry, I've work for my own oxen."

The lyric song emerged as a short improvisation based on the singer's life at the moment of writing, but this improvisation, Murray points out, was prepared for by the poet's mode of living and by the constant exercise of technique. The singer could change his or her mind from song to song, and often within single lyrics several emotions coexisted, in the union of opposites that is characteristic of Greek thought. The lyric was specific, of the present and of the singer; it centered, Fränkel says, on "the personality of the singer, the time of delivery and the particular circumstances of its origin. In a certain sense, the lyric stands in the service of the day and is ephemeral."[10] The singer might reflect on how the song occurred to him and on the paradox of his effort to capture in words a moment always in flux. Mostly, however, the material was presented without evaluation or explanation. The material was drawn from the poet's life and shaped by imagination. The narrative element never disappears in the lyric; as in the epic, vivid detail and gesture express emotion in the poems that have come down to us.

Archilochus is the first lyric singer whose words were copied and preserved. He was working around 700 B.C., but his lyrics were copied from memory and stored in Alexandria when Egypt became the repository for Greek culture in the Roman Empire. The verses may be faulty transcriptions, but a strong personality speaks through them. If lyric has been diluted to mean "poetic" or "pretty" or "graceful," Archilochus was none of those things. The bastard son of a noble and a slave from a marble-quarrying island, he was a mercenary soldier as well as a singer. Like Hesiod, he made money singing his impressions of the hard life he knew. "So my shield, which I left unwillingly—it was a good one—somewhere behind a bush, is now a Thracian's delight," he sang. "Still, I came off with my skin: the shield is not so important. Well, let it go. Very soon I'll buy another as good."

Fränkel notes that Archilochus "takes the first and nearest data of the individual: the now, the here, the I,"[11] and there is an appealing sturdiness to his work. This singer learns from conflict and defeat: "The fox knows many things, the hedgehog one big one. . . . [O]ne big thing I know how to do—terribly repay with sorrow sorrow what is done to me." (All translations from the Greek, except those as noted by Mary Barnard and Guy Davenport, are by Hermann Fränkel.) Archilochus' language was colloquial, clear, and seemed to fall naturally into rhyme.

Of his accuracy and immediacy, Fränkel writes: "The primary data . . . are for Archilochus also the final data. . . . [His] lyric proceeds wholly out of the personality of the poet or leads to it; but it is not subjective in the sense that it wishes to give a picture of life individually shaped or colored."[12] The lyric singers used a transparent language through which reality—of the physical, intellectual and emotional worlds—could be seen. In fact, in a universe animated by the gods, there was no distinction between body and soul, tangible and spiritual; precise detail could embody emotion completely and inevitably.

Accuracy in the expression of one individual life allowed the songs to be personal yet not idiosyncratic. As Fränkel expresses it: "Greek lyric poets did not aim to make themselves interesting by their peculiar sensibilities, but sought rather to demonstrate the general and the basic by the example of themselves."[13] Archilochus makes such an example by saying:

> Such a desire for her love rolled up under my heart, poured a great darkness on my eyes, and robbed from my breast its tender wits. . . . Miserable I lie under desire, lifeless, with harsh pains, because of the gods, pierced to the very bones.

But he's nothing if not resilient: "Heart, my heart, by countless sorrows much bewildered and perplexed, pluck up courage. . . ." At his brother-in-law's funeral he sings:

> Let us sink the painful gift of Lord Poseidon in the deep. [Pain for his death would be lighter] had the funeral fire taken his head and the fair frame of his limbs, wrapped in robes of white, as is seemly. [But] nothing is made any better by tears; nor, if I seek pleasure, company, friendship, and joy, do I make anything worse.

Archilochus is capable of confessing to faults, but, in the same breath, reminds his audience that such failings are human: "I have erred; this very blindness fell on many men before."

Sappho, born about a hundred years later, echoes Archilochus' frankness, humor, specificity and worldliness—and adds her own note of longing, at least in the fragments that have come down to us. In two translations, Mary Barnard's intuitive and imaginative renderings and Guy Davenport's more literal versions, a strong personality emerges from scraps of language. The range represented in the existing fragments—whatever strips of papyrus survived the trash heaps of Alexandria—is extraordinary. Sappho loved gossip, clothes, and both men and women; she could be funny and celebratory and grieving in her songs.

The fragments we have are of songs meant to be sung in public, yet they are intimate, conversational, often addressed to a specific "you." Maurice Bowra says of Sappho's Greek: ". . . [I]t looks like ordinary speech raised to the highest level of expressiveness. In her great range of different meters there is not one which does not move with perfect ease and receive her words as if they were ordained for it."[14] Barnard describes Sappho's style in the original as "spare but musical . . . the sound of the speaking voice making a simple but emotionally loaded statement."[15]

In Barnard's versions, one has the sense of the translator perceiving meaning in the fragmentary details and conversations:

47: I was so happy

　　Believe me, I
　　prayed that that
　　night be doubled for us

13: People do gossip

　　And they say about
　　Leda, that she

　　once found an egg
　　hidden under

　　wild hyacinths

79: Really, Gorgo,

　　My disposition
　　is not at all
　　spiteful: I have
　　a childlike heart

53: With his venom

　　Irresistible
　　and bittersweet

　　that loosener
　　of limbs, Love

　　reptile-like
　　strikes me down

72: Of course I love you

　　But, if you love me,
　　marry a young woman!

　　I couldn't stand it
　　to live with a young
　　man, I being older

In Davenport, the voice is a bit muted, the tone less sure; #32 in his volume *Archilochus. Sappho. Alkman* is clearly Barnard's #72:

> Though you are my lover,
> Take for wife a younger woman;
> Find a newer bed to lie in,
> I could not bear to be the older.

And his #148 is a flatter version of the poem Barnard translates as #13:

> Once upon a time, the story goes,
> Leda found a hyacinthine egg.

Davenport's translations are valuable because he points out missing sections of the fragments by using brackets, and because he translates more of the songs than Barnard does, but he lacks her ability to elicit the poetic argument, the surprising juxtapositions from the elements at hand. Fränkel's prose translations give a sense of Sappho's use of memory and her ability to present a dramatic situation:

> In good faith, I wish I were dead. She left me, crying bitterly, and said to me: "How terrible it is for us, Sappho; truly I go unwilling." I answered: "Go and think of me, happily. You know how I worshipped you. If not I wish to remind you what fair and lovely things we enjoyed. With many garlands of violets and sweet roses on your tresses you sat by me, on your soft neck many necklaces woven of flowers. Your hair you drenched with myrrh . . . laid upon soft coverlets. . . . No sacred grove or shrine was there which we did not fill with the sound of our songs and music of the lyre."

The remembered scene is so sensuously described that it comes to life, putting the present in shadow. In spite of the dubious authenticity of the originals, the spirit of lyric poetry—immediate, precise, personally expressive—survives the barrier of translation. There is a sense of shape, of argument in the fragments: poetic intelligence powerfully at work.

Archilochus and Sappho are still read and translated; the singers who followed them are largely forgotten—probably because they became more instructive than expressive, more general than tactile. External pressures may have brought more public considerations into lyric song; in any case, poets began to talk about "the good," and as Fränkel says, "of 'riches,' 'wealth,' 'poverty,' 'distress,' not of wheatfields, herds of oxen, flocks and sheep, ships bearing produce from country to country."[16] Accepted meanings changed in ways familiar to us from bureaucracy and advertising; *psyche,* which had meant *breath,* had become *soul* by the fifth century B.C.

The last great lyric singer, Pindar, placed a premium on a quality called *kairos* that serves as a crucial element in the continuation of the lyric. *Kairos* has no single equivalent in English; it translates as: "the rules of accurate choice and prudent restraint, the sense of what suits the circumstances; tact, discretion."[17] "Kairos alone produces maturity in any field," Pindar wrote, and showed his sense of balance by setting opposite points of view against one another before making a summation or resolution. Pindar's strategy of argument continues in the sonnet as invented by Petrarch, who set forth his songs of courtly love as dialectics in two four-line stanzas followed by two three-line stanzas, with a rhyme scheme of abba/abba/cdc/dcc. Petrarch's form has been played on in various ways; what seems consistent is the use of argument, the turns and attempt at reconciliation of opposites.

In Shakespeare's sonnets and in Keats's, the sense of lyric poem as argument is particularly clear. Shakespeare's sonnets are objects of such solidity, so well made that they rival the finest watch. Many of the sonnets contain particular information and direct emotion, but they are about the nature of love and of the lover, more than they are directly about the speaker. The speaker separates his own frank emotions from the making of the poem, and attempts to reach a resolution of a conflict he's presented in the poem. In making the formal turn, the poet often moves to adopt the lover's point of view or to work toward a general good as apart from his own needs. *Kairos* is evident in the formal elements of the poem, but also in its vision. The speaker's concern in all the sonnets is how to arrest the flow of time, not how to express personal longing and grief— though longing and grief are often present in large measure. The poems focus on the self only so that the "you" will be better seen, so that the experience will be fully convincing. The "I" is an agent of experience which, if not immediately intelligible to us in its particulars, becomes so as the argument is presented through sound, syntax, and imagery.

Although Milton is a more general, more descriptive writer than the Greek lyric poets, there is lyric emotion and *kairos* in abundance in the autobiographical sonnet "To Mr. Cyriack Skinner upon his Blindness" (Sonnet XXII). The "you" addressed is a specific person; the details come clearly from Milton's life, but the poem is no confession, no plea for special treatment. The concentration is on the poem; the juggled phrases and shifts in expected syntax demonstrate how difficult it is to draw good from misfortune. Milton works from the particulars of his life, but turns toward the poem and ultimately to his friend:

Cyriack, this three years day these eyes, though clear
  To outward view of blemish or of spot,
  Bereft of light their seeing have forgot,
  Nor to their idle orbs doth sight appear
Of Sun or Moon or Star throughout the year,
  Or man or woman. Yet I argue not
  Against heaven's hand or will, nor bate a jot
  Of heart or hope; but still bear up and steer
Right onward. What supports me, dost thou ask?
  The conscience, Friend, to have lost them overplied
  In liberty's defence, my noble task,
Of which all Europe talks from side to side.
  This thought might lead me through the world's vain mask
  Content though blind, had I no better guide.

Milton is always aware of what is beyond the self—the larger cause: of liberty, of reassuring a friend; the guidance of heaven's will. The turns of language make the conflict and its resolution convincing; the reader is drawn into the forging of an argument. *Kairos* is a more discernible element than direct emotion.

The Romantic poets adapted and revitalized the lyric; direct expression of personality, and the use of colloquial diction and of specific detail were part of Wordsworth's aesthetic. In the sonnet to Catherine Wordsworth, his dead child, the sonnet form, the *kairos,* barely restrains the expression of grief—but does shape it. What Maurice Bowra said about Greek funeral friezes applies to Wordsworth here: "Greek art, at least in its archaic and classical periods, so masters its subjects that it passes beyond realistic or naturalistic representation to show another sphere. What might be unbearably painful is so controlled and transformed that it does not distress, but exalt."[18]

Sonnet XXI— Catherine Wordsworth (Died June 4, 1812)

Surprised by joy—impatient as the wind
I turned to share the transport—Oh! with whom
But Thee, deep buried in the silent tomb,
That spot which no vicissitude can find?
Love, faithful love, recalled thee to my mind—

But how could I forget thee? Through what power
Even for the least division of an hour,
Have I been so beguiled as to be blind
To my most grievous loss? That thought's return
Was the worst pang sorrow ever bore,
Save one, one only, when I stood forlorn,
Knowing my heart's best treasure was no more;
That neither present time, nor years unborn
Could to my sight that heavenly face restore.

The poet openly expresses emotion in a tone so intimate it's as if the child could hear him. Although the syntax and diction seem a bit arch at times—"Oh! with whom / But Thee, deep buried in the silent tomb"— we know that Wordsworth used the speech of his time and was criticized for not being sufficiently "poetic." The most direct moments seem absolutely contemporary—"But how could I forget thee?" The poem keeps turning in its propositions, the syntax working against the lines; it breaks apart in questions as the speaker discovers new dimensions to his grief. There is denial and shocked remembrance, but the fact that the poet has actually lost a child is not as important as the demonstration of the ways loss works on the soul. The strength of form enables the poem to accommodate so many turns, to break apart so often in shifts of tone, and yet to be all of a piece in its expression.

Keats, too, was able to use the stuff of his own life and at the same time to find form and language to express not the facts of that life but his concerns. We know of Keats that he watched two brothers die of tuberculosis and that he may have noticed symptoms of the disease in himself by the time he wrote the sonnet "When I Have Fears." The poem is located in a moment, a specific "when," but this very designation shifts the focus away from the poet, as it wouldn't so quickly if he'd begun, "I have fears," and then gone on to detail them. The *when* broadens the approach to include everyone—assuming almost conversationally that others share those fears—and sets up a sort of argument; if there's a *when* clause, the expectation is that a *then* clause will follow and possibly resolve the proposition. A sense of balance is established, not only by form but by syntax; if *this* is true, then *that* must follow, at that moment. We read, drawn by argument, by music, by syntax, by image—but there is finally, movingly, no resolution of the fears. The turn is down, to the revelation that the mind is unable to comprehend its own death, even as it knows that death is inevitable.

When I have fears that I may cease to be
    Before my pen has gleaned my teeming brain,
Before high-piled books, in charactery,
    Hold like rich garners the full ripened grain;
When I behold, upon the night's starred face,
    Huge cloudy symbols of a high romance,
And think that I may never live to trace
    Their shadows, with the magic hand of chance;
And when I feel, fair creature of an hour,
    That I shall never look upon thee more,
Never have relish in the faery power
    Of unreflecting love;—then on the shore
Of the wide world I stand alone, and think
Till love and fame to nothingness do sink.

The poem is the object Keats puts in the way of oblivion; the only resolution to the fear of no longer being able to trace the shadows is to trace them. The sonnet is remarkably specific and personal, yet it also speaks for us; we go beyond sympathy for the speaker to the sense that the speaker is ourselves.

Akhmatova, too, wrote poems that are scenes from a specific life in a particular time and place, but her interest is not in the self. Rather, she focuses on relationships between people, and on the relationships between sounds and images that make a poem. In her best poems, though this is hard to see in even the most sensitive translations to date, there is a sense of unity, an interlocking structure of images that brings to mind the quote from Donald Justice that Michael Ryan uses in his essay "Flaubert in Florida"[19] to describe Justice's own work:

In a good short poem a fine sense of relations among its parts is felt, word connecting with word, line with line: as in a spider web, touch it and the whole structure responds.

This could be an echo of Aristotle's: "A thing whose presence or absence makes no difference to a whole is not part of that whole."

It's said that readers memorized Akhmatova's poems and would recite back to her the lines she'd forget when giving a reading; the degree of identification is high, because there is just enough detail to create an experience that may be the speaker-poet's, but is also known in essence to the reader. In Akhmatova's poetry, complex histories—personal and often public—are conveyed by precise details, but these specifics are also general, available, and analogous to the reader's experience, as Lowell's details are not. Akhmatova, like a Greek lyric poet, exemplifies the personal without being idiosyncratic. Her sense of what the poem demands supersedes any concentration on autobiographical data.

In the 1917 poem usually translated as "We Don't Know How to Say Goodbye," the speaker addresses a specific "you." The couple's predicament is particular, their relationship is outside convention, but the inevitability of the parting resonates beyond the particulars. The poet takes the reader on the couple's wandering, and ends with an image of illusion that becomes clear in its implication as the "you" draws it in the trampled snow. The reader's imagination is elicited to complete the picture, and does so because the poet has also made the poem an experience to be entered as a participant.

> We don't know how to say goodbye—
> we wander all over shoulder to shoulder.
> It's already starting to get dark;
> you're thoughtful, and I keep quiet.
>
> Let's go into the church, watch
> a funeral, a christening, a wedding;
> let's leave, not looking at each other . . .
> Why don't we live like that?
>
> Or, let's sit in the cemetery,
> in trampled snow; let's breathe lightly,
> and let you trace with a stick palaces
> where we will always be together.

> (Aleshire translation)

Akhmatova is the reader's representative; she articulates what we have known. Along with Mandelstam and her first husband, Nikolai Gumilev, Akhmatova believed that poetry would find resonance in the immediate and concrete; the Acmeist movement which they founded was a reaction against the static abstractions of Russian symbolism in the late nineteenth century. "Long live the living Rose!" Mandelstam proclaimed, tired of flowers that were merely representations of ideas. Both Mandelstam and Akhmatova were classicists and made the lyric tradition their own.

Although I have no evidence that Yeats was familiar with the Acmeists in Russia, he made a conscious break with the French symbolists and, at the same time in the early twentieth century, began to write poems that were clear and expressive of personality. In "Discoveries," an essay published in 1906—just a few years before Mandelstam celebrated the "living Rose"—Yeats wrote:

> ... [W]hat moves men in the arts is what moves them in life, and that
> is, intensity of personal life, intonations that show them ... the
> strength, the essential moment of a man who would be exciting at the
> market or at the dispensary door. They must go out of the theater
> with the strength they live by strengthened from looking upon some
> passion that could ... strike down an enemy, fill a long stocking with
> money or move a girl's heart.[20]

He began to write directly out of his own life, in a conscious shift from his earlier, more fanciful and more distanced poems. With "No Second Troy" of 1910, Yeats forges a poetry that is particular in personal detail, that deals clearly with the poet's self, but which focuses on the poet-speaker's relationships with the world, with others. In "No Second Troy," the poet is speaking to himself, acknowledging anger and sorrow, but he concentrates on the beloved, opposing reason and sympathy to anger and pain. But then Maud Gonne—the undisputed "you"—becomes not so much the subject of the poem as does her experience, which is then, through the dimension of simile, set in the context of myth. The "I" transmits experience but almost disappears in the process, indicating that the self, where the poem began, is not as important as the story. The poem moves through the particular life of the "she," and then shows that life as history, as part of human endeavor, is more than an individual life.

Why should I blame her that she filled my days
With misery, or that she would of late
Have taught to ignorant men most violent ways,
Or hurled the little streets upon the great,
Had they but courage equal to desire?
What could have made her peaceful with a mind
That nobleness made simple as a fire,
With beauty like a tightened bow, a kind
That is not natural in an age like this,
Being high and solitary and most stern?
Why, what could she have done, being what she is?
Was there another Troy for her to burn?

If there is anger at the "she" as destroyer, there is also a sense of in-evitability, which subsumes raw emotion. Yeats speaks not only of him-self and Maud Gonne in this poem, but also for Maud Gonne and the nature of her idealism; the poem moves into a dimension of empathy that instructs us and enlarges our sense of human possibility. The argu-ment of the poem—and Yeats believed that a poem is always a quarrel with oneself—is against the part of the self that *does* blame, that is heart-broken and enraged. It is an argument waged in hard, clear terms; the struggle is conveyed in the rhetorical questions—"rhetorical" in the sense that the answer is implicit in the question. "No Second Troy" stops two lines short of being a traditional sonnet, and its rhyme scheme indi-cates a structure of three quatrains—abab/cdcd/efef—submerged in the one long stanza. That the rhymes move outward, rather than repeating or interlocking, conveys the outward movement of the thought: from personal to other, to other's experience and finally to myth. The syntax works against the rhyme scheme to give density and complexity to the strands of the argument.

So far in this discussion, the use of traditional forms has been sug-gested as a way of organizing the material of personal experience—the material that as Mandelstam said, "always resists you." Free verse could be suspected of introducing the self-indulgences I am defining as confes-sional poetry, but traditional forms have not always guaranteed a poet's self-restraint or *kairos*. Poets working in free verse have rather had to cre-ate their own forms, suited to their temperaments and voices. A poem in free verse can—in fact, must—have its own inner coherence, what Eliot calls in "The Music of Poetry," "the inner unity which is unique to every poem, against the outer unity which is typical."[21]

William Carlos Williams, that great improviser, might have resisted the notion that he is a close relation of the Greek lyric singers, but I share Mary Barnard's sense that Williams's immediacy, his attention to detail, and his interest in speech patterns are truly lyric qualities. Also, his sense of the object as conveying emotion, ideas, meaning is particularly in the Greek tradition. "Waiting" is an argument with the self, but it is meant to be overheard. It arises out of a specific moment of sensation and conflict. The poem's focus moves from the poet's sensations to the external objects, events, and human beings that move him. There is a struggle between desire and sense of duty, honesty, and an attempt at balance. The abrupt line breaks, pauses, and swift transitions are expressive of the speaker's state of mind through the poem: his untroubled, sensual solitude; his despair at his children's demands; his doubt and attempt at distance. The poem resolves in a question that takes the focus away from the poet/speaker and into the dimension of self-knowledge and its expression. There is a struggle for balance and for reconciliation, but the demands of love are recognized as demands, and the sorrow is that of inadequate response. The honesty of the exploration is relentless, unsparing of the self.

Waiting

When I am alone I am happy.
The air is cool. The sky is
flecked and splashed and wound
with color. The crimson phalloi
of the sassafras leaves
hang crowded before me
in shoals on the heavy branches.
When I reach my doorstep
I am greeted by
the happy shrieks of my children
and my heart sinks.
I am crushed.

Are not my children as dear to me
as falling leaves or
must one become stupid
to grow older?
It seems much as if Sorrow
had tripped up my heels.
Let us see, let us see!
What did I plan to say to her
when it should happen to me
as it has happened now?

"Let us see, let us see!" The dilemma is insoluble; the natural world is more vivid, more loved than the children, but knowledge—the hard clarity of the truth—arrives, and the poet articulates it. "Waiting" seems at first glance a mysterious title—for whom? for what? isn't directly apparent. But the title indicates that the poem's true subject isn't the poet's moods or his conscience, but the gaining of wisdom. At the time of this poem, the poet sees that he is still waiting to reconcile his opposing impulses; the poem moves from specific situation through turns of awareness to achieve universal resonance.

Louise Glück has been described as a confessional and idiosyncratically subjective poet, but her sense of restraint gives to her poems a mythic dimension. She is interested in "gospel," not "gossip," the experience itself not the literal details. Nowhere is this clearer than in the poem "Mock Orange," which contains a statement of such startling intensity—"I hate them [the mock orange blossoms]. I hate them as I hate sex."—that it may at first seem a confession of the poet's secrets. The poem, however, is more than an outburst; it is an argument between two parts of the self: the one that needs to believe—in love, in union with another; and the one that knows such belief is self-deception, but will go on being deceived. The tension of the argument places the focus of the poem on experience, on human relationship, not on the speaker, who at first seems to be carrying on an actual argument with a "you." The poem begins in mid-argument, with the speaker correcting the "you's" contentions that it is the moonlight that illumines the yard, and that it's the moon, or the speaker's moods, that trouble her. The hatred of the flowers for appearing to be what they are not (real orange blossoms, the wedding flowers, the ones that bear fruit) and for not truly, though they glow whitely, casting a light is not expressed as an absolute statement. It is rather part of an equation: I hate them as I hate sex. The terms of the equation—*as* is the crucial syntactical signal here—give qualification, a sense of degree to the hatred of sex. Sex then is shown in vivid terms as domination by the man of the woman, but it is entered into; the cry of abandonment always does escape. The longing for union combined with the knowledge that union can't be truly achieved makes the poem's argument acutely complex and dramatic. The "one sound," the fusion of longings—the "you's" question and the speaker's "pursuing answer" which is no answer but another searching question—falls apart on the acknowledgement of essential, irreparable separation. And yet, the deception is played out, works over and over on the speaker, pervasive as the mock-orange scent, until the speaker is left with the question of how to reconcile, how to live with, these conflicting pieces of emotional truth. It is a poem not about the poet but the human dilemma. When the speaker says, "We were made fools of," the "you" and "I" and the readers are included, joined in their imperfection.

Mock Orange

It is not the moon, I tell you.
It is these flowers
lighting the yard.

I hate them.
I hate them as I hate sex,
the man's mouth
sealing my mouth, the man's
paralyzing body—

and the cry that always escapes,
the low, humiliating
premise of union—

In my mind tonight
I hear the question and pursuing answer
fused in one sound
that mounts and mounts and then

is split into the old selves,
the tired antagonisms. Do you see?
We were made fools of.
And the scent of mock orange
drifts through the window.

How can I rest?
How can I be content
when there is still
that odor in the world?

This poem is the first in Glück's collection, *The Triumph of Achilles,* a book that shows its roots in classicism and makes the tradition new. It's also possible, though, to see the lyric tradition alive in much less formal, slangy, even gossipy poems like Frank O'Hara's. O'Hara filled his poems with dailiness, with the detail of a particular life of prominence and privilege, but the underlying concerns, the universal passions are almost always apparent. "The Day Lady Died" is a poem of private grief for a public figure in which the power of music and the shock of a death in the midst of life are conveyed with lyric immediacy.

The Day Lady Died

It is 12:20 in New York a Friday
three days after Bastille Day, yes
it is 1959 and I go get a shoeshine
because I will get off the 4:19 in Easthampton
at 7:15 and then go straight to dinner
and I don't know the people who will feed me

I walk up the muggy street beginning to sun
and have a hamburger and a malted and buy
an ugly NEW WORLD WRITING to see what the poets
in Ghana are doing these days
        I go on to the bank
and Miss Stillwagon (first name Linda I once heard)
doesn't even look up my balance for once in my life
and in the GOLDEN GRIFFIN I get a little Verlaine
for Patsy with drawings by Bonnard although I do
think of Hesiod, trans. Richmond Lattimore or

Brendan Behan's new play or *Le Baton* or *Les Nègres*
of Genêt, but I don't, I stick with Verlaine
after practically going to sleep with quandariness

and for Mike I just stroll into the PARK LANE
Liquor Store and ask for a bottle of Strega and
then I go back where I came from to 6th Avenue
and the tobacconist in the Ziegfeld Theatre and
casually ask for a carton of Gauloises and a carton
of Picayunes, and a NEW YORK POST with her face on it

and I am sweating a lot by now and thinking of
leaning on the john door in the 5 SPOT
while she whispered a song along the keyboard
to Mal Waldron and everyone and I stopped breathing

It is hard, finally, to talk about poems that take my breath away. I'm
reminded of Marina Tsvetayeva's comment on criticism: "There is no
approach to art; it is a seizing." In no art form is this seizing more apparent than in the lyric poem, which gives the shock of hearing a human
voice speaking intimately, from the heart.

Notes

1. Jonathan Holden, "Postmodern Poetic Form: A Theory," *Poetics: Essays on the Art of Poetry* (Green Harbor, Mass.: *Tendril Magazine,* 1984), p. 20.

2. Sandra Gilbert, "My Name is Darkness: The Poetry of Self-Definition," *Poetics: Essays on the Art of Poetry* (Green Harbor, Mass.: *Tendril Magazine,* 1984), pp. 99–100.

3. T. S. Eliot, *On Poetry and Poets* (New York: Farrar, Straus & Cudahy, 1957), p 107.

4. Ibid., p. 109.

5. Ian Hamilton, *Robert Lowell: A Life* (New York: Random House, 1982), p. 432.

6. Gilbert Murray, *The Classical Tradition in Poetry* (Cambridge, Mass.: Harvard University Press, 1927), p. 43.

7. Ibid., p. 45.

8. Hermann Fränkel, *Early Greek Poetry and Philosophy,* trans. Moses Hadas and James Willis (New York: Harcourt, Brace, Jovanovich, 1962), p. 13.

9. Ibid., p. 8.

10. Ibid., p. 133.

11. Ibid., p. 139.

12. Ibid., p. 151.

13. Ibid., p. 151.

14. Mary Barnard, *Sappho: A New Translation* (Berkeley: University of California Press, 1958), p. 103.

15. Ibid., p. 103.

16. Fränkel, *op. cit.,* p. 423.

17. Ibid., pp. 447–448.

18. Maurice Bowra, *The Greek Experience* (Cleveland: World Publishing, 1957), p. 146.

19. Michael Ryan, "Flaubert in Florida," *New England Review and Bread Loaf Quarterly* VII, no. 2 (Winter 1984), p. 224.

20. W. B. Yeats, *Essays and Introductions* (New York: Collier, 1961), p. 265.

21. T. S. Eliot, *op. cit.,* p. 31.

Sydney Lea

Making a Case; or, "Where Are You Coming From?"

In the late seventies, I read an essay by Brendan Galvin about poems he called "Mumblings" (in *Ploughshares,* 1978). In such poems, Galvin says, an unidentified first person "tries to tell the reader how he ought to feel about the nonspecific predicament of an often unspecified person." Yes, I thought, or else the poet addresses an unidentified second person about the cloudy difficulties of his or her relationship with that second person, or yet a third (also unidentified). I, too, disliked the verse Galvin attacked, especially for its evident premise: that a Poet, by assuming that title, could automatically lay claim to an interesting inner life. Surely, I believed, an "I" was interesting only if proved to be, which meant, among other things, that he or she must cogently reveal an identity in the writing itself.

My recourse was rash. Goaded by my friends and collaborators, Jay Parini and Robin Barone, I founded a magazine, the *New England Review.* Its poetry, we vowed, would operate from more accessible premises. "Pronouns are not people"—I recall my cautionary dictum on certain early rejections, one that unquestionably smacked of the tyro's glibness, but of whose gist I still approve.

Not that all poets of the seventies "mumbled" in the way Galvin had mocked. Some relied on image, whether deep or shallow, plain or surreal. And yet these writers, too, often seemed to exclude me from their works' deeper resonances—just as I was expecting some authorial commitment, a poet would turn to notice, say, a pigeon carrying a snip of someone's necktie through a rain cloud, or whatever. Subject matter, so to speak, never quite came out in public.

Somebody once accused Edmund Wilson of denouncing as vices all things he couldn't do, elevating his aptitudes into virtues. I want not to be guilty of the same. If, for example, in my own poems I've always inclined, almost catastrophically, to narrative, I've never dogmatically urged the same bent—in part because that would deprive me of a Donald Justice, whose approach I'll never emulate, no matter how deeply I admire it. Nor am I willing to forgo a May Swenson, an Auden, or, more contemporarily, a Jorie Graham, Charles Simic, or William Matthews, to cite a few wildly divergent cases.

Twelve years ago, though, nettled by the self-regard in certain verse of the seventies, I did couch my editorial commentary in narrative terms, initiating, moreover, an annual *New England Review* narrative poetry competition. And by 1982, much time in my own readings was given over to "The Feud," a fifteen-page verse tale from my second collection. The rancor I felt against excessive personalism found a momentary release in story, or perhaps more properly in character, a concern I sensed we might too easily have ceded to prose writers.

My pitch, however fresh in those years, is commonplace now, when many commentators—not all of them clearheaded or well informed—assert that hyperprivacy has lost our poetry a readership. (This despite the fact that verse today is generally less "difficult"—think of Andrew Hudgins or C. K. Williams—than it was a decade ago.) There's also a movement abroad called the New Narrative.

I've recently wondered why—having once stumped so for narrative—I want now, both as writer and critic, to move on. It isn't only that I'd avoid repeating Edmund Wilson's error, as the more doctrinaire exponents of the New Narrative may be doing; more important, my *inclination* to narrative was always of greater moment to me than story line itself. If it served to brake my *own* narcissism (as pronounced as anyone's), it also provided a more positive, and more intriguing impulse: narrative opened my poems to rhetoric, by which I, like Jonathan Holden in his *Rhetoric in the Contemporary Lyric,* mean the language of persuasion—and hence of argument, of testimony, even of the abstraction that Ezra Pound the Ur-Imagist warned us to go in fear of. (I speak of immediately recognizable stuff, not of the rhetorical *gestures* that I think all good poems contain.)

But why was rhetoric, so understood, a goal at all? Having as editor and writer not only lectured but also visited many a workshop, I had noticed, in addition to (and continuous with) "mumbling," a kind of anti-rhetorical rhetoric among participants: "Show, don't tell." Over and over I heard it; and at length I bridled, thankful that most canonical poets had never heeded such an injunction. Consider:

The ceremony of innocence is drowned;
The best lack all conviction, while the worst
Are full of passionate intensity.

Even though Yeats himself polarized rhetoric (made of our quarrels with others) and poetry (made of quarrels with ourselves), he went ahead and composed those great lines in "The Second Coming."

Or, for further example:

Getting and spending we lay waste our powers.
Little we see in Nature that is ours . . .

Time present and time past
are both perhaps included in time future . . .

I have wasted my life . . .

Publication—is the Auction
of the mind of Man—
Poverty—be justifying
For so foul a Thing . . .

I saw the best minds of my generation . . .

The list could be endlessly extended, but whatever our tastes, few would think immediately to send Bill, Tom, Jim, Emily, and Allen back to workshop for the sin of too much "telling." And would any of us really scold John, on the same grounds, for the following lines?

"Beauty is truth, truth beauty,"—that is all
    Ye know on earth, and all ye need to know.

I spent much breath on the virtues of narrative in my early years as editor, teacher, and lecturer; but privately I wanted sanction in my own writing for moves like those above. Indeed, in seven collections, I've composed relatively few pure narrative poems, a fact that surprises me less today than it once might have, since I see that from early on, I sought not so much the freedom to make a story as to make a case—perhaps like Robert Frost's in "Birches":

> . . . Earth's the right place for love:
> I don't know where it's likely to go better.

It was not restraint alone, then, that barred me from cajoling fellow poets into narrative-or-nothing, that made me hedge my bets, proposing a storyteller's "values" instead. Yes, I believed, if I could establish *characters,* including the character called "I," if I could suggest *setting* (historical, political, geographical), if I could at least imply *plot*—if, in short, I could call back to our service some basics of conventional fiction—the reader might accept my mucking around in big issues like the perils of revenge (in "The Feud").

The real goal, however, was to find modes of argufying in verse. And if I still feel that narrative can help a poet make a case, I'm increasingly interested in how poets may do so otherwise, in how we may gain authority for overt rhetoric, for assertion, information, so on, without recourse to fiction's tools. How can Keats write that "Beauty is truth" and impel us to deep thought, whereas, whimsically to choose a seventies' instance, the originator of "Happiness Is a Warm Puppy" impels me to homicidal fantasy—even though that aphorism and Keats's share the exact same rhetorical structure?

I ask you now to remember "Ode on a Grecian Urn."

This poem, of course, will always be inexhaustible to critics, and my quirky responses won't put matters to rest. For one thing, poems can have equal and opposite pulls, as Keats knew better than most. They are not philosophy; nor are they reducible to their "ideas," although they can and do *contain* them. For another thing, I'm reacting here not as critic but as writer. There's nothing scholarly, then, in the following observations:

> —Keats calls the scene on the urn a *love* scene, but it's actually one of intended *rape,* the maidens being "loath," "struggl[ing] to escape," a fact that undercuts the often alleged "calm" of the work.

—The urn is said "to express a flowery tale more sweetly than
our rhyme": if so, to put it crudely, we poets must despair.
—All the questions in the opening strophe concern the referen-
tiality of the urn's images (Where's the scene? What's the legend? Who are the figures? Keats can't even tell if they're
human or divine.), and thus are questions about plot, setting,
and character.
—They're rhetorical questions, the answer to each being "I don't
know."

Let's start with that last point. Keats asks his questions in response to
the urn's images, which "show." The poet will later make clear, prosodi-
cally stressing the word itself, that image cannot "tell." I think this has
consequences, say, for the famous opening of stanza 2:

Heard melodies are sweet, but those unheard
    Are sweeter; therefore, ye soft pipes, play on;
Not to the sensual ear, but, more endeared,
    Pipe to the spirit ditties of no tone . . .

The cheerful reading is that Keats's "negative capability" permits
him to write a poem *even as he recognizes its inferiority to a certain silence*: that of pure image, of scenery transcending "All breathing human
passion. . . ." Never mind that this desire for a stasis removed from pas-
sional life, and from the need to testify till the tongue goes dry, seems
simply un-Keatsian. Consider instead where the second stanza's assertions point: to the turn in stanza 4, with its emphasis on "sacrifice." The
"melodist" of the prior strophe, "happy" in his *quiet,* and the "more
happy love! more happy, happy love!" (Does Keats protest too much?)
Both have vanished, not to return.

Keats, in brief, now recognizes the poverty of his prior claims: that
silence and slow time are superior to human emotion, unheard airs superior to heard, unknowable characters, settings, and legends superior to
knowable. Such contentions lead to a dead end, at least for a poet. If
Keats reverts to his rhetorical questions in this fourth and pivotal stanza,
the answer to each is, still, "I don't know." (Which means, among other
things, "I can make no case.") No longer affirming such ignorance and

powerlessness, nor finding mere image "more endeared" than testimony, here's what he does:

> And, little town, thy streets forevermore
> > Will silent be; and not a soul to tell
> > > Why thou art desolate, can e'er return.

I'd once have claimed that the poet here craves a narrative solution, is "desolate" himself because there's "not a soul to tell"—even on the simplest level—what the urn's depictions enact or signify. Be that as it may, Keats has, by the end, established a dialectic: silence and speech; image and articulation; showing and telling:

> O Attic shape! Fair attitude! with brede
> > Of marble men and maidens overwrought,
> With forest branches and the trodden weed;
> > Thou, silent form, dost tease us out of thought
> As doth eternity: Cold Pastoral!
> > When old age shall this generation waste,
> > > Thou shalt remain, in midst of other woe
> > Than ours, a friend to man, to whom thou say'st
> "Beauty is truth, truth beauty,"—that is all
> > Ye know on earth, and all ye need to know.

The final aphorism is often taken as a further sign of Keats's negative capability: he persists in responding to beauty, even though verbal beauty is *ignis fatuus* compared to that of wrought things. Indeed, some claim that the very stateliness of the ode—its grand rhythms and intricate structures—paradoxically proves this "heard melody" to be as dignified and enduring as the urn's "silent form," which has teased the poet "out of thought," collapsing the dialectical values I've just mentioned. In short, the abstraction "Beauty" destroys the proclivity Keats ascribed to Coleridge—"an irritable reaching after fact and reason"—in the very letter that coined the term negative capability.

Although I'm only a stepchild and not a child of Harold Bloom, this reading does seem sentimental to me. For if the silent urn teases Keats "out of thought," it does so "as doth eternity." This is not, however, to identify poem and urn *sub specie aeternitatis,* but to see eternity as a succubus, reminding Keats (quite understandably) of mortality. To think of the urn is to think of a burial vessel or a grave. Hence, famously, the cold pastoralism that the poet evokes:

> When old age shall this generation waste,
>   Thou shalt remain, in midst of other woe. . . .

Although the phrase I have emphasized is enjambed, the break hints that the urn is itself a woe as durable as "others," so that the silent image—"marble men and maidens overwrought"—is associated with wasted "generation," and thus, etymologically, both with the ruin of genius and of procreation, including its "breathing human passion." If the urn is man's friend, then man as poet needs no enemies.

James Cox once joked to me that Keats must perform an unspeakable act on the "unravished bride of quietness" in order for her finally to speak. It was, of course, a joke, outrageous—but only because the closing pronouncement is surely the poet's. And is it—so nonspecific, so abstract—other than a tepid self-consolation? Even if I can somehow imagine the final aphorism of the poem as the urn's utterance, I'm reminded of a bad parent's response to the child who thirsts for explanation: "Why can't I go outside?" "Because I said so; that's all you need to know."

" 'Beauty is truth, truth beauty'—that is all . . .": the line is also linked by rhyme to "Cold Pastoral!" Reading on, we find it's "all ye know *on earth* [italics mine]." Is there some different venue, then? Yes, but a lesser ode of May 1819 warns against it: "No, no, go not to Lethe," Keats writes in "Ode on Melancholy," "neither twist / Wolfsbane, tight-rooted, for its poisonous wine. . . ." It is wrong, as Keats puts it in the more famous ode to the nightingale, even to be "half in love with easeful death." True, he says:

> Now more than ever seems it rich to die,
>   To cease upon the midnight with no pain,
> While thou art pouring forth thy soul abroad
>   In such an ecstasy!

But here's the conclusion of that stanza:

> Still wouldst thou sing, and I have ears in vain—
>   To thy high requiem become a sod.

Imagination, figured as Psyche in yet another ode, demands votive testimony. Otherwise, she's bereft.

> No voice, no lute, no incense sweet
>> From chain-swung censer teeming;
> No shrine, no grove, no oracle, no heat
>> of pale-mouthed prophet dreaming. . . .

A central issue in all these spring odes, I believe, is the poet's need, precisely, to tell. In "Ode to a Nightingale," Keats dreams of somehow removing himself from passionate speech. But where does that leave him?

> I cannot see what flowers are at my feet,
> Nor what soft incense hangs upon the boughs,
> But in *embalméd* darkness, guess each sweet . . .
>
>> [italics mine]

There is a hint of the grave, once more, in the play on "embalméd." We see how feckless, perhaps even deadly, is visionary image. Indeed, visionary image (*we* might say "deep image") is oxymoronic for Keats; it is "viewless"—i.e., invisible—and therefore, guesswork. It reduces him to passivity, and, worse, it's a fraud:

> Adieu! The fancy cannot cheat so well
>> As she is famed to do, deceiving elf.

If "Ode to a Nightingale" poses different rhetorical questions from those of the urn poem, still their answer is, categorically, "I don't know."

My excerpts are selective, but they dramatize a dilemma of poetry now as then: we must attend to what Richard Wilbur has called "the things of this world"; and yet we cannot be content with them, no matter how splendidly (or grimly) graphic they may be. The music flees if we rely on simple image, as Keats first tries to do in contemplating the Grecian urn; but if we *dissociate* ourselves from simple image and seek some visionary realm, such music as we get is ersatz. We need, as always, a poetry incorporating both image and something nonvisionary beyond it—something that may, yes, involve narrative values but may involve rhetorical ones in addition. Or instead.

I'm campaigning for overt rhetoric, which will not be to the taste of all.

And yet, one way or another, poetry will make a case, or else it will cease to function as verbal art, earning its praise in other terms—making "a good picture," say, or having "good music." In which instances, why substitute verse for an actual picture, or—as Marvin Bell has cogently asked—"if a poem is only music, what chance does it have" against real music?

In what I consider his greatest composition, Keats exemplifies an attitude he had not yet discovered in the great spring odes. Originally composed in September of the miraculous year, "To Autumn" adopts the familiar ploy of rhetorical questioning: "Where are the songs of Spring? Aye, where are they?"—which must certainly include the odes from the preceding May. The answer, however wistful, goes somewhat beyond the familiar "I don't know": "Think not of them, thou hast thy music too. . . ."

This Septembral music, to be sure, is also prepared to "flee." The choir of gnats, the bleat of lambs no longer lambs, the songs of fall insects and migratory birds—yes, these constitute a *memento mori.* Yet the poem itself is mellow and fruitful. One could read the whole renowned last stanza as a gentle Imagist piece, the more imagistic and gentle as it moves to closure. We may think of Wallace Stevens's famous claim that "Death is the mother of beauty." And yet, can we discover a rhetoric similar to Stevens's here?

Let me say that there are many ways to skin the rhetorical cat, and let me swerve momentarily from the strategies of "To Autumn" in order to consider one of those ways: in Robert Frost, whose rhetoric is easy to hear, that's about all there is. "Provide, Provide" is chiefly persuasion, verging on preachiness. It offers four short lines of showing—

The witch that came (the withered hag)
To wash the steps with pail and rag,
Was once the beauty Abishag,

The picture pride of Hollywood

—and seventeen of telling.

The lines that show are narrative, however minimal (and however short, incidentally, on image): famous beauty becomes crone. On the strength of this short-short story, the author moves straight to rhetoric, which begins as wry musing (lines 5–15) and, though Frost doesn't purge the wryness (he rarely does, in any poem), concludes as realist argument:

No memory of having starred
Atones for later disregard,
Or keeps the end from being hard.

Better to go down dignified
With boughten friendship at your side
Than none at all. Provide, provide!

If you agree that Frost here "gets away with" flouting the *show, don't tell* mantra, you may say that he does so exactly because, in that opening mini-narrative, he has shown. My point, however, will be that narrativity is only one of the many ways of skinning that cat. If character, setting, and plot—narrative components—validate the author's point of view in "Provide, Provide," I want to consider other modes of validation. For, however achieved, authorial and authoritative point of view is what is ultimately of moment here: a poet's authority will be the energy persuading us to hear out whatever case he or she may make.

Even though, for example, I took the pronouncement ironically, I heard Keats out when he said that beauty was truth. No, I didn't believe him, nor believe that he believed himself. But the very dialectical structure of the poem, with its attendant tonal changes, told me enough about the speaker that I could share in his ponderings. I witnessed not only how the urn's depictions provoked the loaded questions in "Ode on a Grecian Urn," but also how these mere images could not respond to those unsettling questions. As Stanley Plumly has said, "the image has no voice." It was Keats's own voice I heard: confronted with silence, it articulated an attitude—not "fair" like the urn's but troubled, complex—within the poem. In brief, it summoned me to participate in the author's quarrel with himself, which, for all of Yeats, resulted in rhetoric—and in poetry also. In rhetorical poetry.

We do not participate; we reject or scoff or get angry when we read "Happiness Is a Warm Puppy," because it *has* no specifiable "attitude," is enounced by no identifiable voice, signals no well-grounded point of view. Where, to use the old sixties' phrase that is the subtitle of this essay, is such a proposition coming from? That's another rhetorical question, the self-evident answer being our old, dismaying "I don't know." The puppy slogan is argument, yes, but free-floating argument. It rides off into the distance on an automobile bumper, leaving me, at least, to thunder: Who says so?

Whatever it may do on a bumper sticker, in any case, argument or rhetoric in poems must not hover in such middle air. Indeed, by my interpretation of the "Ode on a Grecian Urn," it was just such hovering that Keats found insufficient, even deathly. Knowing the gesture to be somehow both aesthetically and philosophically wrong, he yet wrote, "Beauty is truth, truth beauty," consciously *allowing* the aphorism to waft upward from its own silent, imagistic context and thus to reveal its desperate breathiness, irrelevance. Only a great poet, of course, would choose so daring a gambit, would trot out the very mistake he implicitly warns against, would permit his rhetoric to "float free" by way of indicating the perils of such a technique.

"To Autumn" moves me particularly in that Keats not only accepts but also affirms the dislocation of his ego, his "I," from the center of his meditation, seeking to fuse it with a greater general process. In the ode on the urn, as I've just suggested, the quest for authority had led to an all but crippling doubt. Indeed, in *all* the songs of spring, Keats's would-be prophet's voice clamored for a spirit's ear—and always unsuccessfully. Now he does not even try to invoke the goddess, doesn't have to: she's already there in what Wordsworth had called "the simple produce of the common day." Far from claiming some Romantic special province for the Poet, then, some insight that only his point of view can muster, the author figures himself as just another observer.

The poem, is, paradoxically, great in its posture of modesty. Its rhetoric is compelling in its hiddenness. For if "To Autumn" does possess rhetoric, it seems strangely unconnected with argument ("Beauty is truth," or whatever). Poetic argument instead relies for its effect on the institution of perspective . . . which, ironically, the poem then seeks to dismantle. This is the greatest paradox of all here: that by first vigorously establishing it, the author persuades us to surrender personal point of view as a vanity. Indeed, the desirability of such surrender is the object of the poem's rhetoric, but it is achieved by exquisitely subtle devices.

Thus, the opening stanza heaps up its imagery, from which the rhetoric—indirect, quiet—takes its resonance. The world is initially shown to be so abundant that the bees "*think* [italics mine] warm days will never cease. . . ." But the irrelevance of even such a comparatively inno-cent ego is made clear by the lines that open the second section of the ode:

> Who hath not seen thee oft amid thy store?
>   Sometimes whoever seeks abroad may find
> Thee sitting careless on a granary floor . . .

That is: I, the poet, have seen the goddess amid all her sweet trappings—but then, who hasn't? Even the birds and beasts are witnesses. The author immediately reverts to images, which now "chime" with the rhetoric just as the rhetoric has chimed with the imagery. But the central point is that neither is sufficient of itself. Let me further attempt to clarify this tricky contention by repeating that "Imagist poem" in stanza 3:

> Where are the songs of Spring? Aye, where are they?
>   Think not of them, thou hast thy music too—
> While barred clouds bloom the soft-dying day,
>   And touch the stubble-plains with rosy hue;
> Then in a wailful choir the small gnats mourn
>   Among the river sallows, borne aloft
> Or sinking as the light wind lives or dies;
>   And full-grown lambs loud bleat from hilly bourn;
> Hedge crickets sing; and now with treble soft
>   The redbreast whistles from a garden-croft;
> And gathering swallows twitter in the skies.

The passage begins in rhetoric, in "loaded" questions, so that the re-turn to imagery—the purest in the poem—remains grounded in the qui-etly argumentative attitude: the very *un*-loading of the language as the stanza progresses suggests the case being made. We have "wailful" gnats that "mourn"; we have "full-grown lambs," sheep ready for slaughter, so that there's some poignancy in their "bleat." But the crickets merely "sing," the swallows "twitter." Keats has moved from images of sight to the cruder one of hearing; but more important, his very verbs of sound grow increasingly generic, almost hackneyed, surely vernacular. His choice of words implies, again, that he is no longer *the* testifier but *a* testifier, common as brutes. Indeed, he wants to extinguish his self's view by conjoining it with a kind of general perspective.

However, in lyric (which for this reason distinguishes itself from certain fictional possibilities, by the way), there can be no general perspective. Lyrical point of view is never omniscient, is always limited; what I'm addressing, finally, is how the limits get established within a given poem. When I say rhetoric must have authority; when I say I want to know where such and such a rhetorical gesture is coming from, be it overt (e.g., "The best lack all conviction") or more latent (e.g., the progressive subversion of images' "significance" in "To Autumn"); when I say I want to know on what grounds a poem's case is being made—it's point of view that actually concerns me.

Whenever we lyricists engage in acts of argument—and I hope we will—or even gentle persuasion, it's a good idea to ask those same slightly wisecrack questions of ourselves, or rather of our poems, that we might ask of the bumper-sticker slogan: *Who says so? Where are you coming from?* For if we let our pronouncements float free, they, too, will be no more than slogans, irksome in their equivocality. Point of view must be earned, as Puritans say. Nor am I saying anything much different: to make our cases in poetic format, we must establish our credentials; that is the crucial end, though the means to it are likely infinite.

In any event, I suspect that every access to authoritative point of view will lead, as each has with Keats, into considerations of voice. And yet voice can be established, too, in countless ways: by the things or images a poem talks about ("To Autumn"); by its grammar or syntax; by exploitation of structure ("Ode on a Grecian Urn" could be studied from this angle and all the others), including responses, obedient or rebellious, to received formal structures (like the sonnet, with its promise of high seriousness, the villanelle, which implies obsession, or the couplet, boding a yen for aphorism), and so on. But vocal authority, however accomplished, is essential. Pronouns are not people. If, having composed a draft of a lyric, we ask ourselves *Who says so?* we must have a more compelling answer than naked "I."

Alan Williamson

Stories about the Self

I.

It might be that, for a literary historian from the future, the most interesting technical development in American poetry in the last two decades
of this century would be the refinement of (largely autobiographical)
narrative. It would be a little surprising, since "confessional poetry" —
almost from the moment that unfortunate term was coined—has been
the whipping boy of half a dozen newer schools, New Surrealism, New
Formalism, Language poetry. Yet it has remained the staple of what
comes near to being poetry's mass audience—the earnest beginners, in
small cities, on college campuses of all kinds and sizes, for whom poetry
is a way of setting their lives in order. On the more sophisticated level, all
the negative attention may well have stimulated poets to approach the
self's story with a tact, a self-awareness, an eye to exclusions and thematic "figure in the carpet," fiction writers have taken for granted for generations (think of *To the Lighthouse*, "Prelude," *A Portrait of the Artist as a
Young Man*). One reads the best of the newer narrative poetry with a
sense of point of view, of strategic timing and delayed exposition, that
makes even the great poems of Robert Lowell and Sylvia Plath feel like
raw lyric by comparison.

Yet I wouldn't entirely agree with Alan Shapiro's sense, in a fascinating recent essay ("In Praise of the Impure: Narrative Consciousness in
Poetry," *Triquarterly 81* [spring–summer 1991]), that recent narrative
poetry, being more social, is in reaction against the concentrated interior
movement not only in High Modernism but even in Lowell and Allen
Ginsberg. That seems to me too absolute an either/or; from another
point of view, all three could be seen as instants along the same vector, an
extension of Ezra Pound's "the natural object is always the adequate

symbol." Heaven knows few poets are working in High Modernist modes at the moment; but some of those who are—Peter Dale Scott, for instance—have made significant contributions, by their very ellipses, to the art of storytelling.

I've spoken of fiction as a model; but it may be useful to notice two other, opposite models, both a little beyond the spectrum of the fictional. One would be movies, which explain nothing, but convey both interpretation and feeling-tone by a series of immensely subtle visual and spatial cues. The other would be the essay, which does nothing but explain, but has a freedom to switch anecdotal subject, setting, and mode of address allowed to almost no other genre. Movies are a model for poetry—as for fiction and so much else—simply because they are our culture's most popular, and most technically inventive, mode of storytelling. Essays may have become a model because of the heated discussion surrounding the term *discursive* after the publication of Robert Pinsky's influential and controversial book *The Situation of Poetry.* (Indeed, Shapiro's sense of a *new* narrative school might be brought into sharper focus by calling it an essayistic school.)

One could trace this mode back to the poets who have most shaped it, poets like Pinsky, C. K. Williams, Frank Bidart. But I'd prefer, in this essay, and the succeeding one, to look at the mostly younger poets who have been able to take the mode for granted, and have brought to it a new finesse, variation, assurance. The title poem of Alan Shapiro's own new volume, *Covenant,* is a spectacular instance of the interweaving of fictional, essayistic, and cinematic possibilities. (I'll concede, at the start, that I have no reason to consider this poem "confessional," other than the similarity of atmosphere to certain poems that are explicitly about the poet's own family.) "Covenant" tells the story of a Jewish family reunion from the terrible perspective of the youngest sister's death "three months away." We know from fairly early on that she will die, but it takes us most of the length of the poem, and many hints, to learn exactly what happens. (Affected, either mentally or physically, by a stroke, she drops a lighted cigarette and sets herself on fire.) But the focus of the poem, while this appalling story is being postponed, is on the inner violence within the family, the tensions around food, around giving and taking, control, intrusion, and contamination. "The oldest sister, her two hands on the table, / about to push herself up," waits grimly while the others go on talking,

> Her gaze so tense with purpose she can almost
> see germs spawning in the mess of white fish
> flaking from the spines, the smear of egg yolk
> and the torn rolls disfiguring the china;
> as if the meal, the moment it is over,
> the meal she made a point of telling them
> she shopped for, got up early to prepare,
> were now inedible, because uneaten.

The long sentence unwinds down through the lines, with a muscular effort that imitates the work of arriving at, and formulating, a psychological insight, as well as the tense insistences of the sister's own harangue. And from the middle of this sentence the horrid, unforgettable visual details flash out—this much, at least, has been learned from the revolt against imagism—with an off-guard vividness they could never have had if the poet's main, declared intent had been to *describe*.

Shapiro is usually a formal poet, but aggressively not a New Formalist. The difference lies between the little lick of self-conscious pseudo-elegance that tends to get laid down on every line when form is an end in itself, and the immense variety of tones it can take, uses it can serve, in the hands of a poet whose eye is on something more serious. At one extreme, there's the puzzled, driving, working-things-out Larkinesque kind of line we've just heard; at the other, the Frostian syncopated line that catches the lilt of colloquial speech by setting it against a metrical expectation. "Listen, she would be saying, listen, Charlie"; "What can you do? What are ya gonna do?" A great deal of Shapiro's poem is taken up with capturing, in pentameter, certain Jewish-American storytelling mannerisms and the emotions they reveal—bewilderment, pain, self-importance, the triumph over experience by reenacting it—more or less the same range of reactions to human misfortune caught by that famous "Yes" in Elizabeth Bishop's "The Moose," a poem Shapiro has written about eloquently.

All of this imitation, and examination, of storytelling reaches its horrid fruition when we finally hear the story of the youngest sister's death in the older sister's voice:

And selfish. She was selfish, that one. After
all those years of living with that bum,
her husband, may his cheap soul rest in peace,
didn't *she* deserve a little pleasure?
And anyway, what could be done for her?
Didn't the stroke just make it easier
for her to sit all day, and smoke, and not care
ashes were falling on the couch, the carpet;
her bathrobe filthy, filthy?

It sounds like the worst Jewish-mother joke one has ever heard: the
youngest sister, it would seem, has died just to burden the older sister's life
more, to "[sit] there, / the queen of Sheba," establishing that "*she* was
there, *she* was always there, / her big sister, to clean up the mess."

Yet at this very moment of grotesque satire, Shapiro's essayistic, ex-
planatory tone comes in to move the poem toward the lyrical, and toward compassion. The bad mother becomes the child, her hostility her
way of defending herself against guilt, helplessness, and self-reproach:

and now they will hear the old unfairnesses,
old feuds and resentments come to her voice
like consolation, like a mother helping
her recite the story of that bad last day—
all that smoke, and running in with nothing
but the dishtowel to beat down the flames

What seems to me cinematic in the poem is the way light and temperature function throughout, both as a foreshadowing—or a reminder—of
the youngest sister's unspeakable fate, and as a subtler emotional index
of the "wavering frail zone it" ("the body," but, by extension, the ego and
its anxieties) "needs / to be forgotten." Early in the poem, "sunlight" is
"only just now *catching* on / a corner of the window [italics mine]"; later
it "burns brick by brick all morning toward the window / like a slow
fuse"; until finally

the sun has only just now
caught in the window, and its bright plaque warms
the air so gradually that none of them
can know it's warming, or that soon someone,

distracted by a faint sheen prickling the skin,
will break the story, look up toward the window
and, startled by the full glare, check the time.

What saves this from being gimmicky is partly that this last, most
brilliant recurrence comes after the flash-forward to the death narrative;
and partly that it so profoundly encapsulates the deepest issues in the
poem. The "figure in the carpet" is "the harm that's imperceptibly / but
surely coming for them," time itself, the unnoticed flowering of causes
and possibilities, always at once too slow and too quick for our attention.
On the psychological level, *control* is the theme the poem settles on, the
impossible wish that makes the claustrophobic atmosphere of this family
comprehensible, even as it also provides an avenue for its aggressions:

Nothing bad, right now, can happen here
except as news, bad news the brother and sister
mull and rehearse, puzzle and fret until
it seems the very telling of it is
what keeps them safe. And safe, too, the oldest sister. . . .
dreaming of how the soapsuds curdle and slide
over the dishes in a soothing fury,
not minding that it scalds her hands to hold
each plate and cup and bowl under the hot,
hard jet of water, if it gets them clean.

Temperature, again. What a savage ending it is—as if the self-
punishing energy in the family became the fire that burns the sister alive.
And yet a compassionate ending, in its willingness to enter, identify
with, and *explain* the labyrinth of motive.

I've loved Shapiro's work—its Larkinesque measures, its truthfulness—
ever since *Happy Hour,* an interrogation of the psychology of love as se-
vere, in its way, as Proust's. This new book is immensely richer and more
varied, turning on our covenants with God and fate as well as the grimmer,
pettier trade-offs within the family. It will please different readers in different ways. Some, I know, are most taken with the Miłoszian poems on historical irony, commonplaceness, and terror. My own favorites, aside from
"Covenant," are "The Lesson" and the series on marriage and fatherhood
running, approximately, from "Owl" through "Separation of the Waters."

The former takes up the explosive theme of child sexual abuse without self-pity, concentrating instead on the glamour the pedophile is able to conjure up for the group of boys. The latter are *healthy*—as the great marriage sequences in recent memory emphatically are not—and for that reason all the more devastating in their sense of the daily bargain with fate.

Tom Sleigh's poem "Fish Story," like "Covenant," has unspeakable violence and pain, slowly disclosed, as its core subject. I take it up as a much clearer instance of the essayistic way of organizing a poem, its oddities and its advantages. (Sleigh's book, like Shapiro's, appears in the University of Chicago Press's Phoenix Poets series, which also publishes Lloyd Schwartz and Anne Winters, among others. The series deserves praise for having identified itself, more than any other publisher, with the best of newer narrative work.)

"Fish Story" begins, in the unapologetically intellectual way Frank Bidart's work, more than anyone else's, has made thinkable to younger writers,

> I was reading *Plutarch's Lives,* about the gods,
> When I remembered someone I once knew, who came to our
>   home
> On Sundays for dinner with his girlfriend Kay

The leap, of course, is anything but accidental. The work of the poem will be to define, through this "someone," what the gods who "come down to us disguised" would be like. At first, the definition seems heroic and uncomplicated, if a little hackneyed. The man, a fisherman, a contrast to Kay's gay ex-boyfriend, is superhuman in his appetites and strength, if also in killing; he talks about

> How the deck gets slimy with scales,
> And the sixteen-ounce steaks you eat morning, noon, and night,
> And how you need that kind of nourishment
>
> To gaff hundreds of fish and club them to death

"A fish story," the speaker thinks, when the man shows his "Blood-soaked socks"; but later, when he himself is seized with the archetypal adolescent ambition of running away to sea, those socks became enviable, the

"badge or token / that I was more than what I seemed," and finally, "As
much an emblem as a thunderbolt or trident." But the moment the
theme of divinity is finally, explicitly articulated, it takes a darker turn—
an unlikeness to, perhaps even a deficiency in, human consciousness:

> So that sometimes I wonder if he himself
>
> Weren't a kind of god: He had the face
> Of a sleepy animal, heavy lids and bushy hair and his eyes
> Went blind when he talked, his spoon hesitating
>
> Halfway to his mouth and the steam
> Off the soup curling upward in the sunlight.
> He talked about the death penalty as a good thing

And here, with wonderful black comic timing, the poem releases its
thunderbolt—

> Which seems strange considering what later happened:
> He was separated from his wife, with two kids,
> When he'd met Kay, and one night, with a flensing knife,
>
> He stabbed his wife twenty-seven times,
> Face, throat, chest, back, stabbed her even in the eye
> Like Marlowe.

(I sometimes wonder what future readers will make of such ostenta-
tiously literary effects as "Like Marlowe." For us, I think, they depend
on the presumption that violence is so commonplace in the news and
popular culture that we need to come on it out of context—in literary
history, for instance—to feel how odd, and how nauseatingly real, it is.)

The murder makes the man even more mysterious, for he seems to
have committed it in a kind of trance, and gets off with "A temporary
insanity plea, which I admit / Seems accurate." In confronting this, the
poem returns to the mythic; and, I would add, to the essayist's freedom
not only of subject matter but of tone, since poetic temperaments are
not expected to be so impressive and so skeptical in the same breath:

> I see him like that, straight-backed in his chair,
> Stone-faced as Ephesian Diana, her throat encircled

> By a necklace of bull's testicles, what poetic temperaments
> Mistake for breasts!

The stakes are high here, for all the cynicism. Is the divine grand and nourishing (the man's "hand . . . seemed gentle and faithful that Sunday"); or is it a rigid atavistic stupidity? From this image the poem cuts directly to its second *coup de théatre*:

> —I think of him at their wedding
> Staring straight into Kay's eyes and her saying, "I do,"

> The flashbulbs gasping in the startled air
> And the air holding still as they drag out the kiss,
> And then his hand clasped hers on the cake knife.

Like Shapiro's last line, this one makes us wince, taking us straight back to the unspeakable crime. Yet the tenderness in it all but overrides that, leaving us, again, with questions. Are human beings dupes—rabbits mesmerized by the snake—or do they discover unbelievably trustworthy powers in themselves, when they fall in love with the ambiguous gods? The slightly heightened tone of the writing—permitted, one feels, by "Ephesian Diana," for all the undercutting—reinforces this double-edged sense of awe, leaving us a little "startled," like the "air!" (Not less so, perhaps, because that phrase echoes a classical scene in Rilke's "First Elegy.")

Reading this poem leaves me feeling heartened, not only about Sleigh's own development (it seems to me the best single poem in *Waking*, though others have even more overpowering subjects), but about the possibilities in contemporary writing it typifies. There's so much more amplitude, of experience and tone, than in the Deep Image style of twenty years ago, the New Critical style of forty. *Pace* Shapiro, it seems closer to the excitement of Modernism, though the means are utterly different. Certainly many unfortunate prejudices have had to be overcome to get to it: that intellect and learned reference are incompatible with emotion; that a speech-based style cannot go with the numinous, or either with any vestige of the formal line. (Sleigh's poem has a much more relaxed metric than Shapiro's, but consider "The flashbulbs gasping in the startled air.") It suggests that we live at a flexible, omnivorous moment in the history of American poetry; and however much discouragingly unambitious work is also out there, that is something to be grateful for.

II.

There is a quotation from Willa Cather that, for all its old-fashioned ring, has haunted me ever since I first came on it:

> If the writer achieves anything noble, anything enduring, it must be by giving himself absolutely to his material. He fades away into the land and people of his heart; he dies of love only to be born again.

It reminds me of a passage Gary Snyder is fond of quoting, from the thirteenth-century Zen master Dogen:

> To carry yourself forward and experience myriad things is delusion.
> But myriad things coming forth and experiencing *themselves* is awakening.

On the face of it, both quotations would seem to be utterly against the idea of personal art. Read carefully, I think both acknowledge that— as the object relations theorist Christopher Bollas has suggested—the self exists hidden within the objects it has cherished, to be resurrected there, in Cather's terms, or awakened, in Dogen's, in a flexible plenitude sometimes lost when we try to examine the self as if it were a fixed object. Another translation of the Dogen passage reads: "Acting on and witnessing oneself in the advent of myriad things is enlightenment."

I think we all know intuitively what goes wrong in art when the self goes out to the myriad things like a conquering army, trying to make them express it (though we might differ enormously as to just which poets and fictionists most embody this failing). Recently, reading the *New York Times Book Review,* I saw someone praised as "the most talented American poet under the age of forty" for lines like the following:

> Now in a gilded apse the celestial globe
> Has rolled to the end of an invisible rope

And come to rest on a cliff in a blue-green garden.
I look up, as if nothing had killed my hope,
At a blue sphere, buoyant in the sixth-century tides
Still surging and dying away through San Vitale,
Where a spring has glinted in the numinous
Fresh-cut grass for more than a millennium.

Now I have nothing against touristic poems about Europe, having written a number of them myself. But how nakedly this one seems to value the cultural objects simply for being cultural objects, able to make things "numinous"! And how it all serves as backdrop for the more than Victorian self-pity of "I look up, as if nothing had killed my hope"—which, one can't help feeling, the poet would have had a harder time bringing off stuck, as Walt Whitman wished us, back among the kitchenware. To me it is a little example of how poetry can deaden the "myriad things," by forcing them into too willed and self-centered a design.

In the last few years I've been struck by a number of poems that, by contrast, simply open themselves, in a lovely, leisurely way, to the world of the poet's affections (usually, but not always, the world of childhood). Only slowly and by inference do we discover that they are also about the making of a poet's mind, or the survival of some crisis—stories about the self. It seems part of the same flowering-out, by experiment and variation, of the possibilities of the personal, that I discussed in my previous essay.

"The Reservoir" is the longest poem in Debra Allbery's *Walking Distance,* the 1990 winner of the University of Pittsburgh Press's Starrett Prize, and a book that would certainly be on my mind if I were doing anything so rash as ranking poets under forty. It is an honest and original chapter in the long history of the love-hate relation between middle America and its artist children. The town Allbery calls Enterprise, Ohio, was also the model for Sherwood Anderson's Winesburg. [When that book came out, it was burned in the public square; now the city limits signs say "(Winesburg)," just as, south of Chartres in the Ile-de-France, one can visit a town called Illiers-Combray.]

"The Reservoir" begins by confessing that the poet's return home, to two comically onerous summer jobs, is partly psychic retreat—"deep

habit, no danger"—and partly a never-relinquished hope that "some of
the endings she needed / might be found, after all, in Enterprise, Ohio."
The sights and sounds of the place are emblems of what Thoreau called
"quiet desperation," and at the same time so deeply messages to the poet's
own self-questioning that there is no escaping the human commonality:

> Walking, she passes these signs
> all summer—one is painted in red
> on a ripped bed sheet and hangs
> from an upstairs window:
> "You've had it? *You're* the problem!"
> And this hand-printed and taped
> to someone's front door: "Day Sleeper."
> In the Christian bookstore window,
> a white-on-black placard: "Does mortality
> limit you?"

The receptiveness of this poem to its world is easier to experience
than to describe. It is stalled and beautiful at once, depressed and full
of affection, like the small-town summer. The poem could easily seem
too long, but somehow doesn't. The severely objectifying third person
alternates with first-person passages in italics, yielding to a dreamlike,
merged perspective the rest of the poem resists:

> *Trains passed through like they were still important*
> *and I'd stand in their wind, reading the flaking names*
> *on old boxcars,* Erie Lackawanna. Chessie, Rock Island.
> *After they passed, the quiet went deeper,*
> *the land lay light green after green, almost seamless.*

Real dreams, by contrast, are reminders of crisis, psychic danger, the need
for change, "the sky of Enterprise filled / with tornadoes, with colored
balloons." Brief scenes with her mother, high-school classmates, an old
boyfriend about to get married—

> the exclusiveness,
> the strange gravity, of his "we,"
> how it tops her halting "I's"
> the way paper-covers-rock

—edge her out of her sense of really belonging, but not out of the sense
that,

> like anyone,
> it's belonging she wants, it's the idea
> of *settled* or *permanent address.*
> And all she's done has been only so much
> rent paid toward that place.

Most of the high lyric moments in the poem are associated with the
reservoir of the title, just outside of town, where "she" goes running. It
becomes the vehicle of the wish to be inside and outside at once, the peculiar kind of distance (implicitly, the distance of art) that permits love
and hate to be held in balance:

> And alongside her, beer cans,
> rubbers, torn cardboard, bleached crawdads,
> and she runs it again and everyday, for it's only
> from this height and pace she can love her town.

(And here I think we can see how Allbery, like Alan Shapiro, is quietly
one of the most inventive of contemporary metrists. That last line *counts*
as iambic pentameter; but it sings as a half-anapestic tetrameter, the
very momentum that glides above the world of counted things: "from
this heíght and páce she can lóve her town." Never rigidly bound by
meter, but tending to return to it at the high points, Allbery restores the
relation to speech, to thinking-things-through, it had in Robert Frost and
Randall Jarrell.)

The poem returns to the reservoir at the end, when the playing back
and forth between the speaker's sense of superiority and inferiority to
her given world, the wish for "distances . . . to try alone" and the wish for
"belonging," have brought it to a point of crisis:

> She's outside of Enterprise, running the reservoir,
> singing to herself *The water is wide,*
> looking past the south and east edges
> of town, at the reach of August sky
> and black clouds moving quickly
> from the west, and she's thinking

Sometimes if I open my eyes very wide
there's this space which is like
room for error. And I see limits,
I see things that can change my mind.

Rather wonderfully, the poem finds wisdom not on either side of its di-
chotomies, but rather in the psychic transaction that leaves both available
as agencies of change. And the ending seems to me equally wonderful.
The poem, which up to this point has found ingenious ways of subordi-
nating narrative to catalog, concludes with a baldly unmediated anecdote:

Long ago, a teacher had told her
about his genius friend, and how
he'd sit with his thoughts wherever
they came to him, thinking them through,
and how he found him once, drenched,
oblivious, sitting chin-in-hands
on a street corner. And this
was the first ambition she could remember,
to not have sense enough to come in out of the rain.

It is a delicately humorous acknowledgement of how the poet has
come to overvalue the outside perspective; the self-destructive potential of that; and at the same time the real value of inner distance, of ac-
tivities that are their own reason for being, of all that goes outside the
bounds of small-town common sense. It's one of the most brilliant and
charming instances of seemingly suspended closure I know of in recent
poetry.

"The Reservoir" makes sparing but skillful use of a musical organization by motif, so that we hear more of *You've had it? You're the problem!*
The water is wide, and other key phrases as the crisis approaches. Such
organization may well be a necessity when divagatoriness, rather than
plot, is the form the love of place cries out for. In Jeanne Foster's "The
Pearl River" (published under her earlier writing name, Jeanne Foster
Hill, in the *Hudson Review,* summer 1985), it is carried to a level more
musical than traditionally poetic. The initial notes have to do with fear
of the world, reassurance, and then discovering the limits of the know-
ableness, the reassurance, of anything outside the self:

This little finger, she reassured,
rolling the baseball-stunned knuckle
of the child's left little finger between her padded thumb
and forefinger, couldn't be broken.
It is so limber, it could be bent
like a sapling under weight of snow to earth
and not snap
. . . .
She is as doe to fawn,
that teacher, who only once
became enraged and broke
the scissors against the desk. The little girl sat
amazed.

But fingers . . .
I've said what I could say
about them.

Against the background of these issues the world of childhood exfoliates. On the one hand, the child's fear, as in Elizabeth Bishop's "In the Waiting Room," of all she is exposed to, made part of, simply by existing—

She in her blue pinafore, trimmed with tiny red and yellow
flowers and green leaves, was afraid
of the very cousins—the red-haired Jim
and the green-eyed Barbara and their hairy friend

—and, even more, of the intimations of death, cruelty, the ultimate indifference of things, her uncle beheading a hen and the body "run(ning) headless under the calm, observant gaze / of the loblolly pines." And on the other hand, the childhood sense of things being simultaneous with their meaning and that meaning, always, intimately related to herself:

And the house was watched over,
its silver-tin roof shooting light from the sun
into the very hearts of those pines.

Certain letimotif phrases, repeated and varied throughout the poem, dramatize the tension of these antimonies. "Nothing would let go"—the sense of trauma, invasion, contamination—plays against the more problematic "Nothing was simply let go," which carries a certain painful promise for the speaker as artist, as therapeutic self-discoverer, as an adult frightened of the total loss of the past, the speaker who will eventually transmute the phrase into

> Everything is kept, but nothing
> is easily recovered.

Another leitmotif phrase is "The Pearl River, the dividing line." Its literal meaning is geographical—between Louisiana and Mississippi—but since the poem nowhere mentions this fact, the reader is left to imagine other borders, conscious and unconscious, childhood and adulthood, life and death. At first the river seems a kind of dream river, something like the collective unconscious, which the child approaches through the back of a closet, like the magic land in C. S. Lewis's *The Lion, the Witch, and the Wardrobe.* Images of mirroring, recognition, condensations, and simultaneities reinforce this feeling. (The psychoanalyst Hans Loewald suggested that condensation is one of the qualities that distinguish unconscious imaginative thinking from rational thinking.) The river is both itself a sign and inscribed with signs, of threats, of dangerous vitality:

> The Pearl River, the dividing line,
> winds like a water moccasin through the red clay soil.
> The moon turns its full face toward
> the upward turned face, and the river shines
> like pearl. Upon its surface
> a water moccasin carves the shape
> of a worker's scythe.

The river is, perhaps most important, the place where "the song" is first heard, a song reconciling the opposed principles of nourishment and threat, value, trauma, and sexual muck:

> Kept all these years,
> a treasure watched over by the pirate's ghost,
> the pearl in the oyster growing in a bed of mud,
> the milk before it is milked from the fangs . . .

The scene, as it is repeated, is very delicately inscribed with the sexual and racial tensions common to Southern writing. The original singer of the song is a "black man"; it is his "upward turned face / shining like black silver," and not just the river's, that the moon mirrors. And the hidden spectator of this otherness is at once the furtive child and the idealized image of Southern womanhood, restrained by her protection:

> A shadow
> white as a madonna lily moves away
> under the dark green cloaks of our forefathers,
> the loblolly pines.

In acknowledging these meanings, and in making the song her own, able "to recall itself / from the labyrinth," the speaker becomes adult: "A slender woman walks out the other side / into daylight."

In the second half of the poem, the adult half, nearly every incident, every phrase, is repeated from the first half—the ego being, in Freud's words, where the id has been. Some of the discoveries are hilarious—

> Uncle Al laid down the hatchet.
> The green-eyed Barbara, the red-haired Jim,
> and Harry, their friend, stood around and watched

—where we realize that the child has misheard the world in the image of the terror and animality already there in her unconscious: "their hairy friend." In the last section, a slightly hostile, challenging blackface voice keeps asking "Is it you, girl?" and the question seems addressed to all the elements in the scene: the hiding shadow, the woman who "walks out the other side," the river itself, shining and reflecting—as if only when all of these larger and smaller selves are acknowledged, will selfhood be whole. Yet the poem never makes this too easy; the adult speaker who can offer the words of consolation to herself remains somehow melancholy in her protectiveness, and the poem ends on the last notes of its overture, the note of muteness, of reaching the limits of the comprehensible:

> Young things are so fragile, she whispers
> and remembers the teacher who stroked the knuckle of her left
> little finger. Only once did she become enraged
> and break the scissors against the desk.

> But fingers . . .
> I've said what I could say
> about them.

Brenda Hillman's "Canyon," from her book *Fortress,* is also a story about a landscape. It's about a park, just outside a city, half wild, half tame, with its "Jewel Lake" and its ducks, but also the high bare slopes, drier, more ignitable as summer goes on, that seem an intimation that "the normal soul / has an extra soul above it." It is a story about feeling, like the landscape, on the edge of ultimates; small and uncertain in that exposure, yet the vehicle of energies at once mystical and mischievous—

> Two fawns in the sun: twin deaths: one
> gazes with unbearable steadiness;
> the other looks up as the id looks up,
> his ears twitching the victory sign

Perhaps it is about a relationship suffused with these qualities—but an impeded relationship, whose obstacles and separations may be the occasion for the solitary wanderings in the park ("I pretended / you were living in another country, not far, / yet impossible to reach. . . . / and I had rushed out here / to be your opposite").

In some ways, the poem talks most powerfully about love by talking about perception. Both have the power to give access to that realm of the "extra soul," where "you are known completely / by seeing, known as if by a secret companion." Both, too, are problematic. In the structure of the poem, the merged immediacy of this particular relationship—

> Thinking I'd feel nothing
> without your hands, their girlish strength (as you
> could feel nothing without my boyish ones)

—is to the work of doubt, tyrannical expectation, finding out who the other person really is, how much meshing is possible (how can it be avoided, one protests, when two people think of making a life together?) as the spider that

> is neither subject nor object, it has no separate
> motions in its realm but lets itself gently down
> into the notch and crack of the inexpressible

is to the birdwatcher who hasn't really seen the bird until he can name it ("oriole"); is to the breakdowns we can make, like Zeno's paradox of the arrow, out of our own "flash" of seeing:

> I recall the illustration in the text, how the solitary
> impulse, like a hiker, hurried down,
>
> disturbed the obstinate whiteness
> of the membrane, climbed
>
> into blockish boats ("receptors"),
> was ferried across the synapse, the little
>
> Lethe between two cells.

No less than doubt, the desire to control the outcome is an almost overwhelming force that landscape must absorb, and eventually alter, in this poem. The fear of loss—loss of the dream, and of the immediate experience, of oneness, no less than loss of each other—almost breaks the psyche, and the bare hills, with the "clarity" of their "lacunae," have their own way of embodying the absoluteness of this claim. Yet the lesson of nature—the hills drying out, the season moving toward autumn—is that things must change, and with change there is always some degree of loss: "the light was changing, and would not change back." Against this, the very divagatoriness of the poem is a kind of defenseless defense. An enactment of the immense creativity, and the stasis, of obsessive love, it prepares for the poem's eventual assent to valuing experience over certainty:

> I can't look too closely at the faces
> of runners; they wear their deaths,
> working out for the long, local races,
> or when they descend the haunted road
>
> after the natural morphine makes of the body
> a stem of soothing light
> . . . .
> I think about the woman in the cap
> who needed water, who staggered like a drunk,
> for whom the cheering didn't matter; she said

she didn't know the difference
between the men in lab coats and the finish line,
but with great yearning,
she spoke of the race as of a beloved tormentor.

Yet it is one of the great strengths of the poem that it never chooses between the "reality" of love and a more disillusioned, or more resignedly experiential, perspective. Instead, after a troubled, inconclusive encounter—the "you," always represented as the more rational, and the more anxious, of the two, sinks into "gloom," and "this mild calm is not the happiness we envisioned"—the poem returns to the image of the fawns:

We shall know without judgment
in the fullness of time—it says that
in some religion. The brave fawn waits
for its companion, and its spots shine

like spilled quarters in the sun.
The scared one steps into the road at last,
becomes the other one;
then the spotted earth becomes the fawn's back.

It's a wonderful summary of all the tensions and hopes, braveries and hesitations, in the poem (the "spilled quarters" refer to a pay phone call, earlier). The last lines—the protective coloration—are at once an affirmation of twinship, both between the lovers and between perception and the world, and a way of leaving open the question whether it can be lived out, short of apocalypse, death, becoming the earth.

What I like best, almost, in these three very lovely, structurally inventive poems, is the happy absence of competition between the "myriad things" and introspection. Enterprise, Ohio, the Pearl River, Tilden Park "com(e) forth and experience(e) *themselves*" in these poems; they remain permanent imaginative landscapes for the reader. Yet they also cause, and/or become equivalents for, very subtly delineated states of feeling and being, states "known completely / by seeing," in Hillman's phrase. Given Dogen's concern with "awakening," perhaps it's no accident that these are poems of self-education as well as self-expression. Landscape, in them, seems to have the power to alter *every* easy, or anxious, or one-sided assessment of reality simply by standing in the face of it. And the selves that emerge at the ends of these poems seem more flexible, more tolerant of contradiction, less anxious about outcomes; surrounded, even, with the aura of a larger, more impersonal creative selfhood, like Foster's river and upturned face.

These poems also interest me intensely as a moment in the history of genres. There are precedents, of course, certainly among the Romantics— "Frost at Midnight" comes to mind—and among Modernist long poems like *Four Quartets*. But in our own time the confessional poem has been so distinct, and embattled, a genre that landscape meditation has tended to hold off, in distant sectors of the map of styles. The interpenetration of their methods is a subtilizing process for both; and one more reason to be glad of the ways American poets have stuck with the personal, the last twenty years.

Joseph Bruchac

The Self within the Circle

In the early seventeenth century, a missionary was speaking to some Lenape Indians, urging them to give up their pagan beliefs and become Christians. They listened politely until he had finished.

"We also believe in God," they told him. "But our God, Manido, does not just live in your churches. Manido does not take the shape of an old white man with a beard."

The missionary was surprised and asked them to explain their concept of God.

One of the men knelt and used his finger to draw a circle in the moist earth. "This is Manido," he said. "Manido is all eye. Manido is all good. We are always in the sight of our God."

In an age of unbelief, in a time when the Western awareness of self dominates above all, that story may seem both naïve and out of date. It also may seem to have very little to do with contemporary autobiographical poetry. Yet, if we are looking at the autobiographical voice in the writing of American Indian poets, the message of that story and the tradition of narrative within which it exists are of great importance. I do not believe it is an exaggeration to say that the idea of existing within a circle, an all-inclusive circle charged by the omnipresence of great spiritual force, is the backdrop of every Native American writer's vision. Coupled with the multitribal heritage of an unending circle of stories that pass from generation to generation is the idea that the circle of narrative borrows each of our voices but survives every one of us. Thus, it is not as easy for Native American writers to take a wholly selfish stance in which the first-person voice and the details of their own lives take center stage in their work.

Note that I said it is not easy for Native American writers to do that. I did not say it is impossible. In fact, some Native poets draw their strongest work from adopting an ironic stance in opposition to the view of life as a circle. Sherman Alexie and Adrian C. Louis often exemplify that approach by consciously going against the grain. But I will say more about them later.

Further, while that ancient circle of good is sometimes envisioned as the "broken hoop" (made familiar to the world in *Black Elk Speaks,* an idyllic world of the past that has been shattered by the imbalance, self-ishness, and greed of white Western culture), the best American Indian autobiographical writing, while recognizing the devastation of Native cultures by the evils of racism, religious intolerance, and a continuing lust for Indian land, does not always lay blame solely on the white man. Things are seldom as simple as that. The Native American as helpless victim is found much more commonly in the work of white romantics than in first-person poems of *real* Indians. We were human beings before the coming of Europeans and we remain human to this day, as capable of bad judgment and incorrect behavior as are the Trickster figures found in every Native oral tradition. Indeed, the Native American self presented in many autobiographical poems has more than a touch of Coyote or Raven or Iktome.

It is also important to note that there is a deep sense of community within contemporary Native America. Many American poets bemoan the lack of community and worry that their words will fall on deaf ears. Our poets, however, know that the opposite is true of their work. For better or worse, if you are an American Indian poet, your poems will be carefully read, not only by those of your own tribe (who will read EVERY word), but also by other American Indian writers and a wide, literate Pan-Indian audience from Alaska to Florida. Words have great power in Indian country and more than one American Indian poet has worried about saying too much or saying the wrong thing in their work. What if, for example, you were to write about your own rite of passage cere-mony. Even though it was yours, to describe it to others might be re-garded as a betrayal by your tribe's tradition-bearers. That is exactly what happened to the late Pueblo essayist Alfonso Ortiz. When he published a description of his own puberty ceremony (*National Geographic Magazine*, October 1991), his Pueblo community was so deeply shocked that the offending issue of the magazine was banned from their community library.

There have been numerous occasions in my own poetry when I have chosen to describe things less specifically, or even to avoid retelling certain stories or incidents I know are not meant to be shared outside a very limited context. Such stories might seem innocuous to outsiders, but to those within the culture they have deep meaning. A poem might be, for example, making clear reference to an ancient petroglyph of a power animal found on the granite wall of a sea cliff somewhere in Nova Scotia. As I have just presented it, no one would object. However, if I were to give a specific description of the actual image and its location, that would be quite a different story. The responsibility of the storyteller in Native American culture is not only to remember and share, but also to know how much to share, when to share, and with whom. As the new storytellers, our Indian poets take on a similar responsibility.

The first Native American writer to emerge as a major literary figure in the second half of the twentieth century was the Kiowa author and storyteller N. Scott Momaday. His novel, *House Made of Dawn,* won the Pulitzer prize in 1968. Distinguished as a poet, novelist, and essayist, it may appear on first reading that Momaday exemplifies the simplest form of Native autobiographical poetry in his often anthologized "The Delight Song of Tsoai-Talee" (*The Gourd Dancer,* Harper & Row, 1976). Hypnotically repetitive, as uncomplicated as a chant, Momaday's poem connects the first-person narrator to the great circle of creation around him:

> I am a feather on the bright sky
> I am the blue horse that runs in the plain
> I am the fish that rolls, shining, in the water
> I am the shadow that follows a child . . .

For eighteen lines, unbroken by any end-line punctuation, the list of "I ams" continues. The second stanza finally breaks that pattern, yet maintains the overall atmosphere of oral tradition:

> You see, I am alive, I am alive.
> I stand in good relation to the earth.
> I stand in good relation to the gods.
> I stand in good relation to all that is beautiful.
> I stand in good relation to the daughter of Tsen-tainte.
> You see, I am alive, I am alive.

It is both deeply personal and enigmatic, a far remove from confessional poetry in the way it defines the self not by standing out, but by blending in, by being "a part of all things." Yet it is complicated. Each of the elements Momaday chooses to identify himself with tie into some aspect of his own life, his family, and his Kiowa ancestry.

That last stanza is both a summation of that catalog (and the resultant oneness that rises out of the poet's wholehearted identification with all aspects of creation) and a connection to a Native American tradition other than Kiowa. It draws strongly on healing chants of the Diné (Navajo) such as the Night Chant which, in its English translation by Washington Matthews, gave Momaday the title for *House Made of Dawn*. This should not be surprising since Momaday's father worked in Indian Boarding schools in the Southwest. Momaday grew up in that enchanted landscape, surrounded by the pageantry of the Pueblo and Diné cultures.

Near the end of the nineteenth century, Old Torlino, a Diné haatali (the Diné word used for a chanter or healer) was asked by Washington Matthews to relate the story of Creation. Here is the personal pronouncement Old Torlino made before he began, in a form virtually identical to that used by Momaday eight decades later:

> I am ashamed before the earth;
> I am ashamed before the heavens;
> I am ashamed before the dawn;
> I am ashamed before the evening twilight;
> I am ashamed before the blue sky;
> I am ashamed before that standing within

which speaks with me.
Some of these things are always looking at me.
I am never out of sight.
Therefore I must tell the truth.
I hold my word tight to my breast.

While certain things are stated directly in both Momaday's poem and the poetic pronouncement of Old Torlino, even more is unstated, implied, or available only to those who know enough to grasp the deeper meaning. Although Momaday does not state it in his poem, he explained to me during an interview for *Survival This Way* (a collection of interviews with Native poets published by the University of Arizona), that Tsoai-Talee is his own Kiowa name. It means Rock Tree Boy. But even that translation needs further examination. It refers to the Kiowa legend of the origin of the rock formation known to most Americans as Devil's Tower. The Kiowas say that it rose up out of the earth after a boy was transformed into a bear and began to pursue his sisters. Seeking to avoid this close encounter of the ursine kind, the frightened girls took refuge on a bit of high ground. The ground rose higher and higher as the bear scratched its sides until finally the sisters stepped into the sky and became stars. Thus Momaday's poem is both a statement of his deep identification with the bear, as well as an evocation of his Kiowa ancestry.

Other Native American poets, most notably the Mohawk writer Maurice Kenny, have used the "I am" form in writing poems of deep personal identification with ancestry and the circle of being that surrounds us. "I am" appears thirteen times in Kenny's poem, "They Tell Me I Am Lost," that ends with the line, "I am the shadow on the field / I am the string, the bow and the arrow." But the form of the chant is far from being the only approach used by Native poets in telling their stories. Some, including Kenny, write many of their poems in an anecdotal form—half travelogue and half meditation on the land and the people they encounter.

This approach is characteristic of the most popular American Indian poet among other Indians—Simon Ortiz. A native of the New Mexico

Pueblo of Acoma, his travels have taken him to every part of North America and led him to conclude that "Indians are everywhere." The "I" in his poetry is often so gentle, so understated, so subordinate to his descriptions of the land and the people he encounters, that his "I" becomes more witness and chronicler than personal confessor. *Going for the Rain: Poems* (Harper & Row, 1976), contains the long poem "Travels in the South," which begins with these lines:

> When I left the Alabama-Coushatta people,
> it was early morning.
> They had treated me kindly, given me food
> spoken me words of welcome, and thanked me.
> I touched them, their hands, and promised
> I would be back.
>
> When I passed by the Huntsville State Pen
> I told the Indian prisoners what the people said
> and thanked them and felt very humble.
> The sun was rising then.
>
> When I got to Dallas I did not want to be there.

Adrian C. Louis, an enrolled member of the Lovelock Paiute Indian tribe, takes a harder look at the roads he has traveled. His hard-edged, unyielding poems, which look straightforwardly at Indian alcoholism and the devastated landscape of reservations, may appear to represent the farthest remove from the gentleness of Ortiz or the lyricism of Momaday. Unlike Old Torlino, whose reference to being "ashamed" was meant to state his humility in the face of a great and good creation, Louis really *is* ashamed of the bitter reality many American Indians are forced to survive. Here are a few lines from "Elegy for the Forgotten Oldsmobile," which appeared in his 1989 collection, *Fire Water World*:

> But nothing is static. I am in the reservation of
> my mind. Embarrassed moths unravel my shorts
> thread by thread asserting insectival lust.
> I'm a naked locoweed in a city scene.
> What are my options? Why am I back in this city?

When I sing of the American night my lungs billow
Camels astride hacking appeals for cessation.
My mother's zippo inscribed: "Stewart Indian School–1941"
explodes in my hand in elegy to Dresden Antietam
and Wounded Knee . . .

A "naked locoweed" is a far cry from a "feather on the bright sky,"
and calculatedly so. There's no question that Louis is aware of Momaday's
"Delight Song of Tsoai-Talee." However, Louis's bitter spin on it (showing an Indian totally removed from the nurturing nature Momaday celebrates) does not invalidate the old systems of belief. They stand as a
contrast to the blasted landscape. Louis's poem is one of rebellion against
the failed promises (or outright lies) made to Native Americans. Later
in the poem, repeating the phrase "the reservation of my mind" for the
third time (incantation, chant) he writes:

Here I am in the reservation of my mind
and silence settles forever
the vacancy of this cheap city room.
In the wine darkness my cigarette coal
tints my face with Geronimo's rage
and I'm in the dry hills with a Winchester
waiting to shoot the lean, learned fools
who taught me to live-think in English.

Women writers are among the strongest voices in contemporary
Native writing. Kimberly Blaeser, Diane Burns, Anita Endrezze, Nia
Francisco, Joy Harjo, Linda Hogan, nila northSun, Wendy Rose, Leslie
Marmon Silko, Mary Tallmountain, and Luci Tapahonso are among
those whose books have received critical acclaim and whose poems are
often autobiographical, focusing on the self and the lyric "I." Here, even
more than with the male poets, we find that the poem of the self becomes the poem of the family, the tribe, and the people. Intimate personal histories flow into both larger oral traditions and chronicles of
tribal survival through 500 years of colonization. Here are the first lines
of Joy Harjo's poem, "Autobiography," from her 1990 book *In Mad Love
and War.* Harjo's Creek ancestors were among the many tribes forcibly
relocated to Oklahoma, the backdrop of this poem:

We lived next door to the bootlegger and were lucky. The bootlegger
  reigned.
We were a stolen people in a stolen land. Oklahoma meant defeat. But
  the
sacred lands have their own plans, seep through fingers of the alcohol
spirit. Nothing can be forgotten, only left behind.

Last week I saw the river where the hickory stood; this homeland doesn't
predict a legacy of malls and hotels. Dreams aren't glass and steel but
  made
from the heart of deer, the blazing eye of a circling panther. Translating
them was to understand the death count from Alabama, the destruction
  of
grandchildren, famine of stories. I didn't think I could stand it.

The word "we" appears in this poem twice before the "I." Family
history and the larger history of the Creek Nation come before the individual appears in the poem, and even then the presence of the first-
person narrator is that of the dreamer, the visionary, the survivor who
sees the pain of the past and recognizes it as part of her own life. There is
a great deal of pain in this poem, but it is not the pain of the lonely soul.
It is the pain of the people and the pain of the land.

Who are the newest voices in American Indian poetry? They are many
and their work often exhibits the strength drawn from regaining the
connection to the ancient circle. After decades of relocation, unequal
opportunity, racism, and denial, Indian poets continue to find their
way home. There is, for example, Janice Gould, a Koyangk'auwi Maidu
writer whose two books of poetry deal not only with the urban Native
experience in California, but also with being a lesbian of Indian heritage.
In "Blood Sisters," Gould talks about the process of rediscovering personal identities as she tells a friend:

    . . . about the Maidu song my mother Sang
    in a scale I could never learn,
    and about the tree on an old dirt road
    where the white men lynched my people.

and then concludes:

> We glance at one another,
> fall silent.
> Americans do not know these things
> nor do they want to know.
>
> But each of us knows stories
> we have never even whispered.

Of all the emerging Native poets, none has burst more forcefully onto the literary scene than Sherman Alexie. An enrolled Spokane/Coeur d'Alene from the Spokane Indian reservation in Wellpinit, Washington, his first book of poetry, *The Business of Fancydancing,* came out in 1992 and was followed in rapid succession by a half-dozen more volumes. His first book of short stories, *The Lone Ranger and Tonto Fistfight in Heaven,* was the genesis of his screenplay for *Smoke Signals,* often described (somewhat inaccurately) as the first Indian-directed and -written feature film. "Sherman Alexie," Adrian Louis would state in a blurb on that first book of poems, "paints painfully honest visions of our beautiful and brutal lives."

It's true. I don't know of another poet who does a better job of telling it as it is with such style. Modern as he is, new as his voice might be, he still holds a deep reverence for those things that were best about the American Indian past, those things that survive with new shirts over the old skins. The self-mocking tone of such poems as "Basketball," quoted here in its entirety, is yet another way of being humble before Creation:

> After a few beers, every Indian is a hero of "unbroken horses." Some-one always remembers I was the Reservation point guard with the Crazy Horse jump shot. Someone always wants to go one-on-one in the alley while Lester Falls Apart balances on a garbage can, his arms forming the hoop. Someone always bets his ribbon shirt against mine, and we play, and I win. Someone always finishes the night bareback, like it should be, while I go home, hang another shirt in my closet, an-other Crazy Horse dream without a skeleton or skin.

Yes, the circle in this poem is only a basketball hoop, formed by the arms of a half-tanked Spokane Indian on a garbage can, but (like the great Lakota hero Crazy Horse) it is the goal for which Alexie aims, a goal that connects him to the dreams of his people. Yet another circle within which a Native American writer finds himself.

Billy Collins

My Grandfather's Tackle Box:
The Limits of Memory-Driven Poetry

Since the broad subject of this piece is autobiographical or "post-confessional" poetry, I should begin by making a confession regarding the above title. As far as I know, my grandfather never owned a tackle box, and if he did, somebody must have thrown it out. Because my parents married late, all four of my grandparents were already dead by the time I was born, so if one of my grandfathers did own a tackle box, I would have no memory of a grandfather to connect it to. Plus, my grandfathers were Irish immigrants who were probably too poor to afford such sporting gear. And even if such an object actually existed, it would be lost on me since I myself do not fish, a point I made clear in a poem titled "Fishing on the Susquehanna in July." I settled on "My Grandfather's Tackle Box" because I thought it was a good title to open a discussion about poems that are primarily driven by the engines of memory rather than the engines of the imagination. More narrowly, I thought the tackle box might epitomize the proliferation of contemporary poems being written—and sometimes read—on the subject of family relations, especially poems on the subject of deceased parents or grandparents, and even more particularly, poems that reveal a fixation with some fetish-object such as a grandmother's apron, a mother's kitchen scale, a father's favorite hat. My complete lack of experience with grandparents probably accounts for my minimal participation in producing such poems.

At one point, I was considering "Milton's Mother" for a title because I thought the subject should be approached historically. Milton never wrote a poem about his mother, or his grandfather, or any other relative for that matter—not even a sonnet about his daughters who worked so hard taking down in dictation much of *Paradise Lost*. Imagine a blind poet of today *not* writing anything on the subject of his dutiful, sighted daughters reverentially scribbling so many thousands of pentameters. Milton's silence on the subject is due to the heavy hand of poetic decorum, that cultural force which sets down for any given age certain guidelines governing acceptable artistic expression. Decorum is at work in every historical period, whether silently in the background or loudly in a theoretical foreground as is the case with neoclassical theory where models for literature were derived strictly from classical forms and then elevated to rules governing style and subject. Ben Jonson's advice was to imitate the bee and to feed on "the best and choicest flowers" so that all would be turned into honey—the most pungent sources of honey being Horace and Virgil. Up until the end of the eighteenth century, poetic decorum would remind an author that he must keep himself subordinate to his subject matter, which would be determined by his choice of genre. High matter for the epic, verbal coyness or plangent sincerity for the love lyric. For a poet to write of his own life—his discovery of daffodils in a field or his grandfather's tackle box in the attic—would be not only self-indulgent but of no value to an audience interested in its own edification, not in the secrets of the poet's past. W. H. Auden, perhaps feeling the touch of an older decorum, was heard to bark after attending a poetry reading: "Who the hell cares about Anne Sexton's grandmother?"

All of the above is offered as a reminder of how recently autobiographical expression came to occupy a central place in poetry. Were we to trace the history of the ego in Western literature, we would be done with our subject shortly after breakfast; for if we started with Augustine's *Confessions* (c. 400), we could traverse the next 1,365 years with hardly an egotistical bump in the road until we arrived at a work of the very same title by Rousseau, which he began writing in 1765 while staying at the home of David Hume. It was during this extensive period that Milton did not write about his mother, or Pope about his abusive father, or Dryden about his venomous, alcoholic first wife. Remember that the opening sentence of Rousseau's *Confessions* declares that the author is about to embark on an enterprise which never before has been attempted in literature and which probably will never be attempted again: that is, to disclose fully and candidly the story of the author's personal life. Too bad he couldn't have hung around for Ed McMahon's autobiography, or Meatloaf's.

It is with Wordsworth that all this changes. The autobiographical entity of the ego saunters downstage and never leaves. If Wordsworth had not created a new decorum centered on the ego, someone else would have, it is easy to say. But we have only one history, and so we can declare with some confidence that the preoccupation (I am putting it as mildly as I can) with personal experience in poetry today begins in 1798 with the publication of *Lyrical Ballads*. Affixed to this short collection of poems (not without significant contributions by Coleridge) was the now famous "Preface" in which Wordsworth presents himself as a writer of experimental (his term) poetry that is bound to leave its readers struggling "with feelings of strangeness and awkwardness." One cannot help but think of more recent kinds of experimental poetry or linguistic edgework after hearing Wordsworth predict that the readers of his poems "will look around for poetry and will be induced to inquire by what species of courtesy these attempts can be permitted to assume that title." Such expressions of humility are rare these days—rarer still from the quarters of artistic experimentation—since what was once called "humility," as Wilfred Sheed has pointed out, is now a dysfunction known as "low self-esteem." Wordsworth will cleanse poetry of falsely elevated diction (a fish will be a fish, not a member of "the finny tribe") and the poet will feel free to write about his "passions and volitions," what he feels and desires. Not to mention his family and friends. Milton's daughters are not likely to make a surprise appearance in the middle of *Lycidas*: but sure enough, toward the end of the mini-autobiography that is "Tintern Abbey," who walks in from the wings but Wordsworth's sister Dorothy—to save the day, it might be added. At this point in English poetry, Grandfather's tackle box is just visible on the horizon.

The English Romantic poets were philosophically encouraged to base poems on personal experience by John Locke's notion that each individual's consciousness is uniquely formed. Instead of coming into the world with mind and spirit already shaped, our infant cerebrum is a blank sheet of paper, a *tabula rasa*. Experience leaves its marks on the paper, and the more we experience the more the page begins to fill with the doodles of our exposure to the outside world. The implication is that no one sheet of paper contains the exact same pattern of markings. Thus is established the premise of personal uniqueness that subsequently will be examined and celebrated through acts of poetic recollection. But who needs Locke when you have Freud? Lowell, Sexton, Plath, and other poets made to huddle under the "confessional" umbrella will drop the masks of Yeats, the personae of Pound, and the impersonality recommended by Eliot to achieve a more direct, less mediated form of personal revelation, often with wiggy psychiatric effects. Under the assumed name of Prufrock, Eliot may confess his acute self-consciousness, but this hardly comes close to Lowell divulging his time on the ward holding a "locked razor" or Plath reduced to singsong by a Nazified father. But who needs Freud when you have William Blake, a supply of Benzedrine, and some good reef? On an adjoining stage, individualism was being taken to new extremes by the Beats with their revved-up typing, visionary hysteria, and pants-dropping exhibitionism.

All of which is meant to bring us to the scene today. Contemporary poetry is a house of many rooms. Never mind that the inhabitants of one room show little interest in what is going on in the adjoining ones. The house is still large enough to accommodate the stitch-work of formalists, the showmanship of performance poets, and the affirmations and grievances of minority poets. The poets working in the room of autobiography might be imagined to share a distinct set of concerns, not the least of which is how to produce a poem that is more than just a nostalgic memory dressed up in figurative language and set in lines. If you have a memory, write a memoir, the austere advice goes; and if you have lived a freaky enough life, try an autopathography. To put it more practically: if what you want to say in poetry can be said as well or better by some other means, be it a memoir, a travel piece, a diary entry, a short story, a phone call, or an e-mail, by all means stop writing poems. The key risk in writing the memory-driven poem is a failure to take advantage of the imaginative liberty that poetry offers. A poem suffering from such a disadvantage wanders around in the past and may amount to little more than a record, an entry in the log of the self's journey, a fond reminiscence, a photo in a family album, or worse, a carousel of color slides.

In *Triggering Town,* Richard Hugo suggests ways of "getting off the subject, of freeing yourself from memory." His well-known formula is that a poem has two subjects: a triggering subject that gets it going and a generated subject that the poem discovers along the way. The first subject is finally just a way of accessing the poem's true subject. The first subject is the map, the second the treasure. In a poem of recollection, the trouble often is that the memory itself can exert so strong a grip on the poet that the poem never leaves the confines of the past, never achieves the kind of escape velocity that would propel it into another, more capacious dimension. Such a poem may end up doing little more than reiterating its starting point. Examples are so abundant, it is hard to settle on any one, but let me offer in as benign a spirit as possible the following, a poem by Bonnie Minick chosen from a stack of recent journals in a manner just short of throwing a dart:

Raspberries

The raspberries used to hang dark and moist
in our neighbor's woods, if you climbed over
or under the fence you could pick them.

Reaching through the dusty sunlight and tangled brambles
made my mouth water. The day my brother and his friends chased
the neighbor's daughter in and around the trees

until she was cornered, breathless, I watched. They threw
raspberries at her, each one staining her white blouse.
It was beautiful: her cheeks shining wet, legs quivering,

the awkward way they stood around her, wanting.
Their laughter stopped, hovered above us, still. I wanted to be their
    want.
When our father found out his belts clanged and rattled on the tie rack

like bones, like the floorboards as he moved from my brother's room to
    mine.
We knew the pink rash, anger. My brother stayed quiet the rest of
    those weeks

of summer, while I moved through the darkness picking more and
    more

of those berries. Eating them alone, I let the juices drip off my chin,
I let the pink juices stain my tongue and hands. I kept eating
while the night became swollen with fireflies. I kept eating

while the night throbbed with the white pulse of stars.

OK, the poem provides us with a display of weighty themes as it
broadens from the central image of dark forbidden fruit to include suggestions of sexual awakening, guilt, paternal authority, and autoeroti-
cism. But the poem never really escapes its own past setting. The event
feels over and done with. There is no call to read the lines again. The
last-minute transcendent gesture toward the stars is not enough to save
the poem from being primarily a vehicle for the past, an expression of
ambivalent nostalgia. What is missing is a sense of the poem's own present. Even a poem based on a past event can give off a feeling of immediacy if it manages to convey an awareness that it exists in the present
tense of its own unfolding—an awareness, ultimately, of its own language. A sense of the poem's "running time" as opposed to its narrative
time can convey immediacy, even urgency. Such poems—the Romantic
lyrics are my best examples—exist in their own zones of time. They
sound fresh the way Charlie Parker and Miles Davis sound, as immediate today as they did in 1947. As readers, we may be looking into the
poem's rearview mirror where a little movie of the past is showing, but as
the poem's passengers, we are simultaneously aware that we want to be
moved forward by the thrust of language and by the steering of the
speaker's consciousness into fresh, unexpected territory.

A poem about a past experience can transcend the mere circumstances
of its triggering event through many different kinds of maneuvers. The
poem may turn down an alley into another part of the poem's town; it
may develop a disproportionate interest in some feature of itself; it may
get sick of its own reminiscence and throw up its hands. Or it may bend
time and space as is the case with "Double Exposure," a poem by Jeffrey
Harrison, also chosen as randomly as possible. It opens thus:

> My great grandfather's photo albums
> from his trip around the world in 1905,
> their suede covers printed with his name
> in gold capitals, and their brittle pages
> torn loose and out of order, show him
> in the Philippines with William Howard Taft . . .

The tone of sentimental mustiness is not promising and echoes other poems in which a speaker broods over family memorabilia. But a stanza later, the poet spots a photograph of Varanasi (formerly Benares), a city he himself has visited, and the poem begins to move, first as the speaker is joined with the great-grandfather

> . . . and all at once I'm looking
> with his eyes through the viewfinder
> of his camera with the black bellows extended.

The photograph—now animated into a moving picture—is of a "body in flames / crumpling as the pyre underneath it / collapses," a scene that burns its way into the body of the speaker/great-grandfather who is now summoned into the present tense:

> [he] gets up and leaves me on the stone steps
> in the exact spot he rose from, while he
> wanders off along the ghats, ghostlike,
> in the shadows of temples piled like stalagmites,
> to join the multitude of spectral figures
> who have traveled here for centuries,
> disappearing behind a hazy veil
> of smoke rising from the funeral pyres
> and the emulsion's silver sheen.

The final effect of the man disappearing into history after his moment of reanimation is achieved by Harrison's taking advantage of the poetic plasticity of time and space. Instead of getting stuck in an historical backwater, the poem moves into more expansive territory through a set of smooth imaginative manipulations. Up, up, and away.

Another matter that might concern poets working in the room of recollection has to do with fidelity to the past, with things as they really

happened. That memory is a creative act can be proven by simply scruti-
nizing a few of our favorite stories about ourselves and then admitting
how slight the connection is between them and actual past events. We
are, after all, the sum total of our own stories, our reiterated fictions, our
auto-discourse, if you like. In poetry, the imagination is not just free to
add the light that never was, it is *expected* to carry the poem beyond the
precincts of ordinary veracity.

Of course, current wisdom tells us that a poem must be true to itself,
not to the facts. In writing a poem, one is pursuing an aesthetic truth
(which may be a total lie), not a journalistic or historic truth. Binjamin
Wilkomirski's Holocaust fantasies, which he outrageously passed off as
an actual memoir (*Fragments,* 1995), remind us that there are cases where
it might be well to respect the line between truth and invention. But we
are within our rights as readers to expect memory to act in poetry as more
than an agency of reminiscence. Memory is often well employed as a
starting place for a poem, a springboard into zones more exhilarating
than the strictly personal, zones where language, not history, is king. In
poetry, recollection mixes so easily with invention that many of the maneuvers we have come to associate with modernist poetry (the un-
expected "turn" or "volta," for example) are really devices designed to
escape the narrow confines of memory, to fly over history on the wings
of the imagination. Borges put it this way: "When I write, I try to be
loyal to the dream and not to the circumstances [which] should always
be told with a certain amount of untruth. There is no satisfaction in
telling a story as it actually happened. We have to change things, even if
we think them insignificant; if we don't, then we should think of ourselves not as artists but perhaps as mere journalists and historians."

At the time of its appearance, Wordsworth's "epic autobiography,"
The Prelude, was by far the most ambitious poetic excavation of a personal past ever attempted, the verse equivalent to Rousseau's *Confessions.*
Throughout the long poem, Wordsworth is acutely attentive to the op-
erations of memory. In fact, to a reader of today, the most intriguing
parts of *The Prelude* deal not so much with the headlong narrative of
Wordsworth's life as with his self-consciousness about attempting such a
feat of poetic recollection. On the island of memory, he is as alone as

Robinson Crusoe. At many points in the poem, we see Wordsworth stopping to wonder what he is doing and how he is doing it. In one of these pauses, the complexity of the process of memory is admirably expressed through the extended image of a man bending over the side of a "slow-moving boat upon the breast / Of a still water." The autobiographical man can see under the clear water "weeds, fishes, flowers / Grots, pebbles, roots of trees and fancies more," but he has difficulty distinguishing these things from the surface reflections he also sees, not just of the mountains, sun, and clouds above him, but of his own face, a "gleam / Of his own image," superimposed on the watery tableau. It is impossible to view the past, the image suggests, without also seeing the present and in it the mirror image of the self. The observer is an ingredient in the observed. This triple vision so well reveals the complicated nature of a poetry based on memory that it might act as a signpost, a warning for poets who assume that the past is easily accessible and that their play in the country-garden day school of nostalgia is a sufficient form of poetic activity.

The poetry of memory walks a vibrating line between the demands of history and the impulses of the imagination. In these postmodern times, when such fundamental terms as "author," "reader," and "text" are considered unreliable and problematic, surely there is room for poetic falsification. Fernando Pessoa's multiple "heteronyms" may be precedents for other kinds of autobiographical splittings. If poetry is a combination of fire and algebra (Borges), why shouldn't the fire burn the past? Yet when we turn (reluctantly) from theory to practice, we find that readers of contemporary poetry still make deep emotional investments in the poets (not the "speakers") whom they love to read. Despite our care in discriminating between the voice on the page and the biographical poet, despite our ability to distinguish linear memory from spatial memory, and willed memory from *mémoire involontaire,* we retain a felt, post-Romantic attachment to the author as a reliable self-expressive source—an equivalent to the human voice we hear arising from print. We may say one thing in discussion but feel something different when we are alone with the page.

In that light, let me close with an illustration of the reader's need to believe in the reliability and veracity of the person who wrote the poem. In a poetry workshop I oversaw this year, a loose discussion of memory and poetry arrived at a sound but familiar conclusion: poetry is not bound by the ties of historical truth; it must be true only to its own aesthetic integrity. As long as the poem is a good poem, what's the difference if it is true to fact or not? And, yes, the lowest defense for a poem is that it actually happened. Lots of nodding around the table. But then I asked the group how they would feel if I told them that Sharon Olds's father was not really dead. True, she did devote an entire collection *(The Father)* to her father's dying and death. True, the book is a startling series of poems that pushes the elegy into new psychic territory. But in fact, her father is living in Phoenix where he plays golf three or four times a week with his buddies. Mr. Olds, I happened to know, was a 17 handicap. Even though I presented this as pure hypothesis, I could feel a sudden drop in the room temperature, a barometric shift. The students were more than a little stunned even to have to consider such a possibility. My inner elf urged me to continue. What if I told you—I told them—that Philip Levine, so widely and justifiably celebrated for addressing working-class life in poetry—was not raised in Detroit at all but in Beverly Hills, the son of a wealthy orthodontist no less—make that the orthodontist to the stars! The students begged me to stop. Even on this level of fancy, they felt a sense of betrayal. They had agreed that Olds's and Levine's poems would be just as powerful if invention were their only mother, but they were now forced to admit that they also wanted the poems to be true in some reliable and ingenuous sense. When all the chips were pushed into the center of the table, they didn't want to hear about "the speaker" or "textual distance." They wanted to believe in a real Sharon, a real Phil—a human source.

Our relationship with literature has long been a mix of the clinical and the passionate. We tend to go public with the clinical while keeping our passionate attachments to ourselves; thus, the double life of the reader. We may say that we value "aesthetic distance" while what we really cherish is the opposite—what William Matthews called "aesthetic intimacy." It is a paradox that slides easily into the foreground of any discussion of autobiographical writing. We are not talking here of poets whom we know from reading one poem or a half a dozen poems, but about poets with whom we have formed long-standing alliances. The more we read of any one poet, the more clearly a human shape begins to emerge which we come to recognize as the human Berryman, the human Bishop. Eventually we develop—sometimes against our wishes—a kind of interior soap opera, or call it a wax museum of poets—figural images we can visit and even commune with. The writer may be "best on the page," as the wife of Ruskin said of him, but the reader cannot help taking as claims to truth and as acts of good faith the words that make up a favored body of work.

Who else can take the blame for this head/heart paradox except the young nineteenth-century Romantics? They demanded that poetry allow into its inner courtyard something close to the sense of the self that we walk around with every day of our lives. We may not need to believe in an actual, living-and-breathing John Milton; *Paradise Lost* can get along fine without him. But don't try to take away our frail, tubercular John Keats. The Odes, we might say at the seminar table, stand by themselves as aesthetic monuments: we might even go on to call them self-consuming artifacts or frozen discourse. But all the terminology in the world cannot diminish our enchantment with the white handkerchief, the sudden flecks of blood.

II

Our Better Halves:
Autobiographical Musings

David Graham

Voluminous Underwear;
or, Why I Write Self-Portraits

I am somewhat surprised to realize that I have been writing self-portrait poems, with varying degrees of obsession, for about twenty years. Easy enough, I suppose, to resort to Thoreau's quip on the first page of *Walden*: "Unfortunately, I am confined to this theme by the narrowness of my experience." Even more to the point, however, may be his astringent remark on that same page regarding his liberal use of the pronoun "I," which in the context of early nineteenth-century literary proprieties, required at least a *pro forma* apology:

> In most books the *I*, or first person, is omitted; in this it will be retained; that, in respect to egotism, is the main difference. We commonly do not remember that it is, after all, always the first person speaking.

A great deal of misguided discussion of confessional poetry could begin to be cleared up, I feel, by attending closely to the truth, even the truism, of what Thoreau is saying here. For personas, third person, and various dramatic devices are no warrant against egotism and self-enclosure; nor is the first person invariably a limiting or solipsistic option. As I will suggest, also, I tend to think of "the self" as something akin to a persona.

Of course, Thoreau immediately proceeds to muddy the waters when he calls for a writer to offer "a simple and sincere account of his own life," as if such a thing were possible. The romantic extravagance of this call to sincerity certainly dates the passage nicely, grounding it in a typically American strain of Romanticism. Yet before we condescend to Thoreau and other idealistic writers of his era, we should attend to the complexities, even the contradictions present in their works. Certainly I would be reluctant to apply either adjective—*simple* or *sincere*—unreservedly to Thoreau's book. Its simplicity is belied by numerous kinds of stylization and literary artifice, including the usual omissions and shadings common to every memoir; its sincerity is questioned on nearly every page by Thoreau's habitual irony, hyperbole, and wordplay. But we don't have to go so far to undercut this famous call to simple sincerity. Let me complete the sentence I quoted selectively from a moment ago, and take it to its ironic conclusion:

> Moreover, I, on my side, require of every writer, first or last, a simple and sincere account of his own life, and not merely what he has heard of other men's lives; some such account as he would send to his kindred from a distant land; for if he has lived sincerely, it must have been in a distant land to me.

My own reading of this famous jab is that it does more than suggest that sincerity is a rare commodity, or that Thoreau himself lives among particular hypocrites. It implies a huge and inevitable gap between what we ask of a writer and what any given writer can accomplish. (I would not exempt Thoreau himself from this generalization, and doubt if he would have claimed absolute sincerity for himself, either, though there are certainly passages in *Walden* that could be taken to do so.)

At root in all the controversies that swirl perennially about the lyric "I" and its particular embodiment in so-called confessional verse is this inevitable gap between what we as readers typically want—including honesty, truth, and reality—and what a poem can provide, which is at best some stylized version of such things. It is not merely the unsophisticated common reader who fudges or forgets the difference between map and territory, either; witness the many reviews of Ted Hughes's *Birthday Letters* that concentrated not on assessing the poems but on reviewing the life, frequently bestowing great moral approval or disapproval upon its author for matters that, strictly speaking, lay entirely outside the book proper.

Like most poets, I suppose, I began writing with a certain innocence, attempting to capture the uncapturable flux of experience, often enough taking as subject my own paltry experience and rendering it melodramatically. To this extent, I guess that many of us begin in a raw confessional vein. Long before I had read Robert Herrick, or even Anne Sexton, Top 40 radio had provided me with a fairly clear understanding of the lyric mission—and not an entirely naïve sense of things, either, for from the start, I instinctively grasped the fictive nature of the enterprise. I knew quite well that the tuneful lovesick groans of the pop singer stood for a certain emotion; they didn't mean that the singer was actually weeping in the recording studio.

Some two decades ago, having outgrown, or so I hoped, my adolescent self-absorptions, I conceived of a poetic experiment, an open-ended series of self-portraits. As far as I can sort out my motives at this remove, I think my impulses were not very confessional. In fact, they were rather aggressively the reverse. My immediate inspiration was not my own life, but a book that collected Rembrandt's lifelong series of self-portraits, which struck me as a fascinating project. During his working life, Rembrandt painted, etched, or drew his own likeness as main subject nearly one hundred times. We can watch his image pass through a rich variety of moods and postures. He takes palpable pleasure in trying on an array of often sumptuous costumes, including swords, gold chains, velvet gloves, furred capes, and an amazing collection of hats. He scowls, preens, laughs, holds up a dead pheasant, and lifts a beer in toast. And while some of the later paintings in particular are haunting in their portraiture, fearless in documenting the effects of age on the artist's body, quite a few would have to be called frivolous. Paging through the book, my first impression was that this was an elaborate game of dress-up.

For which is the essential Rembrandt? Is it the deep-eyed old burgher calmly looking at us from some of the late paintings, or is it the impish young man practicing facial expressions like a boy at the mirror—joy, surprise, anger, and so on—in a series of tiny etchings? How do we reconcile the severity, even the spirituality of the 1659 portrait in the National Gallery in Washington, D.C., with the foppish figure in The Hague's 1634 painting, with his glittering ear ring, feather-plumed silk hat, and not quite convincing expression of courtly charm?

I hope it is obvious that we reconcile such moods and attitudes according to Whitman's timeless brag—for Rembrandt, too, is large, and contains multitudes, including a capacious taste in hats. So do we all. I was attracted both to the experimental nature of Rembrandt's project—its variety of style, stance, and medium—and also to its open-endedness. So I embarked on my own poetic version, aiming to try on as many metaphoric hats as possible, and with no plans to cease until the poetry itself does. If, along the way, I successfully document elements of my own changing body and soul, that certainly will be a personal inducement, if not sufficient reason for persisting. If one motive remains inescapable self-regard—and if in a sense I remain a boy in front of his mirror trying on different expressions—the technical challenge of theme-and-variations has from the start engaged me just as deeply. My subject has been readily at hand, just as Thoreau suggests. What better way to focus on elements of poetic craft than holding up the mirror repeatedly to one's most familiar realities? In a very real sense, I see my self-portraits as among the least revealing poems I have done, not simply because they are all as posed and static as a wedding photo, but also because my goal in writing them has been to explore aesthetic more than personal issues.

Well, of course no one believes this. And I confess I only half-believe it myself. No one believed it when John Berryman claimed not to be Henry, either, but I did; or, at least, I half-believed it. It is that very ambiguity that has often felt like the animating spark of my self-portraits, in which I conceal by selectively revealing, and vice versa. Few would care to sort out these paradoxes even if they could, and it's true that the details of my actual or poetic lives are seldom rich with the sensational. If any of my self-portraits have succeeded as poems, I believe it must be because they have managed the dramatic sleight of hand that has always been at the heart of the lyric, which engages the personal and the local in order to illuminate and animate something larger. My poems are little dramas, stylized and shaped as best I can; they are also full of intimate explorations. In them, I literally confess that I am no confessional poet. Good luck sorting out the tensions here; I can barely do so myself.

Here is one of my earliest self-portraits that was conceived as such.

American Gothic

I was christened from a telephone directory,
because my parents wanted a name no one had,
at least in this family. My first word was "bug."
Left in my playpen to drool and chatter
I posed stuffed animals for imaginary photos.
Soon I was singing songs invented
according to traffic signs. I loved
"yield," "go stop slow," and "squeeze left,"
all of which were possible in the back seat.
Down by the railroad tracks I churned hot gravel
fist to fist, awaiting the five-car freight.
In stores downtown I said "Charge it"
and my father's name. My school grades
were printed in the daily newspaper.

Mom kept her old address book a secret,
hidden under her voluminous underwear
in a dark oak dresser. Of course I peeked,
I was meant to, but I do not think
I was supposed to fall in love
with the brown-gray photos of that college girl,
strange as late night movies. I was young
but her truth was younger. And Dad
kept his secrets some place I never found,
though it's possible I didn't look hard,
as I turned away my eyes each time
he rose dripping from the bathtub.

And if I memorized sex manuals,
and if I caressed pillows and
practiced kissing mirrors, I can't remember.
What I remember are the dogs,
Eager, Loyal, and Foolish—teaching them
to worship the hoops they leaped through.

When I look at this poem now, twenty years after composing it, I recognize some details lifted directly from my own life, some recomposed from family stories, some made up from whole cloth, and some I'm not entirely sure about. No one but me and perhaps my immediate family will recognize one of my nieces masquerading as me in this poem, and me masquerading as a beloved family friend in an episode from his own childhood. As near as I can recall, the poem's gentle spoofing of Freudian readings of childhood was grafted onto some memories of my own that were perhaps too precious for me to deal with in anything but an ironic stance. And as the title's echo of Grant Wood's deeply strange painting was meant to indicate, the whole performance is conscious of itself as performance, even as it hoped to create something iconic out of the raw materials of my own small-town childhood.

Naturally, this was the poem that my college magazine chose to represent my book *Magic Shows* when it appeared; and unfortunately they reprinted it under the headline "Oedipus at Home." This occasioned a mock-angry phone call from my mother, after she had endured some fierce ribbing from family and friends, some of which was no doubt occasioned by the magazine's focus on the Oedipal aspect, but much of which was fastened on my sonorous adjective in the phrase "voluminous underwear." Of course, I chose the word for its sound as much as for its meaning, but this was no defense, nor should it be. My attempt to justify it in terms of point of view fared little better. Much as I protested that I was simply dramatizing a boy's sense that *everything* about his parents, including Mom's underwear, is of mythic size, I was only half-convincing. My airing of this particular dirty laundry was and was not forgiven, as it was and was not serious in the first place, as my mother was and was not mad at me. I do not claim that this is a great poem, a complex one, or even one of my best, but it strikes me as a fitting case study about the difficulties of sorting out the strands of reality and sincerity in what is called confessional.

Similar mixtures of fact and fiction occur in most of my self-portraits, naturally. Looking over the poems now, I note that the degree to which they are even *about* my life varies considerably. In "Self-Portrait with Stage Fright," for instance, I reveal almost nothing of my intimate life, and the poem relates only tangentially to my actual experience.

Self-Portrait with Stage Fright

This isn't my real personality
standing up half casually
to talk about myself. Usually
I'm sparrow-skittery,
shy as water through
my own fingers—
just ask my mother,
if you can find her; that's her
hunched in the back row
or two steps from the door.

Usually dew glazes my lip
when everyone's looking,
sleet thrums my stomach,
a regular hailstorm
in my knees.

What can I give you
but dark inklings
you already know
or a twinge or two
out of history? What is
my stammering hello
but code for farewell?

Wouldn't you rather watch
buzzards circle their roosting tree?
Without past, without regard
they swirl as black snowflakes
in one of those bubble villages
that live on coffee tables.

Shake them and they perform.
Shake me and I'm gone.

Like every teacher, poetry reader, or other public performer, I occasionally experience nervous feelings when I stand in front of an audience,
but in truth, I have never suffered from true stage fright; for if the term
means anything, it must refer to something extraordinary, a nearly paralyzing resistance to performance. In any documentary sense, then, this

self-portrait is a blatant fib. This is true even though there are, as usual, some details drawn from my life. My shy mother, for example, often does prefer to sit near the exit at a concert or lecture, in case she is overwhelmed by the desire to flee. She rarely is, but that is probably because she is sitting comfortably near an exit. In any case, at the time I wrote this poem, she had never heard me give a poetry reading.

I made up a case of stage fright, I suppose, in part because it seemed a convenient metaphor for the strangeness of self-portraiture, the complicated dance of revelation and concealment involved in writing in an autobiographical vein, and then, of course, presenting such a dance in public. I don't experience stage fright, exactly, but I do feel the absurdity and self-promotion inherent in the practice of the poetry reading, along with the usual self-doubt about the quality of both work and performance.

When I have read this poem publicly—and I also wrote it, in part, precisely to read aloud to audiences—listeners have tended to assume that it is a piece of confession, or at least that I *used* to suffer from stage fright. I allow them to think so, even though it seems to me that the poem tries to ironize the pose of sincerity so common at poetry readings, as the poet with genial and often self-deprecating humor presents what we are meant to understand as lyrical profundities. It seems to me that the confessional impulse itself is an odd blend of vulnerability and brazenness. This poem conducts its ironic commentary in the form of that most comfortable ritual of the contemporary poetry reading: the between-poems banter in which the poet attempts to charm the audience and deflect any impression of undue egotism or self-absorption that the poems themselves may justifiably have created.

And finally, a recent poem that began in the self-mocking vein of "American Gothic" with some writerly whining, but arrived, much to my surprise, at a wholly different tone:

Self-Portrait as Runner Up

I've never been a shoe-in. I'm always flappable,
and when I make a joke it's like fumbling
for change. My motto is Yes, But.
I'm everyone's third choice, and rightly so,

because I couldn't blaze a trail
in butter. Most of my twenties
I spent paging through catalogs,
my thirties struggling with a stuck zipper.

Now, in my cruise-control forties,
I seem to watch the weather channel
in my sleep. I've never gone
without saying. Believe me, I need
plenty of introduction. When the comet
everyone's mad about appears
in the northern sky, I see lint,
a dim and vaguely luminous idea,
celestial smudge on my glasses.

Still, more and more mornings I wake
and let the cracks and cobwebs
on the ceiling swim for a moment
in my blurred, dread-stirred eyes.
Then rise with a relish past fame
to tend a fire as common as it seems rare.

In this case, my sincerity was accidental. I simply intended to write
a jokey poem about being so frequently an also-ran, an honorable mention, or a semi-finalist—an experience I find that most contemporary
poets are apt to jest self-consciously about. And yes, it did occur to me
that this might also be a fun poem to present at poetry readings. But in
the process of writing, improvising on my theme, I more or less blurted
out the final stanza, thus ruining the joke and veering away from any sort
of a punch line. It didn't take me long to recognize that I had inadver-
tently veered into honesty, though it was an honesty that probably could
not have emerged from intention. I let it stand. Although the poem originated from a desire to charm, I find that whether it is touching, funny, or
even successful to anyone else doesn't matter much to me now. Of
course, no one will believe this. Nevertheless, the poem does seem like a
gift to me. I imagine that Rembrandt, too, in the process of trying on all
those silly hats, might have occasionally had a similar experience.

Stanley Plumly

Autobiography and Archetype

I.

When Wallace Stevens writes that you must become an ignorant man again, and see the sun again with an ignorant eye, and see it clearly in the idea of it, he is focusing one of the things basic to an archetype, which is its original sense of itself, its almost primordial apriori sense of itself, while suggesting, at the same time, another basic thing, which is an archetype's dependence on recurrence, reenactment, return. Seeing the new in the old, the old in the new; seeing that, at once, the archetype is original and familiar, ancient and present, eternal and mortal; recognizing that its ghost cannot be summoned except in a living, particular moment—for the writer, the soul of that moment is the common life we call autobiography, since our identities depend so much on that with which we identify and that which identifies with us.

Yet just as there are no straight lines nor corners in nature, there can be no easy lineation between the archetype and the named experience. If there is too direct a connection, the archetype usually degenerates into allegory. When I say a bird flies between the cover of the woodland understory and the exposure of the open field, I'm aware, at some point, that a bird is also a symbol, more often than not a symbol, through its song, of longing, or through its flight, of life's brevity, as brief as a sparrow darting the length of a mead hall. When I say that a tree is a green complexity of time and change, mystery and clarity, I know that trees, by their silent natures and sentinel presences, are the nobility; and that the fountain branching of the elms that once lined both sides of the street, meeting in the middle, describes a vaulted, cathedral ceiling. When I evoke one of my parents, say my father, I want the experience in the poem to be fair to memory and larger than life, since *father* is a word as well as specific flesh.

Archetypes, in the abstract, have a genius for generalization. But to be of any use they must be arrived at inductively. Autobiography, as remembered experience, is inductive; in fact, it is the first definition of inductive. Nevertheless, we may have had the experience, says T. S. Eliot, but missed the meaning, as if meaning were inherent in, concomitant with the experience. Seeing, or remembering, is a way to get the meaning, the idea as well as the image, just as experience itself repeats and returns, becomes general, common. Archetype is the machinery through which autobiography achieves something larger than the single life; and autobiography is the means by which archetypes are renewed.

Who am I, we sometimes ask ourselves, *to have a life?* We call it a gift, I suppose, because we didn't ask for it. But because it is a gift, it has a price. *Who am I?* "Death is the mother of beauty" is a matrix of archetypes— three very big ideas linked in a logic that makes a single powerful idea, an idea that requires us to see in the old, something new; and out of new connections, a first idea. *Who am I?* is an old archetypal question, to which the answer is—regardless of who I think I am—my autobiography. Or would my biography as written by someone else better answer the question? Self-biography draws on resources that require us to see the archetypal within the actual, the eternal within the mortal, the parental within the beautiful. And to that extent, archetypes are autobiographies of the imagination.

I once wrote, in "My Mother's Feet," that "Someone who loved her | said she walked on water." The poem is both an appreciation and a panegyric, an elegy to vulnerability. However ancient and mystical walking on water is, when I heard the comment in conversation as a boy, I knew that the expression was familiar and the idea rather wonderful but understood that it could also be either praise or put-down. For my mother, from the tone of what was said, I realized it must be praise, praise that, as an adult, I treat with a certain affection and irony, since my mother's feet were working feet, like a bricklayer's hands. Feet here become the synecdoche of an archetype, just as the action of the feet, in the auditory imagination, becomes the verbal act itself, which is central to the archetype as well—the literal metrical feet of the way the line walks the line and the way the caesura ("Someone who loved her | said she walked on water") marries the act to the internal rhyme. Words linked to words enact the oldest archetypes; they darken the breath with original knowledge.

II.

Stevens further writes that the first idea is an imagined thing—not so much made up as made visible. Insomnia has been an image in my poems from the beginning, an image of the terminal kind, the kind that causes you to wake up far earlier than you should, the kind that becomes like a dawn patrol. If sleep is *terra intermedia* (Jung), then terminal insomnia is an abrupt edge. It is one of those fundamental conditions that lends itself to transformation, and that echoes a first idea. Lazarus, the ultimate insomniac, is a manifestation of the myth of resurrection, just as resurrection is the sun rising. Sleep, of course, is always death; less threatening to some than to others.

Lazarus at Dawn

Your whole life you are two with one taken
away. The inadequate air and fire,
the inadequate joy, the darknesses
of the room so gathered at the window
as to fly, wing on wing on wing open
against the glass, opening and closing,
bone, blood and wrist. But nothing happens but
exhaustion and evidence of the eyes,
the red-gold cloud-break morning beginning

with the objects that floated in the dark
draining back to the source, floating back to
the surface tension of things, those objects
struck the way the first light starts suddenly,
then slowly in relief across the room,
the window's shadow garden come back one
last time once more from the leaves. Waking now,
the door half-open, open, the doorway's
blindness or blackness silence to be filled.

A man was sick, a sickness unto death.
All he wanted to do was to lie down,

let the light pick him apart like the dust.
He wrapped himself, in his mind, in his own
absence. He did not want to hear the rain,
with its meaning nor the moment after
rain, nor the sound of Jesus weeping, nor
the dreaming, which is memory, though he
lay a long time cold, head against the stone.

You see the wind passing from tree to tree,
thousands of green individual leaves
silver and fluid at the surfaces,
the long nothing narrative of the wind.
The wind is the emptiness and fullness
in one breath, and the holding of that breath,
restlessness and stillness of the spirit.
You see your dead face in the gray glass close,
and see that it is already too late,

that death's blood nakedness clothed white is smoke,
the father standing in the doorway white,
whom you see in part, the way the morning
gathering is part in the slow degrees
of rectitude, a kind of twilight dawn.
Nothing is said, though he knows you love him.
Nothing is said, though you know he loves you.
Longing, as a sickness of the heart, is
invisible, incurable, endless.

I wrote this poem after a series of stark early mornings. I'd wake up at three, sometimes before, sometimes after, and if I was really tired, closer to four. At those hours you drift in time—do I wake or sleep?—your eyes closed within a visible stone-gray space, often cold, sunlight still so distant, so under the lip of things, that whatever light exists seems refracted, leftover from the day before. This particular time it was probably March, slow spring, sunrise earlier and earlier. I had large windows, with myrtle trees backed up by large hardwoods, in layers of shadow that, with the dawn, advanced to bring the outside in, but at invisible speed. After a while my eyes would open, adjust, and begin to pick apart parts that were being revealed—edges, angles, and known detail, shapes that I knew by heart, yet were now distorted. And in the long hour before the sun would actually break, the room would change, and change again, a different space entirely.

One thing: across the one-room apartment from my bed there was a doorway leading into a deep walk-in closet. The closet door seemed, always, to have its own notion of opening and closing, and in dawnlight, halfway between open and shut, disappeared into the dark, a dark which, when you looked at it long enough or caught it, surprised, at an angle, resembled the rectilinear height and width of a grave, as vertical as a man standing. Among all the grays and emerging bric-a-brac color of the room, the doorway stayed solid; solid black. Lying there, inside time, you had to ask yourself—or it felt like the question had been asked for you—whether this was void or an emptiness filled.

The idea of the figure in the doorway came to me *after* the stanza in which I project the figure of the sleepless Lazarus, who wants only to lie down. The figure in the doorway had to be a father, my father. For the living, sleep may be a little death, but for the dead, as I imagine it, there is no sleep. Perhaps dreaming, then, is not so much a death wish as a life wish, a desire to return, since the dream is a memory of life, its richness, confusion, strangeness, randomness. Lazarus wants to sleep in order to rest. Inevitably, he dreams his resurrection, his coming back to terms, his reconciliation with the father, who, for me, becomes the life principle, no less confused and contradictory, but passionate, even violent; while the mother is inconsistent, withdrawn, even aloof, manic-depressed, calling from death.

III.

Muse figures are complicated, and a great part of their complexity is that they tend to choose us rather than the other way around. They are involuntary sources of the work they tell us must be done. Jung characterizes three foundation archetypes: the shadow, the anima, and the animus. He says that they each have equal numinous power, perhaps combining powers: antagonistic dark shapes delineated by light, as if one were seeing one's own shadow, whose source of illumination is just off periphery.

My father has been, in differing degrees and intensities of magnitude, such a muse—a shadow stained darker in his combination of anima and animus. If Nature is the guarantor of our imaginations, our parents, and those who sometimes take their places, are the collaborators of our emotions. The muse here is an animating principle, an inspiritor, and a conspirator of content. The drunken god in my father, the vulnerable, wounded animal in his heart, the passionate, generous, violent dimensions of his mind are all aspects of his divided personality. On the other hand, my mother, the familiar, is like the form in my poems—half-measured, precariously balanced, quietly obsessive. She is the selector and separator, the organizer of space, the civilian, the compromiser, but fragile, and—depending on the poem's content—threatening to fall apart.

My father was like a thief in the night, a housebreaker, intruder, trespasser. He worked long hours, factory hours, and more often than not spent the evening at Bing's or another beer hall, as my mother called them, and then, in a state somewhere between stump drunk and depressed sober, drove home. He was like the horse who knows the way, rain or shine. Almost every night, in fact, he was out in the world, in bar-life. He could not make a quiet entrance, and sometimes he would be suddenly hungry, hence kitchen noises and the usual muffled, corrosive arguments with my mother. Occasionally, though, if it were really late, say 2:00 to 4:00 A.M., he would enter the house with stealth in order to keep his secret. I never failed, regardless of the hour, to hear him. Some nights, clearly, he needed to be heard, and the fight that followed was his way of rejoining the group. Some nights he needed to remain the alien, the outsider. Either way, he was the reverse of the rule of childhood: the one heard rather than seen.

The next morning, whatever the hour of his nightly arrival, he would be up at dawn and on his way back to the gray grind and cycle of the day. He was a foreman, which meant that he could be late to work if needs be, so long as he didn't push his luck. And in many ways, except for the burden of his family, my father was a lucky man. People were drawn to him, which was surely one of the reasons he loved bar-life so much: the family of his buddies. Alcohol was the oil of affection. But he

was popular at work as well, among the sober business of great machines, tool-and-die, molten steel, cast iron, welding, assembling. He
had the humor and innocence of a man who understands men, and he
never lied, except to my mother. He had fierce physical strength, the
kind other men look up to. As a boy I spent Saturdays at his elbow at
Bing's. As an adolescent I worked summers at the same factory, like a
distant relative, someone who must prove himself. On weekends, from
my childhood until the year I left home, we both worked the garden and
the few animals on our small farm at the margin of the town. Work was
my father's salvation—work for the sake of work as a transcendent virtue: a purifier, rectifier, and, finally, an apology. For my father, work
made up for all the other failure in his life, almost. The Depression and
World War II probably had something to do with my father's (and my
mother's) emotional attitudes and limitations, just as *his* father had
proved to be an overbearing antagonist. Events and parents teach us how
large fate is and how small we are. Life taught my mother fatalism, but it
taught my father luck. Drinking was his way to live in luck.

By the 1950s, my parents, like most adults of the time, had adopted
the protective coloration of Cold War repression, a posture that lent
itself to latent, implied, or otherwise accepted domestic violence. My father's various frustrations often exploded, especially when the demon was
encouraged. Drinking was the prime encourager, but so was my mother,
and, by extension, so was I. The bully in my father would take over, and
the best you could do to deal with it was to bully back or else melt into
the wall. This terrible dance takes its toll. By the time I left home, I never
looked back. Somewhere in my twenties, however, I began to identify,
even empathize, with my father. Somewhere around the time I turned
twenty-three and realized that I had been born when *he* was twenty-
three, a fact of life that would have sunk me. That was the moment I
began to wear my father's body.

IV.

I was out of the country, and out of touch, when he died. I missed the funeral, in fact, missed his death altogether until I stepped off the return

plane and was greeted with the news. The muse is ultimately a figure from the dead, which is why lyric poetry, whatever its announced subject, is so elegiac. Love, fear, anger, longing, any number of sources of joy or pain may drive the fever, the cool fever, of the poem, but the result, the overtone, will always return—if sometimes in the silences—if sometimes only in the language—to reconciliation with loss. The narrative of the lyric bends to shape some part, or all, of a circle. In Ohio, when a funeral is successful, they say you could have sold tickets. From what I'm told, you could have sold tickets to my father's funeral. Even those of us who might have hated him, also worshipped him, as my mother, once he was gone, was fond of saying. Something about him did compel attention; you felt more alive in his presence. Which is why, as a boy, I loved his company so much. His rough affection was larger than life, certainly, and powerfully larger than I when he would pick me up and carry me under his arm like a carpet. I remember Nellie Otte, my high-school English teacher, asking me about him—many times—asking me to say hello. Your voice, she would say, is just like your father's. She loved me too, I think.

Thus, archetypes are never abstractions, whatever general ghost forms they fill. They are our feeling sources, and in the lineup behind the figures in our dreams they loom, like parents, at the end of the line. Perhaps only one parent at a time can dominate our inner lives, while the other becomes the one we suffer for, as if we were doomed to perpetuate their marriage within our own hearts. In our time, we have turned these classic parental sources and struggles into an industry of illness, like a sickness to be solved. But who would medicate the muse? My father and I have colluded to create my limitations; as he is my resource, I am his representative. I don't see myself as having written father poems or not-father poems, tree poems or bird poems, country poems or city poems, love poems or elegies. The heart in my poems belongs as much to the muse as to me—double-hearted, as it were, or one's heart of hearts. When I hated my father, I was dead; when I learned to love him, I came to life—I wish it were that simple. I know that when he died I was free to love him again.

You cannot write alone, no more than you can be alone inside your poems. The muse is not only, in contemporary vernacular, an inspirator, but a facilitator. As the acknowledged or unacknowledged antagonist—that is, the opposition that creates the energy and story of the poem—the muse is both the need and means. It provides the imagination with context, and, when all is said and done, the text itself. The treeness of our trees, the birdness of our birds, the pity of our forgiveness, the beauty of our longing—our paralysis, our prevarications, our palaver—all may saturate the colors and textures of our poems, but they are masks over the singular face of the archetype. The famous loneliness of the writer, like the long-distance runner, is just part of the reason we invite the muse; when it is good, when writing is like breathing, the muse has invited us. That moment near the beginning of Keats's last poem, *The Fall of Hyperion,* when he is struggling to identify "What Image this, whose face I cannot see," is a moment "That made my heart too small to hold its blood." It is a recognition scene. The goddess he is looking at may be Moneta, but the face is his dead mother's, the muse unmasked.

> Then saw I a wan face,
> Not pined by human sorrows, but bright-blanched
> By an immortal sickness which kills not;
> It works a constant change, which happy death
> Can put no end to; deathwards progressing
> To no death was that visage; it had passed
> The lily and the snow. . .

And that moment in Delmore Schwartz's seminal short story, "In Dreams Begin Responsibilities," when the narrator is sitting in a darkened movie theater, rerunning, on the movie screen in his mind, the film of his parents meeting on a boardwalk by the romantic sea—that moment when he stands up in the empty theater and shouts at the screen not to do it, not to meet, not to fall in love. . . .

The film of my parents' meeting shows my father driving across Ohio in his new, yellow, Ford convertible coupe, 260 miles between Barnesville and Piqua. He is twenty-one, the car is a birthday present, and he is about his father's business. It is 1937 and the far side of the Depression. All-in-all, farming and lumbering have been less affected than urban economies, so my father's car is more a gift of generosity than a glare of ostentation. My mother's mother is a single parent raising two daughters, of which my mother, at eighteen, is the younger. They run a boarding house, where, fate will have it, my father will stay. He is supposed to be marrying, within the year, someone else. Instead he meets my mother, who, without ever having driven anything on wheels larger than her grandfather's bicycle, wants to try the yellow convertible. She is a Depression child down to her soles, and this car looks like a chariot. My father comes from Welsh Quaker rectitude, my mother from soft Methodist fires. They will, in the years ahead, together and singly, wreck many cars and walk away as if they had never been there. This time, of course, is my mother's first, and most meaningful, wreck. She is barely down the road one hundred yards before she runs dead into a tree, from which she will forever wear, under her right eye, a small, barely visible scar.

Colette Inez

Family Talk: Confessional Poet? Not Me

Of course, there have been countless dissertations about the family with a capital "F" written by sociologists on their way to Ph.D.s. While it's been an American tradition to idealize family life—I think of Norman Rockwell's *Saturday Evening Post* covers and his classic *Four Freedoms* as symbols of that—its reality has certainly fallen on hard times.

The changing matrix of our complex society has a good deal to do with it, as well as the lifestyles of numerous subcultures and changing gender roles. Nowadays, Dad may be presiding over the microwave while Mom is checking out her e-mail. Sunday dinner in America is just as likely to serve up enchiladas, takeout mu shui shrimp, or lasagna as once chicken and peas were doled out by our real or imaginary grannies.

In late-night *Andy Hardy* movies, the elderly judge and his teenage son wear suits and ties, mother and daughter are dainty in dresses. When gathering for dinner, all pass the biscuits and spoon gravy over pot roast and mashed potatoes. That's how Americans lived, and the Hardys were real Americans, right?

Growing up in Long Island and Cleveland, I bought that image of family and hankered after the cupcake mother, the apple-cheeked grandma kneading dough, the respectable dad doling out wise counsels. That was not my reality.

My own origins, to say the least, were unconventional, and these are the hard facts. I was born the illegitimate daughter of a French American priest (later elevated to Monsignor), and his French protégé, a scholar he had hired in Paris to research church documents for papers and books he authored on Aristotle and Stephen Langton, Bishop in the Reign of King John.

The liaison hardly came at a liberal and forgiving time, and the confidence was sealed in the confessional. I was conceived in Paris and born in Brussels, a city to which my mother came in secrecy. Not even her only sister, with whom she had a strained relationship, knew of my birth.

As an infant, I was parceled out to the Sisters of Charity in a Brussels orphanage with the proviso that I would be kept ignorant of who I was and where I came from. My status: a ward of the state. There I stayed under religious tutelage among one hundred or more children, a child with filmy recollections of being visited by a gloomy woman introduced as a family friend or a distant aunt, but who was, in truth, my mother. At age eight I was collected by two American men and brought to the United States for reasons I did not then understand. I had hoped to be reconnected with my rightful parents.

The Monsignor had since died, and these men, his student-colleagues, honored my father's last testament by retrieving his daughter. I was to be brought up as an American in the care of a prearranged adoptive parent, also a former student, whose first name was Inez—a pious Catholic unhappily wed to a Swede working in Hollywood.

For reasons I'll not go into, the adoption didn't happen. But under pressure to place the girl *somewhere,* I was farmed out to a Merrick, Long Island, family looking for a child to heal its alcoholic and emotional maladies, and, I suppose, to parallel the *Saturday Evening Post* family seated around a table of heaped-up, home-cooked food. Incidentally, I later learned that my blood mother had already arrived in this country and was working for a professor of medieval studies at Princeton. She would confirm the arrangement before returning to England. Hitler was on the march. War in Europe had been declared.

My life was split. America gave me penny candy, Jones Beach, school friends, library books, and a shiny blue bicycle, but family life was to be shattered by drink, bankruptcy, and death. One-and-a-half years after my arrival, my foster mother died at thirty-two. Cirrhosis of the liver and complications, the doctors said. Widowhood didn't agree with hotshot salesman, foster father Ray, who soon married a college dropout ex-chorine he met at a bar near the New York World's Fair.

Restless, trapped in suburbia, Ray's drop-dead good-looking boozing pal—she was twenty years younger—proved to be a sadistic hellion who found me to be the perfect victim. At age seventeen I was thrown out of the house; my books, poems, clothing, and ragtag scraps of this-and-that were burned in a backyard bonfire. Left adrift, but never without friends, I made do as I could.

What followed is another story, more apt for a passage on the dust jacket of the memoir I've now completed and that rests in the hands of an agent. A year as a split-shift "B"-board operator with the local telephone company was followed by years on the Bohemian scene in Greenwich Village and as an office temp on dull corporate jobs—more colorfully with *Figaro* in New York City, and with a theater magazine called *IT* while living with an artist on West Tenth Street. After earning a night-school degree at Hunter College, I taught junior-high students in the Bronx and people in federally sponsored poverty programs. A spirited, persevering self had been fortified by these experiences and stood me in good stead.

These were early rites of passage, bootstrap efforts during my twenties while being driven by what is common enough among orphans: the search for family, the blood lust—in this case, with little more evidence in hand than a French birth certificate stamped "Status Illegitimate."

There were clues to pursue: the names of the men who escorted me to America, hints about my father's mysterious identity. Letters were sent to various dioceses and universities, and to the president of Hunter College who I learned had befriended my father in Paris. Later, with my birth certificate in hand, I discovered my mother's name, her birthplace and hometown—Nérac in Gascony in southwest France. And that was a powerful lead, but I'm getting ahead of myself.

During the tedious retracing of names and numbers over the years I contacted and visited one of my escorts to America, a lawyer from Virginia, and he identified my mother and her whereabouts.

Pieces of the puzzle fell into place during a pilgrimage I made as a backpacking tourist to Europe. My first encounter with my mother came during an unannounced visit to her lodgings in Oxford, England, her second home. A scholarly, withdrawn woman, she spoke and wrote English fluently. I still remember her early words to me: "I have no money to give you." She thought I'd come as a blackmailer, but a door that might have slammed shut was left ajar. My mother agreed to correspond but I was not to refer to our relationship.

I guess that involvement in a process of reconciliation is typical among family outsiders, an effort to come to terms with those who wronged them in the past, to resolve, in some sense, the unresolvable, to attempt an understanding of one's own self before absolving others.

I've learned something in my life about the institutional family, the false family, the foster family, the wasted family destroyed by booze and its addictive counterparts. And I've come to know the futility of rejoining a French family who wears my flesh and bones, although I've recently reconnected with Maurice, an octogenarian blood cousin in Paris, a charming relative and generous storyteller whom I met by chance during a last visit to my mother in Nérac. I've learned that *my* close family is centered around my husband and ally, Saul, with whom I share Sunday dinners, occasionally of mu shui shrimp, enchiladas, or lasagna. And this family also extends to a clutch of faithful, like-minded friends and the larger guild of poets and writers to which I've belonged for more than twenty-five years.

For me, what is born from this through the process of writing is an affirmation, an "I write therefore I am" that can be translated into art, not as an alternative to personal solace, but as way to share common experience in a search for what we find or *should* find in ourselves: empathy, endurance, and humanity.

And over the decades, learning to be one's own trustworthy guide while drawing on memories, fantasies, and desires finally leads to compassion after rage. What gradually followed was not a reconciliation with those who wronged me, but an intensified self-regard that, little by little, accommodated the spirit of clemency.

✦ ✦ ✦

Confessional poetry is defined in Longman's *Dictionary and Handbook of Poetry* (editors, Jack Myers and Michael Simms), as "an autobiographical form of poetry whose name was created by twentieth-century literary critics." It is applied to poets such as John Berryman, Robert Lowell, Sylvia Plath, Anne Sexton, and W. D. Snodgrass. Although often resented by those defined as such, the term is not pejorative, per se, but is meant to classify a genre of poetry which, some critics maintain "is limited to the self in nature and subject matter."

Reviewing Anne Sexton's "All My Pretty Ones" in *Poetry* magazine (March 1963) Richard Howard alludes to "the catalog of ills" in Sexton's work. "She has," he writes, "in Mr. Lowell's choppy wake, restored to our poetry . . . the lyric of self-dramatization that had hidden out in the novel . . ." He goes on to praise her as "tough-minded and too honest to extol mere wretchedness for long." Howard is sympathetic, but the term "confessional" seems to raise the hackles of other reviewers and invites opprobrium and disdain.

I'm reminded of a story from *The Wise Men of Chellem* that tells how ghetto Jews petitioned their rabbi to rectify an injustice. "The rich drink sweet milk while we are condemned to drinking buttermilk," they complained. The rabbi appeased his supplicants by having them call buttermilk "fresh milk." Couldn't we satisfy confessional-poetry haters with the same sort of felicitous renaming?

William Packard asked Anne Sexton in a 1970s interview *(New York Quarterly)*: "How would you define confessional poetry?" She tossed the question back to Packard, who replied, "We'd probably say it was autobiographical—and associated with a certain purgation, and sometimes classified as therapy." In turn she responded, "Was Thomas Wolfe confessional or not? Any poem is therapy. The art of writing is therapy. You don't solve problems in writing. They're still there. I've heard psychiatrists say, 'See, you've forgiven your father in your poem.' But I haven't forgiven my father, I just wrote that I did."

I hesitate to compare myself to Sexton, one of the literary goddesses who, along with Plath, gave women of my generation permission to write of the macabre, of bedlam, abortion, depression. Interestingly, in the midst of a family in steep alcoholic decline, I was writing poems about sunsets on Lake Erie. The beauty of nature was a proper subject for poetry; I then believed what I'd been taught in school.

Although I don't think of poetry as therapy, as a prescribed remedy for sorrows, the act of writing can bring clarity to what seems blurred, and may sometimes rescue us from the edge. Keeping journals, and writing and receiving letters are vital routines to me as an artist. But poetry is not a cure-all nor does it promise compassion or forgiveness. It's an art with verbal music and intensities that may or may not reveal a parallel universe of insights and well-being.

And so, back to the subtitle of this essay: *Confessional Poet? Not me.* I'm not confessing. I don't extol wretchedness. I'm not after absolution for, or remission of my sins as in the confessional booth of my childhood. Even though my last collection of poetry is called *Clemency,* I'm not seeking it, but rather dispensing clemency to others who misjudged or disdained me in my past.

Most of my personal "villains" are joined to that great number of the dead who outnumber us, as Annie Dillard writes in *For the Time Being,* her new and grimly brilliant book. In short, I'm neither spilling the beans for titillation, nor telling all to exact revenge, although a few reviewers have suggested that as a motive. Revenge may reside on the shadow side, in the undersong of my poems but not as a judgmental and overriding disclosure, not as a *mea culpa* or you're to blame.

I'm concerned with language, with the clarity of telling the emotional truth, and where possible, getting at the facts of my story, a good, ongoing one, after all, although surely one doesn't have to own a dramatic life story to be a writer. In writing autobiographical poems, I'm after an array of voices, vibrant, high-wired, somber, calm, even detached. Please, no "falling upon the thorns of life" and bleeding self-pity, which makes for bad art, as does a holier-than-thou stance.

I don't possess the single answer, and fear those who profess to know all that's knowable. I'm no Santa Inez. What absorbs me are words, using them to make art out of what moves me, and out of the strangeness of those events that shaped me. As I conclude in "In Every Sense Corrective Ink Is Running Out," "I write it down to get it straight, to redeem my life." In the process I hope to move the reader with my story. In this connection, I'm reminded of a quote from Gustave Flaubert that is pinned to my bulletin board at home: "Human language is like a cracked kettle on which we beat our tunes for bears to dance to, when all the time we are longing to move the stars to pity."

As it happens, I'm curious and interested in many things beyond my exotic chronicle. I'm interested in stars, the celestial ones, although the Hollywood screen images of my childhood are still dazzling. Rapture is where you'll find it, in anthropology, birds, jazz, folk and classical music, in Asian poetry, biography. As such, I consider myself a narrative poet, and increasingly so despite the somewhat deceptive titles of my two most recent books: *Family Life* and *Clemency.*

Over time, seasoned by a growing self-esteem, of a sense of entitlement (one needs that to confront and respect the emotional tangle of difficult material), and an attempt to make coherence out of hints and specks, unkempt and tattered bits of knowledge, letters, photographs, I've plunged more and more into straightaway storytelling. Using the metaphor of archeology, perhaps I could say I've begun to piece together a fossil history from disparate clues and artifacts, and achieve clarity, or its approximation, using words as implements. I trust their power to light dark paths.

Returning to my chronicle, my personal narrative about being a love child conceived in Paris has some of the drama of Héloïse and Abelard, though none of its physical violence. My story was filled with secrets and stratagems for keeping me concealed.

The secret of my birth was kept until the death, in 1992, of my mother, whose small family thought her eccentric, reclusive, a pious virgin. Making myself visible, having my say, has always been grounds for writing autobiographical poetry, although not without some ambivalence for fear of offending or alienating whatever family members I might subsequently approach.

Perhaps now is the moment to explore some of my autobiographical poems and to give them some background, influences and methods of orchestration.

My narrative style, infused with some lyrical passages, shows up in "A Story" (1993), composed after reading one of my favorite collections, *Poems of the Late T'ang* (A. C. Graham, translator). The lines that spurred me on appear in the poem "To My Young Brother" by Tu Fu, written, the editor tells us, "high in the Yangtze's gibbon-haunted Yuei-chou region."

Rumors that you lodge in a mountain temple
in Huang-chou, or in Yueh-chou for sure. . .

The word within those lines that moved me most was "rumors." That ordinary word burned on the page. My cousin, Maurice, had recently announced my mother's death in a letter. When I disclosed the truth about myself, telling him something of my story, he wrote back to me: *"Il y avait des rumeurs d'un prêtre Américain."* There were *rumors* of an American priest.

Unlike much of my work, which arrives piecemeal, the poem below was bursting to be written, and came into being almost full fledged, inspired by that exchange with Maurice. Composed in quatrains, it relates my parents' meeting in Paris, my birth, my mother's resolute denial of that birth, and their deaths. The poem shifts toward a more involute diction with scenes of my father's imagined regret, and my being bundled off to live with nuns.

I try to empathize with my parents' burdens as they parted in 1931, she, to my Belgium birthplace, and he, to Paris to continue as a priest-scholar gathering medieval texts for a compendium on Aristotle. He would die three years later.

A Story

There were *rumors* of a priest old enough.
to be her father. She was the Latinist
he needed for his work on medieval texts.
Her family had no reason to suspect

her deference to a learned man.
She wrote she was swayed by his fame
as an Aristotle scholar
after I asked had she ever loved him.

When her clothes strained at the seams,
both may have talked of crossing
the border into Belgium.
I don't know. No one must know,

they agreed, except their confessor,
and a colleague or two.

Dust on cathedral windows,
gathered in bouquets,

shook out again in wind and rain.
Birds migrated, wedge-shaped shadows
on deltas and plateaus.
In the sacristy, among surplices and robes,

he paced, a man clouded over with regret
for the child he might not hold.
And the woman lodged in another country?
My father did not hear her screams

pierce the leaves as I unfurled.
Clouds like bridal veils drifted above the city.
Hidden with the Sisters in an outlying part,
I grew where flowers took root in dry fields.

Soon the priest will be buried near the sea,
but my mother would grow old recording parchments
and tomes on the history of the church.
After she slides into earth, nothing

of his name, nor mine, not a scrap
will be found in locked boxes or her vaults.
None will guess a child had slipped out
of those delicate thighs. And I will have my say.

Again, I'm having my say, as should any intrepid narrator. And I've had that say in different kinds of autobiographical poems. The next I'll share has a more dense texture, a more luxuriant style than "A Story." I'm attracted to a variety of voices in poetry.

Some background: when teaching at the Aspen Writers Conference in 1992, I asked students to list their obsessions, observing that poems arise out of these fixations. One of my own long-standing obsessions is that imaginary moment when I was conceived in Paris. Born in June, I count back nine months to summon up October for my entry into a Belgian summer in the early 1930s.

I'd been reading Jane Hirshfield and Mariko Aratani's *The Ink Dark Moon* (Vintage Books, 1990), translations of love poems by Izumi Shikibu and Ono no Kamachi, women of the ancient court of Japan. I wrote down questions posed by the poets, and asked my students to make a poem, in any form, out of answers to one or more of these questions quoted from Shikibu and Kamachi:

> "Do they recognize autumn in the sound of the blowing wind?"
> "Did he appear because I fell asleep thinking of him?"
> "What should I do with this body that lives stubbornly on?"
> "Is that how you want me to follow you?"
> "Which shouldn't exist in the world, the one who forgets or
>   the one who is forgotten?"
> "If I live, what more can I do?"
> "How can I leave a world that includes this child?"

Sometimes I work the assignment along with my students, and in one case, chose to paraphrase, "Do they recognize autumn in the sound of the blowing wind?" with a modified title reading, "How Did They Recognize Autumn in the Dark of the City?" It's a poem I began in 1991 and completed two years later after ten revisions, likely more.

> A crucifix over the bed,
> a tremor of shadows and the moon
> flying low like an owl into their room,
> gave no hint I might arrive, purple and curled,
> a child begun in a reverie
>
> of autumn. Like a rain cloud he burst
> into the dream from which she woke to Burgundy
> masked by peppermint, silver bristles
> of his chin rubbing her cheek, neck.
> Inhaling her scents, lavender and library paste,
> he barely guessed she longed to straggle after birds
>
> over the Seine, away from the Bibliotheque that penned her
> in rooms whose knowledge he desired as he longed for her
> flesh to tremble beneath him. She did not confess
> to doubts of ministering to his needs.
> When she wept, he kissed her flight
> of tears, pressed his hand to her lips, gesturing
>
> their secret. Summer had vanished like a wafer
> on the tongue at Mass. Both knew time by chrysanthemum
> stars blowing quills of light on the city,

from the wind's rasp and pulp of leaves,
by the stir of a child they would barely know,

one who would celebrate the union of heaven and earth,
and their coupling in the shadow of Notre Dame
whose gargoyle-gabbled waters sounded waves
of applause resonating in an autumn squall.

Here, I'm a chronicler, a storyteller sidestepping tear-jerking excess. Sometimes it's exhilarating to deal with fury and pain by creating another persona. In "Thinking of My Parisian Mother's Discretion (Only Her Confessor Knows) in Not Telling Her Sister or Hardly Anyone about My Birth," (That's only the title, not the full poem), I assume the guise of a gossipy, theatrical Southern woman chatting about her mother's love affair.

In the same spirit of role-playing, the dialogue poem depends on two voices, neither mine, and yet, both belong to me. One, the narrator, me, speaks in a tough, sarcastic Cockney, while the other, using standard English, suggests the remote and refined mother. The poem was prompted by two phrases in one of my mother's arid letters: "This is a crucial election. Giscard d'Estaing represents our highest aspirations." D'Estaing was then running for office as premier.

Crucial Stew

Crucial, that's me mother's word;
"this is a crucial election."

Christ's been banged
on the crucial with niles,
it were a bloody saight.

"Giscard d'Estaing represents
our highest aspirations,"
me mother writes,

she what
dumped me in an orphanage
in Beljum

is very neat about er person
and as been corresponding
with an English nicetype
for 28 years;
they ain't ever met.

Crucial, Comrade Crucial.
Communist atheist and Kulak killer,
she'd ave said of im.

We're two tough ducks, me and me mum,
she what dumped me with the Catolick Sisters.

Still, crucial, the word, seems a bit
thick and damn the bloody Pope
if I care what wins.

I lost me mother from the start
when they had me stabbing mutton fat
in that groveling pit
of highest aspirations.
Not an eyetheist in saight
but plenty of crucials with niles.

We was very neat about our persons.

"Stabbing," "nails," "killer," "crucifix," and "bloody" are words that
spurt undeniable rage, and yet, written years before I entertained the notion of clemency, the poem keeps anger in check through its mocking
tone and working-class dialect. As the speaker, I intended to rally behind
the victimized and chafing "I" of the poem, and say *j'accuse* to my high-
minded mother—all the while acknowledging her durability and singularity of purpose, to account for and to praise the faithful and scholarly
life pursued so steadily apart from mine.

My mother would not have welcomed this praise nor, for that matter,
any intrusions on her privacy. Before she died, I sent her a copy of *Eight
Minutes from the Sun,* a book of nature poems she dismissed as too modern. The journey of the soul, devotion to the Almighty, concerned her
more than issues of poetry, confessional or otherwise.

From early on, I have had the impulse to write intimately of my life, and I came to believe that my story might be understood by those who have surmounted childhood obstacles. I imagined autobiography might be transformed into literature.

I have tried to write about my family with compassionate detachment and discretion; easy enough, I suppose, when one's parents are not alive to comment on secrets revealed. Of course, we live in an age where little separates the exhibitionist, pornographer, or betrayer of secrets. Yesterday's shunned immoralist is today's blockbuster-book author.

In *The Making of a Poem,* Stephen Spender writes that "Maine de Biran in his *Intimate Journal*. . . reflects that perhaps the worst crime is all this interest in oneself." Reading Jean-Jacques Rousseau's *Confessions* in high school, I was riveted by his passionate narrative of self-interest. I *became* Jean-Jacques. I empathized with his quasi-orphaned state, sighed with relief that he, too, had pilfered small objects and fervently disavowed his misdeeds. The account of his failings gave me immense solace and provided me with an early revolutionary sense that one could be absolved while having one's say.

But the writing of poetry is not about the unburdening of angst. It is about paying fierce attention to language and its exactitude. It is a long labor. W. B. Yeats said it best in "Adam's Curse":

> . . . Better to go down on your marrow bones
> and scrub a kitchen pavement or break stones
> like a pauper in all
> kinds of weather
> for to articulate sweet sounds together
> is to work harder than all these . . .

Thylias Moss

My Better Half

It so happens that Thylias the writer is the better half of this marriage if talking dollars and sense, dominant versus recessive, fifteen minutes of fame, and number of listings in *Books in Print*. Properly, I defer to her achievement; she is the one certain of life, though hers is papery, and certain that words are the means to all ends; she is the one whose doubts, if any, are insignificant and don't threaten the ideologies that she will take to any forum, accepting honoraria for the visits where not much is required of her, just the reiteration of her writings. For these occasions, I lend her my physiological ability to produce sound; her voice is merely the articulate manipulation of thoughts. An audience would not be satisfied with an exhibition of her thinking which, though active, is not memorable to watch. So while I contribute only anatomy's menial service, she realizes the difficulty she'd have proving hers the greater contribution, since she would need me to assert that proof, and some words I refuse to type for her, claiming carpal tunnel syndrome. There is necessary fraud involved. There would be nothing universal or personal without deceptions.

Her certainty of much that I question makes our debates useful; I'd like to win one. Since I can't explain her existence, she doesn't feel subject to boundaries, physics, or my guilt. Her sympathies are with the inexplicable, the death-defying, cold fusion. Having the exemption of angels, she doesn't need, as I would, to allow the possibility of regret to censor her publications; she says anything. If she persists, there won't be any secrets, none of the mysteries she reveres and exposes in the most unsavory places—tabloid news shows, sports, shopping malls, motels, music videos, the Psychic Friends Network, Sumo suits, *The Birth of a Nation*.

If problems arise, they're mine; I'm the one feeling mortality's pinches; I can be caged and harassed while she remains free to write, deriving at least that strange pleasure from anything.

The distance between us widens as she becomes something I can't be—someone I struggle to emulate, moving while I stand still, wondering by now, why she married me, and thinking about leaving—so I offer the seduction of details from my childhood that she can use for poems. See, I think to myself, she doesn't want you only for your body, those vibrating vocal chords, those agile fingers. Predictably, she seizes any thoughts I have, for there is no way to conceal them from her; she's swift, enterprising, compelled, and limited to that one duty of word-mongering. She knows she is better at saying anything I might have to say.

These began as my thoughts, but she, the articulate one, is more likely their arranger. She is hungry for ideas and it's my responsibility to feed her since she is more mine than I am hers, the way it always is with offspring. Who should get possession of this should we separate? The reader; of course, the reader. She has much to say about that, but my carpal tunnel syndrome is flaring up and changing the subject to inconvenience, the only subject, really.

Frank Bidart

Borges and I

We fill pre-existing forms and when we fill them we change them and are changed.

The desolating landscape in Borges' "Borges and I"—in which the voice of "I" tells us that its other self, Borges, is the self who makes literature, who in the process of making literature falsifies and exaggerates, while the self that is speaking to us now must go on living so that Borges may continue to fashion literature—is seductive and even oddly comforting, but, I think, false.

The voice of this "I" asserts a disparity between its essential self and its worldly second self, the self who seeks embodiment through making things, through work, who in making takes on something false, inessential, inauthentic.

The voice of this "I" tells us that Spinoza understood that everything wishes to continue in its own being, a stone wishes to be a stone eternally, that all "I" wishes is to remain unchanged, itself.

With its lonely emblematic title, "Borges and I" seems to be offered as a paradigm for the life of consciousness, the life of knowing and making, the life of the writer.

The notion that Frank has a self that has remained the same and that knows what it would be if its writing self did not exist—like all assertions about the systems that hold sway beneath the moon, the opposite of this seems to me to be true, as true.

When Borges' "I" confesses that Borges falsifies and exaggerates it seems to do so to cast aside falsity and exaggeration, to attain an entire candor unobtainable by Borges.

This "I" therefore allows us to enter an inaccessible magic space, a hitherto inarticulate space of intimacy and honesty earlier denied us, where voice, for the first time, has replaced silence.

—Sweet fiction, in which bravado and despair beckon from a cold panache, in which the protected essential self suffers flashes of its existence to be immortalized by a writing self that is incapable of performing its actions without mixing our essence with what is false.

Frank had the illusion, when he talked to himself in the clichés he used when he talked to himself, that when he made his poems he was changed in making them, that arriving at the order the poem suddenly arrived at out of the chaos of the materials the poem let enter itself out of the chaos of life, consciousness then, only then, could know itself, Sherlock Holmes was somebody or something before cracking its first case but not Sherlock Holmes, act is the cracked mirror not only of motive but self, *no other way*, tiny mirror that fails to focus in small the whole of the great room.

But Frank had the illusion that his poems also had cruelly replaced his past, that finally they were all he knew of it though he knew they were not, everything else was shards refusing to make a pattern and in any case he had written about his mother and father until the poems saw as much as he saw and saw more and he only saw what he saw in the act of making them.

He had never had a self that wished to continue in its own being, survival meant ceasing to be what its being was.

Frank had the illusion that though the universe of one of his poems seemed so close to what seemed his own universe at the second of writing it that he wasn't sure how they differed even though the paraphernalia often differed, after he had written it its universe was never exactly his universe, and so, soon, it disgusted him a little, the mirror was dirty and cracked.

Secretly he was glad it was dirty and cracked, because after he had made a big order, a book, only when he had come to despise it a little, only after he had at last given up the illusion that this was what was, only then could he write more.

He felt terror at the prospect of becoming again the person who could find or see or make no mirror, for even Olivier, trying to trap the beast who had killed his father, when he suavely told Frank as Frank listened to the phonograph long afternoons lying on the bed as a kid, when Olivier told him what art must be, even Olivier insisted that art is a mirror held up by an artist who himself needs to see something, held up before a nature that recoils before it.

We fill pre-existing forms and when we fill them we change them and are changed.

Everything in art is a formal question, so he tried to do it in prose with much blank white space.

Claudia Rankine

The First Person in the Twenty-First Century

Is it fair to say there is, in the twenty-first century, a greater consensus toward the notion that true coherency is fragmented? For me, for example, if the movie star goes to the bathroom I feel better about the movie. So what if the action-packed narrative is broken into, fragmented. Each toilet flush suggests someone is invested in seeming real. Bathroom time, phone calls, recalled events, chats, and naps after all, contribute the fragments that altogether we recognize as experience. "Human Beings for the Collage That Is Life," the subtitle could read.

The poet Paul Celan wrote, "Reality is not simply there, it must be searched and won." The search includes reintroducing all that has been broken off to make the narrative smooth. Most of us have been around enough to know that the "I" ultimately has a responsibility to the intelligence (think humanity) of the "you." Some might say that recognition of responsibility on the page is what makes use of the first-person social. It recognizes that we are always being broken into (visually and invisibly) by history, memory, current events, the phone, e-mail, a kiss, calls of nature, whatever.

The languaged self, then, in order to keep itself human, in order to cohere, has to fragment. The notion that coherence is itself not fragmented is what lands a certain kind of "I" into a singular subject position. But behind that position is this truth: the "I" exists in time and is married to biological, personal, historical, and cultural meaning. Not to realize this is to commit a blink of omission. For example, *I am a black girl in a yellow dress.* The adjectival insistence in this sentence immediately reminds us that words have social and political currency. Black does not generally suggest the presidency, Marilyn Monroe, or *The Simpsons*.

Yellow could look good against black skin. Yellow dresses are gender specific. Black girls have a "public story." Cowards might avoid yellow. Soon, I am both closer to and farther from myself due to my mind's-eye association to the colors yellow and black. Chip away enough, and I am bouncing off social and cultural generalities complicating the first person's association with hue (read you). So what that the initial thought was simply: *I am a black girl in a yellow dress?* There is clearly a more fractured and complex reality behind this sentence.

And the complexity doesn't necessarily lead me to what I recognize. *I am a black girl in a yellow dress. I want to light up my life.* Exactly how much agency does the "I" of the second sentence have? Does it matter what the "I" wants if cultural prejudices disallow black girls from wanting anything in a society that constructs them as victims? In a cultural minute that "I" becomes "Everyone." *Everyone* (Where did they come from?) *wants to light up my life.* In my imagination of the neighborhood where all the little black girls grow up, a yellow dress makes me more visible to the gun-slinging drug dealer. I could exploit this cowboy reality in the name of . . . what? Urbane authenticity? (fragment, no suggestions) Sentimentality? (fragment, no suggestions) Racism? (untold fragments, never suggested) Clearly more fragments are needed. Clearly, even more is needed if "I" am to begin to cohere. Together let's think, "Love is all around, why don't you take it." Remember her, Mary Richards? Put her next door to the black girl and maybe a swing set would come to mind. Or maybe Lorraine Hansberry's *A Raisin in the Sun.* Or, maybe, a handshake? Which is to say—so many times should "I" shake hands with the times I live in.

The investigative play above enacts how a strategy of fragmentation can be used to complicate the scripted assumptions connected to identity. Not to investigate subjectivity is to reinforce cultural stereotypes, erasing the compromises and assertions that compress the languaged self. All assertions of self have consequences of meaning greater than the typographical space an "I" inhabits. The writer's attempt to insert into, redirect, juxtapose, or interrupt the first person, demonstrates a desire to write with awareness and integrity within the knowledge afforded us in the twenty-first century. The construction of self, then, becomes a process in motion determined by indeterminacy through a strategy of fragmentation.

In other words, when I use the first person, my wish is to expose the implications of what it means to speak from the seeming coherency of that position. I write to encounter the accidental privileges and anxieties of my "I's" assertions:

> I am all of me feeling I am in constant paraphrase.
> loosely. without the fence of time. in time losing to form
> absorbed. swiftly caught
>
> by my own resistance to the completed sacrifice to
> the long line arriving me. bringing everything I mean.
> unmistakably personal. to this same feeling of loss. lost
>
> far from here though I am here aiming. though every
> plot has prodded. each driven drama digested by this
>
> world. a dawning giving back so much to the self. in
> reflection darkening so much. the day might call it night.

(excerpted from Plot)

As fictionalized as the space of poetry and prose can be, I still feel the construction of a self must demonstrate a consciousness of its scriptedness. In my own work, fragmentation is the strategy I use to keep in play as many possibles as possible. In time, the path of the first person crosses borders, strays, pauses, and repeats to cross borders, stray, pause, or repeat. The ruptured syntax and the fragmented text are used to suggest, and perhaps reflect, the process by which existence (being in time) is enacted—which is to say, the text engages irruption, interruptions, and discontinuities in order to approach the initial silence of being.

The veering variable of the "I" diverts the self from its eventual ability to exist in silence. Our own physicality, the body, its flesh and bone, is the only solid. Its solidity, a solidity that can never be truly languaged, is what's sure, and yet, at any time, it is what will break down in soil or be made to turn to ash. In truth, no one exists behind the languaged self. I myself am nothing, though feeling everything. It is this nothingness that tries to cement itself into a singular subject position. It reaches out in the lie of the linear, continuous, and coherent line toward solidity. It reaches out in the lie of the fractured, fragmented, and dueling line toward nothingness. This nothingness is breaking up all the time. *I am a black girl in a yellow dress.* Is every adjective not a betrayal? *I want to light up my life.* Is every verb not an interruption?

Despite its unruly status, the use of the first person is as steady as I get to be. Those lines of ink adhere to the page and are my assertion of self. As such, my "I" is authorized to stay ahead of me in time: I, I, I . . . to infinity. To abandon the fragmented text—this is the fantasy—is to encounter a world of homogeneity, a single "I," the stillness of it fixed by time; this, we are to believe, is a privilege. But not to recognize the instability inherent in any assertion of the first person is to believe that the gated community of the text is a place suitable only for fantasy worlds.

The "I," the first person, is lost though I am here. Is not my "I" on the page, my languaged self, like the body? I appear to be of a piece. But what do I really inhabit to inherit? Am I not the life and the death of my "I's" assertion? Does not my every word, on its way to a sentence, gather together my being, its presence, in order to lose it? *I am a black girl in a yellow dress.* Isn't race, gender, and position (arrived at by the preposition "in") dressing and redressing me for public and private consumption? By the time we arrive at the period in my sentence, my assertion of self, haven't I been encapsulated, by the death of arrival, into the illusion of meaning? To break away from this nonbeing, don't I have to fragment, split apart, be ruined?

It seems crazy to choose a ruined subjectivity to a coherent one, but what happens to a coherent subjectivity that has mythologized itself through privilege as privilege? No "I" in my mind's eye is the whole of anything. I am a part and so, torn apart by the aggression of the uninterrupted. Hyperbolic as this sounds, I look around and see the illusion of wholeness and surety inciting the Crusades, slavery, the Battle of Little Big Horn, *Shoah,* Hiroshima, Pearl Harbor, Vietnam, etc. . . . We cannot be committed to any version of the first person to the extent that we are unwilling to interrupt, diverge, or reroute in the name of known and unknown truths. This attempt, the constant investigation of subjectivity, should be what it means to be human. Paul Celan wrote in a letter to Hans Bender on May 18, 1960:

> Craft means handiwork, a matter of hands. And these hands must belong to one person, i.e., a unique, moral soul searching for its way with its true poems. I cannot see any basic difference between a handshake and a poem. . . . We live under dark skies and—there are few human beings. Hence, I assume, so few poems.

I think it is all right to want to be moral. And I think it all right to be searching for a way. It is that search, that moral search, that pulls me up short to reroute midstream; that search that interrupts and dissolves; that search that fragments me. Simone Weil wrote, "I am also other than what I imagine myself to be." Her statement is the act of an "I" asserting itself against itself—against the illusion of a whole self. I try to keep her words in mind as I think, as I act, and as I write:

> The full thickness of my tongue forces itself to
> part, to call
>
> I segue under
> the rouged opening of the boneless jaw
> because green clings to the leaves
> because the idea remains
> fresh
>
> All day I will record
> And never convince
> With such luck we

(excerpted from Plot)

Annie Finch

Coherent Decentering: Toward a New Model of the Poetic Self

Like many contemporary writers, I find the Romantic poetic construct of the fixed, central self and its point of view to be extraordinarily limited. Whether or not one accepts the Buddhist insight that the true self is a non-self, unconnected to transitory thoughts and emotions, if we look closely we are not likely to perceive our selves as discrete entities. I am aware that my own selfhood, let alone the self voicing my poems, is not a clear and simple unit, separate from everything else in the world. Our selves, insofar as they seem to exist at all, are more likely to come to our awareness as a shifting progression of moods and thoughts, contingent on circumstance, culture, and context, and open to many interpretations.

When I was a child, my family would spend several months a year in an isolated cabin in the Maine woods without car, phone, radio, TV, or even electric light. Each summer, several weeks into my hiatus from "civilization," as my family called the outside world, I found the boundaries I kept around my supposed self beginning to dissolve with the long months of silence and simplicity. At the same time, I was noticing how each hour of the lakeshore's life had its own personality and presence, how nature's cycles and patterns were coherent and connected, always continuing in the field of their core necessity. These experiences had a lasting effect on my forming consciousness as person and poet. Following the push of sunrise, the pull of my breath, over pebbles and ripples, intuition and awareness moved me through the day. The centered self I had built during the winter months became a distraction. Eventually I left her piled on porch or shore like my sandals and shirt, so I could connect more directly with what lived around me.

Just as nature was a place where my younger self could dissolve without fragmenting the world, I now see language as a place where the poetic self can dissolve without throwing the world the poem represents into chaos. I appreciate poems that "problematize" the self, to use one common critical term, rather than pretending that the selves of the speaker of the poem and its reader are simple, solid entities. But, as the deconstructionsts argue, the most apparently coherent syntax does not *really* create a simple point of view. And conversely, the usual avant-garde markers of the decentered poetic self—disjointed syntax, floating margins, random signifiers, clashing dictions, collage structure and found language, shifting or unidentifiable points of view—are, it needs to be said, literary conventions themselves. I believe that when contemporary poets disrupt syntax to convey the decentered self, it is the world, not the self, that they are representing as incoherent.

The incoherent worldview that is a *sine qua non* of much contemporary avant-garde poetics can be viewed as a direct descendent of the Romantic notion that Truth is a distant, absolute, and unreachable goal that is best approximated through some kind of "systematic derangement of the senses." My own experiences in nature have made me skeptical of such strategies. The contrast between my summer and winter lives was so great that it was hard for me not to romanticize what I experienced at the lakeshore. I remember that I would sometimes be caught up in a trancelike state that could last for hours. But I believe that I was not "transported" by the sight of the world around me in the Romantic sense, because there was at those times no self to transport. The Buddhist scholar Robert Thurman has captured this experience in his book *Inner Revolution*:

> It seems paradoxical that having decisively dissolved our absolute, independent sense of self we should now be so aware of the essence of each and every thing . . . Everything seems dreamlike and illusory, yet things seem present in a way no longer separate from their dissolution . . . Far from dwelling in some sort of mystical state of disappearance, I am now at home in reality . . . At last I am immune to any temptation to mystify some extraordinary state of dissolution, some absolute nothingness or absolute beingness, and make it the goal of my existence.

During those long adolescent summers, the decentering of my self became a key element in my poetry. Since I had not yet been exposed to the conventions of avant-garde discourse, I gradually devised my own poetic strategies to convey the decentering experiences I was having. I had been writing poems since the age of eight and had already been published, but in 1974, the summer after my freshman year of college, I wrote what I felt was my first *real* poem and called it "First Poem." Reading it now, I think the reason it felt like such a breakthrough was that the speaker of the beginning of the poem cannot bring herself to inhabit the traditional, Romantic, lyric self:

First Poem

The honest spirit is bewildered
by the going of the night.
Bruised back by morning's light squares, she laments:
"I've settled in a clan of waking ghosts.
There's no more solid thing for me than light."

But here the flick of evening opens
her who let stars' spider trails
run quick cold sticky errands through her night.

Day breaks into a pomegranate,
or some night of leaping patterns,
and she breaks to hear your words,
and now she's dialogue:

Attent me! Let the syntax crack!
(my voice in an old tangle of synapse)
You will tug at the old strains daily
(I'm a mirror, and a sieve)
So sift and scald the ancient cups. Don't sleep;
give your blanched filters back for homage.

The young, "honest spirit" who wrote this, well-versed in the Romantic poetic tradition, is bewildered by the apparent need to act as a coherent central lyric self to write poems. Yet nature's manifold connections show her a way to blend outward and still remain centered. She lets the flick of evening, the sensitivity she has felt in the safety of night, begin to

inhabit her day—so the day, like the night, becomes a network of connections, of selves: a decentered place. When her hellish, ghost-filled
day "breaks into a pomegranate," the poem seems to imply, she can eat
its seeds and remain there—or half-there, as part of a dialogue. Who is
the "you" of this dialogue? Another part of the speaker? The reader?
Either way, the "I " is not unified. And, though there is room for the syntax to crack at the strange word "attent," it doesn't crack. The language is
tugged, sifted, and scalded, but finally "given back" to itself, to the necessities of meaning and syntax.

The more I developed my poetic approach to subjectivity, the more
the idea of the self as the point of reference around which everything
else revolves—the lone conscious subjectivity in an objectified world—
seemed wrong to me as person and poet. In those years before I had read
theory, feminist or poststructuralist, I might not have had the framework
to continue exploring this new poetic self had it not been for my father,
a scholar of Weil and Wittgenstein. All through my high-school summers and into college, he and I would talk, sometimes sitting for hours at
a time during the summer evenings, gazing through the rusted screens
and faded wood of our little porch, out over the lake. The main subject
of these talks was the theme that most occupied his mind and writings
during those years: subjectivity or, more accurately, the falseness and un-
necessariness of the subject-object distinction.

The rest of the year I was well trained in the Cartesian logic that per-
meated school, television, journalism, all the voices of my winter life.
But in the summer I heard my father's voice, explaining patiently, "That
idea you have of being separate from the world is a habit. It's just an illusion! It's a way you have of thinking *about* experience, and it gets in the
way of true experience. It's not necessary for the self to be separate." Already I knew he was right, because in my quiet hours in nature I had felt
the consciousness of a rock, a berry, a leaf, just as I felt my own consciousness, each occupying its own place and also being completely connected with the rest. I had never known how to talk about it before, but
now I took that newly conscious knowledge into my unfolding adolescent selfhood, like rain swelling the growth rings of a thickening tree.

Years later, when I began to study feminist poetics, I recognized the feminist critique of the traditional Romantic self of lyric poetry. I loved Keats, but I couldn't put my own lyric voice in that position with a straight face. As a woman, I knew too much about how it feels to be something—nightingale, urn, woman—that is an object in other people's eyes. And, as my father's daughter, I knew that philosophy had a different way to conceive of the self. The more I thought about these themes, the more I found myself writing poems that turn object into subject, such as "Still Life" (1978), where a woman who seems to be in a Vermeer painting suddenly turns, drops her pitcher, and "betrays Vermeer"—and poems that turn subject into object, such as "Inside the Violet" (1991), where the speaker tries to contemplate a violet as a Romantic poet would, but finds herself drawn into the flower until she herself takes on its point of view.

Once I became more aware of poststructuralist theory and post-modern literary conventions, I experimented with pastiche and frag-mented syntax in an attempt to convey the decentered self. But the more I worked with language, the more I wanted to accept all of its common limitations. An effective shaman is able to return from a vision and live normally, to talk coherently and do business intelligently, to follow the laws appropriate to each world. It seemed to me the strongest strategy was to work within the honestly conventional and artificial constraints of the language, twisting and turning their qualities to my advantage, rather than to pretend that those constraints didn't exist.

The French philosopher Simone Weil wrote that "a fixed point of view is the root of all injustice." But she also wrote, "God consigned all phenomena without exception to the mechanism of the world" and "ne-cessity is the veil of God." Weil's first statement asserts the importance, now familiar in postmodernist thought, of a multiple, shifting, frag-mentary perspective. Her other statements stress the inevitability, and the sacredness, of the coherence in and of all things.

A truism of today's avant-garde poetics is that Weil's statements are contradictory—that a fragmentary and disjointed style, defying the common mechanisms and necessities of language, is the only way to avoid positing a falsely unified self. This largely unexamined belief is one of the key dividing points between experimental and mainstream poetics. One of the tasks of my poems and criticism is to explore a third possibility: that Weil's statements are not necessarily contradictory, that the decentered, multiple point of view that Weil advocates can thrive in the "mechanisms" of syntactic coherence—arguably the most crucial and uncompromising "necessity" of language.

The coherent methods of decentering the lyric self that I have explored include: syntactic density and innnuendo; lexical and metaphorical subtext; and the questioning of "objects" and use of multiple speakers. Most of all, I have found my tools in the defamiliarizing repetition of conspicuous word and sound patterns, or "form." When I began to write in patterns, I found a nonverbal vocabulary of coherent decentering and vatic containment that could channel the balance of energy and form, chaos and pattern, which I felt in nature and in language. The density and weight, the inward turning of words, the rhythm, and the imagery in the following poem aim to problematize the lyric self within the conventions of syntax.

Wild Yeasts

The bubbles riot in my kneaded bread
as the soft-fleshed breath of wild yeast starts to roar;
then my slow touch rumples down their wild heads,
pushing my airborne daughters towards their core.
They clutch with peaked foam, weaving into light
stretched sinews gasping. They fall under the arch
that stiffening dough concludes. They sing with tight
linked whistling stops of hot dark from the starch.

In the end they quiet, through the vaulting loaf
that murmurs its only longing empty sound
from their arching lust. They terrace this drying roof.
In resonance their voicing flights rebound.
The cathedral-savage trails their bodies trace
have roared sun-thin and died to dome this place.

In this poem, I wanted to create a voice so open to the yeasts and the loaf that it is located partly where they are, and partly in the words themselves, as if language itself were talking. I wanted the reader to lose track of the self, and then to startle back and realize the self was there all along—not as the central, shaping consciousness of a post-Romantic poem, but as a reflection of a coherent syntactic context.

I am aware that my method of coherent decentering substitutes one set of literary conventions for another. But for me it has two advantages over the accepted avant-garde practice. First, it avoids the mistake of confusing a fragmented worldview for a decentered self, and so it feels truer to my deepest experiences in nature. Second, it accepts consciously the artificial and contingent nature of language. All poems, however incoherent their syntax, posit a central self or speaker *because* poems are made of language. By defying common syntax, a fragmented poem focuses the reader's attention even more intently toward meaning-making. A coherently decentered poem, by contrast, respects the boundaries of common syntax and thereby addresses the reader's inevitable need for coherence—while, at the same time, pushing the boundaries of syntax so far that the reader's self may become unmoored, floating free within the confines of the poem.

A syntactically fragmented poem tries to depict the decentered self directly through language, an inherently impossible task no matter how much the language is broken and altered, because the decentered self is like the head of Medusa; if you try to look at it directly, you will turn to stone and be thrown back into the egotistical self. By contrast, coherent decentering uses the common syntactic capacities of language to create the *experience* of the decentered self for the reader.

As a poet, I find syntactic coherence a key element in the beauty and strength of the language. And as a postmodern woman, I want to honor the core of my experience as a self that I know is not a self. If our language grows syntax as a tree grows blossoms, if our words communicate as a tree bears fruit, if we heed the ordinary, conventional habits of grammar, does it really imply that our selves are not also aware of the wild, fluid capaciousness of possible selves? If we open our mouths and eat when it is time, does it really mean that we don't remember how to kiss? Much more precious to me than aleatory dynamics or primary process, now, is the counterpoise of energies that incorporates, as all balance does, opposing forces: center and circumference, coherence and incoherence, boundary and core.

Yusef Komunyakaa

The Autobiographical "I": An Archive of Metaphor, Imagery, and Innuendo

When I was sixteen, I went looking for Walt Whitman, and I finally asked the high-school librarian if *Leaves of Grass* was checked out or lost. It wasn't on the shelf but it was listed in the card catalog. Hadn't I learned my Dewey decimal system?

"No," she said. "You have to sign it out; we have it here behind the checkout desk."

Do I still remember her curious stare into my unknowing eyes, or is this also a part of my autobiographical imagination? To this day, I can still see this nameless soul, a light-skinned African American woman with the soil of Louisiana in her voice, gazing up at me squint-eyed as if I'd crossed some boundary of the flesh. This little scene is part of my emotional biography: almost every time I open *Leaves of Grass,* the librarian's voice is there. Of course, this happened before I knew Whitman would help me discover the undivulged mysteries of my surroundings—his terrifying, lyrical vibrancy that exacted an allusive beauty in life. He told me that my own rough song could also embrace a believable, shaped lyricism made of imagination and experience. As a matter of fact, imagination, not only what's observed, also counts as experience. And, since the artist, the poet, isn't just a reporter of the so-called facts, Whitman, as journalist, seemed keenly aware of this. His brave, robust "I am" seems like an act of conjuring. He reinvents himself on the page, singing his imagined self into existence, into immortality through a lyrical urgency. Whitman's a frontiersman, and it isn't surprising that Ralph Waldo Emerson says, "And we must thank Walt Whitman for service to American literature in the Appalachian enlargement of his outline and treatment." Indeed, there's a bigness in Whitman's vision and voice.

William Wordsworth's personal pronoun "I" is different than Whitman's. More self-centered and egotistical, Whitman reaches for a crescendo driven by the sheer force of will like a birth-cry and death-cry woven into one impulse. Whitman's "I am," a self that embodies imagination, travels beyond the personal. His poetry, made of intellect and body, is shaped fresh from the forge. This self is so all-encompassing, it can only exist as a "we." Here, however, I'm drawn to what Martin Buber says in *The Way of Response*:

> For the typical man of today the flight from responsible personal exis-
> tence has singularly polarized. Since he is not willing to answer for the
> genuineness of his existence, he flees either into the general collective
> which takes from him his responsibility or into the attitude of a self
> who has to account to no one but himself and finds the great general
> indulgence in the security of being identical with the Self of being.

As poets, many of whom accept Whitman as his or her forefather, we might at first feel uneasy with Buber's statement. We hope the Bard wasn't (that we aren't) speaking to a generalized "we," the other as object. We know that language is important to Whitman. Buber also says this:

> Language never existed before address; it could become monologue
> only after dialogue broke off or broke down. The early speaker was not
> surrounded by objects on which he imposed names, nor did adven-
> tures befall him that he caught with names: the world and destiny be-
> came language for him only in partnership. Even when in a solitude
> beyond the range of call, the hearerless word pressed against his throat,
> this word was connected with the primal possibility, that of being
> heard.

Whitman wanted to be heard, and so do we—it's something basic. The poet wishes to share. Even when the dialogue is with part of oneself, spoken to a corner of one's psyche, one would hope that he or she isn't Echo. For me, the speaker is often a universal "I" whose feelings have been shaped by experience and/or imagination, an empathetic witness.

Since the human being is an act of becoming, the "I" is *cultivated,* shaped, and nurtured—from first breath to last. The "I" possesses will: "I am" is an action, and so is the act of writing poetry a sustenance. Like any of the other arts, poetry isn't a career or a job. Neither is the poet the

mere keeper of an emotional logbook, nor a reporter, curator, or docu-
mentarist. Although he or she may keep a journal, jotting down the daily
mishaps, observations, and blessings, cataloging glimpses into the past
and present, straining to see the future, the poem is still "a made thing."

Robert Atwan, in his forward to *The Best American Essays 1995* says,
"The center of 'auto-bio-graphy' isn't 'self' or 'writing,' it's 'life' in the
fullest physical meaning of that powerful ancient Greek word." For the
writer, maybe it is really a combination of the three. A self embodies
imagination. We humans have the ability to bridge the past and future
while living in the temporal present. Emily Dickinson's statement seems
to have come out of lived experience when she says, "Tell all the truth /
but tell it slant." *Slant* seems to suggest that the poetry has to enter the
telling. For this recluse in Amherst, there are hints of the personal woven
into her poems, but one has to go to her letters to untangle musings
about Charles Wadsworth and Samuel Bowles. Did she have emotional
attachments to these two men? When we hold Dickinson's poetry up to
this question, her work, that box of poems her sister Lavinia found in
Emily's bedroom after her death, the poetry is what counts. In that sense,
William Gass's statement seems so right: "Autobiography is a life writing
its life."

Nowhere is this more apparent—how imagination and autobiography dovetail, one influencing the other—than in the life of Frida Kahlo.
When I stood in her house in Mexico City, with images of her past–the
mirror over her bed and the Victorian garments–I thought about the
brightness of the colors in most of her paintings. I wondered if she'd in-
corporated a sense of the tropics into her psyche to survive the ongoing
pain. Carlos Fuentes in his "Introduction" to *The Diary of Frida Kahlo:
An Intimate Self-Portrait,* writes:

> She is capable of coming back to her original sources and transform-
> ing them. She animates her father's photographs while reclaiming
> some of their stilted flavor. She also takes his calendars and fills them
> with an interior time, a subjective experience of night and day, summer
> and fall. "September" is her "September," not the ninth month—birth,
> perhaps miscarriage—of a successive year. Time stands still only to go
> underground and reappear tinged with the personal images of Frida

Kahlo. Not a painter of dreams, she insisted, but a painter of her own reality. "I paint myself because I am alone. I am the subject I know best."

In my *Autobiography of My Alter Ego,* a long poem, whose narrator is a Vietnam War veteran, the ideas and feelings the persona experiences rise out of a certain privileged position based on his white skin. The speaker in the poem disrobes his psyche, but I wanted a tone that authenticates him, that parallels the artist: a tone shaped by decorum and aesthetics—an observer as artist who happens to be a bartender, a veteran. He is not a character who impersonates the artist for the social moment or a stage, nor a performance artist who has fallen in love with the mike, but a character who has been wounded by his observations.

Perhaps, in many ways, this is close to what Bruno Dossekker did when he invented himself as Binjamin Wilkomirski, narrating *Fragments.* He says, "I have no mother tongue, nor a father tongue either," and goes on to say:

> My language has its roots in Yiddish of my eldest brother, Modeskei, overlaid with the Babel-babble of an assortment of children's barracks in the Nazi death camps in Poland. It was a small vocabulary; it reduced itself to the bare essentials required to say and to understand whatever would ensure survival. At some point during this time, speech left me altogether and it was a long time before I found it again.

Where Dossekker becomes his own fictionalized character or facsimile, with an invented biography, I wish for my character to speak from his personal history, from inside his own skin—a composite of a few veterans I've known. But it isn't nonfiction. At times, it seems as if I'm there at the Chimera Club, facing him, listening to his ruminations.

The artist is audacious enough to remember his or her beginnings in the womb—fully engaged in the present, but also a seer into the past and future. Willing to embrace some aspects of the embellished autobiographical "I," I am compelled to agree with Tomas Tranströmer when he says in *Memories Look at Me: A Memoir* that "Our earliest experiences are for the most part inaccessible. Retellings, memories of memories, reconstructions based on moods that suddenly flare into life."

Sometimes the autobiographical "I" invents itself because of ego or need for affirmation, but, usually it invents itself out of action: it defies silence. Death. Tension keeps it alive. Poetry doesn't exist without tension. In *Knots,* R. D. Laing's patterned sayings that fall between poems and prose passages, there's a moment that comes close to capturing the twists and turns of the "I" as artifice:

I am doing it
the it I am doing it
the I that is doing it is
the it I am doing
it is doing the I that I am doing it
I am being done by the it I am doing
it is doing it

In this little tussle of pronouns, the "I" as its own object, is something more than narcissistic. Laing attempts to create a template of the "I's" conscious action. It almost devours itself through action.

The intensity by which we remember an incident seems almost biological or chemical. Sharing a common history does not mean that siblings remember or recall identical facts. Things that may happen when brothers and sisters are in the same room at the same time are often recalled through contradictory details. Of course, the artist, especially the poet or fiction writer, feels that he or she is the *real* truth-teller or griot in such a familial gathering. But as that old spiritual suggests, "It ain't necessarily so." The plumber or seamstress might possess the sequential facts. The artist often shapes events and situations into art; we heighten the moment. Finding the shape embedded in language, we discover the possibility of the autobiographical "I" through our imagination. That is truth for us. So when the realist or pragmatist asks, *Did that really happen?* we can look him or her in the eye and say, *Yes.*

III

Degrees of Fidelity:
Ethical & Aesthetic Considerations

Kate Sontag

Mother, May I?: Writing with Love

My mother, in her own mixed-message way, once gave me permission to write about our family. I was visiting over the holidays, and we were having one of our customary late night heart-to-hearts: "Write about us all you want," she said, "but make sure you write with love." Years later, her statement still rattles my nerves, and yet if I think of someone else writing about me, I might be tempted to ask for similar consideration. For who cherishes public humiliation or blame? Who among us wishes to have some part of our life sensationalized at the whim of a fellow artist?

Robert Lowell's exposure and alteration of Elizabeth Hardwick's personal letters to him in *The Dolphin,* his book of sonnets detailing the demise of their marriage and his affair with Lady Caroline Blackwood, provides a provocative case. Many would agree that his friend, Elizabeth Bishop, was right to hold Lowell accountable, as she did in her correspondence with him, for what she called a "cruel" artistic decision. In "Rereading Confessional Poetry," Susan Rosenbaum cites the following note from Bishop to Lowell as illustration of the murky moral waters into which Bishop felt Lowell had plunged: "One can use one's life as material—one does, anyway—but these letters—aren't you violating a trust? IF you were given permission—IF you hadn't changed them. . . . But art just isn't worth that much." Clouding the waters further, for Bishop, was her belief that Lowell's use or *misuse* of Hardwick's letters, in addition to violating a private trust with his wife, had violated a public trust with his readers. Rosenbaum, again, cites the following as illustration: "The letters, as you have written them, present fearful problems: what's true, what isn't; how one can bear to witness such suffering and yet not know how much of it one needn't suffer with, how much has been 'made up,' and so on."

As the tide of autobiographical writing continues to flood the world, issues of responsibility toward the people about whom we write poems, as well as our contract with the reader, naturally arise. Many books of contemporary poems contain almost exclusively first-person lyrics, and a growing number of poets have adopted the narrative structure of memoirs or novels in verse. One recent example is Jane Shore's *Music Minus One,* which moves through each successive stage of the poet's life as she comes of age and matures—from childhood and adolescence to motherhood and the loss of her own parents. Sharon Olds's *The Father,* which chronicles, in graphic detail, her father's dying from the onset of cancer to reflection in the years after his death, is another example. And the subtitle of Andrew Hudgins's *The Glass Hammer: A Southern Childhood* speaks for itself. In addition, Carolyn Forché's 1993 anthology *Against Forgetting* has popularized the notion of a poetry of witness: poems that address the self in relation to history, particularly to crimes against humanity and other political extremities; the term is also used in relation to more purely private experiences of sexual violence, illness, abuse, and suffering. Such poems of witness or testimony constitute an important subset of autobiographical lyrics, including works as distinct as Forché's own *The Country Between Us,* Czeslaw Miłosz's *Rescue,* Sharon Doubiago's *South America Mi Hija,* Linda McCarriston's *Eva-Mary,* and Alicia Ostriker's "The Mastectomy Poems" from *The Crack in Everything.*

Of course, not all poems written in first person are necessarily autobiographical. They may be written in persona, or they may be a collage of personal, observed, and imagined experience. The boundaries between fact and fiction are as fascinating and complex in poetry as they are in prose, and deliberations about the truth, lies, and consequences of the lyric "I" can be as intellectually subtle as they are emotionally charged. Consider Philip Levine's statement from an April 1999 *Atlantic Monthly* interview: "Sisters walk in and out of my poems, but I don't have any sisters. . . . Why be yourself if you can be somebody interesting? Imagine a life. Imagine being something other than what you are." Or this from Larry Levis as remembered by a former student: "The more I lie, the closer I get to the emotional truth." Or this from David Yezzi in "Confessional Poetry & the Artifice of Honesty": "All poets use their lives for poetry, but not all lives are used similarly." Still, the question remains: to what extent do we need permission when we reveal family secrets or use as subject matter the personal lives of our relatives and friends, and to what extent do we *own* the material once we transform it into poetry?

In "Nonconsensual Nonfiction: Writing About Those Who Don't Want to Be Written About," Robin Hemley raises issues equally relevant for poets:

> Intention seems to be crucial in what one divulges about others. Are you willing first of all to divulge as much about yourself as you are about others? Are you able to realistically examine your motives? Are you trying to be the hero or are you trying to educate yourself? . . . .
> I often think the true nonconsensual participant in one's writing is some part of oneself that resists being revealed, like some secret inner personality.

In my more forgiving moments, I tell myself these insights about intention and self-discovery are what my mother was asking me to consider—certainly a task with more integrity than prompting me to paint a "beautiful" picture. "Make us look pretty as a picture," the mother of a poet-friend of mine once said to her.

I must confess, however, I often succumb to my own desire to create a beautiful surface. I am also aware of how such a surface can mask emotional turbulence underneath, especially when I write about my family. The following poem, whose external landscape is *beautiful,* is the first in a sequence of ten poems that addresses the fractured inner landscape of growing up as a stepdaughter in a time period when divorce was neither as common nor as openly discussed as it is today:

The afternoon we go rowing
swans bring us no closer
to perfection. Nor do reeds
bowing their heads downwind.

> My parents argue which stroke
> will turn our borrowed boat around,
> which method reverse this drifting
> into the Long Island wake

of another daughter's story,
her whole family capsizing
as storm clouds break
over the site of their future cottage.

> What are we doing here with them
> in the middle of this pond?
> Say the swans brought us
> or the reeds bowing their heads.

Last summer my stepfather
brushed a bee from his mother's hair
without her knowing. *What is it,* she asked,
touching where his hand had been.

> *It's nothing,* he said. *It's nothing.*
> Like the sound the oars will make
> dipping in and out of the water
> when this argument is over—

my sister on the dock
among the white glide of birds
and green bend of grass
motioning us toward her.

Later in the sequence it becomes clear that the sister in the last stanza
and the speaker are half-sisters, and the family that drowns is a projection of the speaker's original family that split apart when she was a young
child: her mother, her blood father, and herself. It was written with *love*
for the lost family that becomes idealized, just as the sister in the last
stanza becomes idealized because she, unlike the speaker/stepdaughter,
is the offspring of both parents in the poem. The sister also becomes a
projection of the speaker herself who remains forever in mourning for,
and separated from, her birth family.

In any event, to write with *love* or with *beauty* means something different to poets than it does to moms. Love of the poetic idea, the image,
the line, the surprise and permutations of individual words, music and
lyrical structure—all of these figure into a poem taking on a life, a truth,
and a beauty of its own, beyond the people who inhabit it or who provide the narrative impetus. Furthermore, because emotional truth is sub-

jective, many would qualify my mother's requirement of *love* to include *emotional honesty,* a potential source of conflict for both parties. In "Degrees of Fidelity," Stephen Dunn asks, "Is a poem ever worth the discomfort or embarrassment of, say, the family member it alludes to or discusses?" His answer:

> Certainly many poets have thought so, especially since the advent of so-called confessional poetry in the late fifties. My loosely held rule for myself is that if my poem has found ways to discover and explore its subject, if it has on balance become more of a fictive than a confessional act, then—regardless of its connotations—*I* will not be discomforted or embarrassed by it.

Despite the extent to which we may delve into the subject in unexpected ways—the day I went rowing with my parents, my sister was not even there with us—or alter certain details for the sake of musicality—the "bee" in my poem was actually a tick—the emotional truth remains and can elicit, in both the poet and the reader, a feeling of actual confession. Was my mother wearing a pink or a white nightgown the night we spoke about *writing with love?* Was my father sound asleep next to her or wearing headphones and watching TV? Was it Christmas, spring, or summer break? These facts seem trivial compared to the dead weight of my mother's words that, when I remember them, make the room go cold and my mind draw a blank even though I know she was asking me to be fair, which seems a fair enough request. If I were writing this scene into a memoir, my contract with the reader would oblige me to tell you that I cannot remember what happened next. Perhaps I left the room, feigning sleepiness, or changed the subject entirely. If I were writing a short story, I would feel free to pick a fight with her but challenged to make it *feel* true. If I were writing a poem, say a pantoum, I would feel equally inspired to be true to the form. The calling of truth, the necessity of invention, or the responsibility of love, however we interpret our role when writing about others, remains a central concern for poets as well as for fiction and nonfiction writers.

I think of a friend who, when making final revisions before her first book was published, agonized over a phrase in a poem about her dead uncle in order to spare her still living aunt's feelings. We shared an office and, as I bent over her shoulder to look at the computer screen she asked, "What do you think of my calling him a 'boogey' man instead of a 'drinking' man?" I felt as divided as she, as divided as I know many of us feel when we make public our own and others' personal lives. "'Boogey' is a great word," I said, trying to be supportive. And so she changed it. Recently, when speaking to a creative writing class she asserted, "There was already enough drinking in the book." Ultimately, each of us has to make a decision we think we can live with, both personally and aesthetically. For poets, the sounds and connotations of individual words or phrases are often the currency with which we weigh such decisions.

Balancing the potential feelings of those we write about and degrees of disguise, against our own reasons for and comfort level with making private lives public, comprises one ethical arena. Another is our contract with the reader with respect to literal truth. Should readers feel cheated if Sharon Olds, for example, had fabricated abusive parents or a dying father, or had done what Ted Kooser condemns, in his essay of the same title, as "lying for the sake of making poems"? While his position that poets not "exploit the trust a reader has in the truth of lyric poetry in order to gather undeserved sympathy to one's self" is an important and provocative one, it reflects the increasing blur between author and speaker. It also presumes that poets can control the reader's response and that readers can ascertain the poet's motive. The issue here is subject matter: when are we obliged to make clear the distinction between poet and speaker, fact and invention? Why does the poet Ai sometimes use the disclaimer "a fiction" directly beneath the titles of her newer persona poems, and sometimes not?

Say we write from the perspective of a rape victim but have not experienced rape. Perhaps we have a sister or close friend who has been raped but we choose not to reveal her identity, or perhaps we simply feel compelled as writers or as women to explore the subject matter. Are we morally bound to make clear the poem is written in persona? Kooser would say yes, and many who seek wisdom from fellow survivors in dealing with traumatic events through poetry might agree; for them, and for other readers, the politics of such identity shape-shifting may well be an issue. But don't poets have a long and healthy tradition of lying in order to tell the truth, just like fiction writers? Isn't our primary obligation to the poem itself, to make it *ring* true, no matter how factual or fictional? For if a poet elicits the reader's genuine sympathy or empathy, this usually attests to the imaginative force of the poem, part of the craft of which may be the artist's choice not to call attention to the "I" as a persona but to speak to the reader directly and intimately. A significant tradition of the dramatic monologue exists, but where and how do we draw the line, especially given that poets often discover their persona poems contain as much, if not more of themselves than do their poems that originate from experience, since wearing the mask can be so liberating.

Although she did not pair them in the same breath to make this point, Carol Frost, at an Associated Writing Programs panel in Albany in 1999, offered two intriguing examples that help illustrate the complexity of the issue. About Hilda Raz's powerful collection of breast cancer poems *Divine Honors* (which, it's interesting to note, includes an invented daughter), Frost admitted she would feel deceived if the poet did not actually have cancer. Yet about her own memorable poem "To Kill a Deer," in which the speaker tracks, kills, and guts a deer, Frost remarked, "Am I really a hunter? None of your damn business!" One thing seems clear: the rise of the poetry of witness, confession, and autobiography has made more complicated the negotiation between poetic license and the contract with the reader, between invention and interpretation, between the mother of the poet and the poet herself.

Ted Kooser

Lying for the Sake of Making Poems

I once knew a husband and wife, both aspiring poets. He had a young son from a prior marriage whose face was badly scarred. One evening, the stepmother showed me a poem in which she described her husband's first wife cutting the child in a drunken rage. Horrified, I asked, "Did that really happen?" and she answered, "No, it was an innocent accident. I just thought my version would make a better poem."

How could somebody write something like that, I wondered, just to "make a better poem?" The child's natural mother was libeled, and who knows what damage might be done to the child to have this distorted version of history on record? Did we really *need* that poem, that lie? Has it become acceptable for a poet to exploit the misfortune of another in this way, and by so doing quite possibly gather something for herself, some credit for taking on the difficulties of raising a "damaged" child?

I've changed the details to protect the identity of these people because I don't believe this poet intended any malice toward the natural mother, nor was she looking for sympathy for herself. She simply hadn't thought through all the implications. She was young, just starting out as a writer, and, most important, from her reading of contemporary poets she'd gotten the idea it was acceptable to fabricate something to make a better poem.

Perhaps I am hopelessly old-fashioned. Perhaps I should accept the possibility that what the poet says happened really didn't happen at all, but I'm going to have to make a painful adjustment in the way I read poetry and honor poets. I grew up believing a lyric poet was a person who wrote down his or her observations, taken from life. I have always trusted the "I" of Walt Whitman as he dresses the wounds of fallen soldiers; I trust Mary Oliver to tell me what birds she saw as she walked through a marsh; I trust Stanley Kunitz when he describes two snakes entwined in a tree.

When "I" says something happened, I believe it happened, and if something awful has happened to "I," I feel for the poet.

There are, of course, conventional poems that use the "I" in a very general manner: "I love you because . . ." In those poems, the "I" customarily suppresses specific autobiographical detail and defers to the subject, love in this instance. Shakespeare's first-person sonnets would fall into this category. And there are those poems that clearly are flights-of-fancy, as in "I leap the mountain in a single stride." I leave such poems out of this examination.

Nor do I include persona poems that are identified as fabrications by their context. The poet Ai comes to mind. When her persona poems are set side-by-side in one of her books, it is evident that these "I" speakers cannot be the poet, for no one writer could have had the wide variety of experience the poems present. But when her poems appear alone in magazines, the distinction may not be so clear. I would feel more comfortable with persona poems if each poem would in some way advise me that the experience presented may not be the poet's own.

I am most concerned about poems in which "autobiographical" information is presented in such a way as to affect the reader's feelings *about the poet*. In such poems, the speaker, calling himself or herself "I" (and without forewarning the reader in any way), builds a poem around what *appears* to be autobiographical information, but that is untrue. A childless man writes with great skill and tenderness about a schoolyard experience with his small son, engendering sympathy in the audience. Another poet writes with touching sadness about the suicide of a brother, and we pity her until we chance to learn from some other source that she has no brother. Hundreds of readers may be moved by these fabrications, moved to pity the poet, moved to praise his or her courage and candor.

Poets defending this kind of poem sometimes take the position that they are writing "dramatic" poems, thus sidestepping the ethical questions. Just the same, I prefer that the poet prepare me. If a poem is framed in such a way as to inform its reader, at its onset, that the situation presented is a fictional dramatic monologue, that seems to me to be honest and forthright. If a poet named Melissa writes a poem entitled, "Rebecca Speaks to the Elders," we know this to be a persona or dramatic poem. We'd all agree that the bishop in "The Bishop Orders His Tomb at St. Praxed's" cannot be confused with Robert Browning. Or if a poem is contained in quotation marks, we know that someone other than the poet is speaking. There are all kinds of ways to prepare a reader for a dramatic poem, and I think poets are obliged to do so.

I was recently asked to review a collection of poems, some of which were good examples of the kind of deception I am concerned about. I know a good deal about this particular poet's life, and I knew that the autobiographical information was fabricated. When I expressed my concerns about this issue to an acquaintance she said, "I don't have a problem with that. I've written a poem in which I talk about my disabled son, and I've never had a disabled son." She continued, "People sometimes come up to me and say that they are sorry for me, and I have to tell them that I made it all up." She went on to say that, curiously, those readers seem taken aback. Clearly, those readers have been cheated and deceived, and they have a right to be taken aback.

Weldon Kees seems to have been tinkering with this issue more than fifty years ago. His short poem, "To My Daughter," begins by speaking of "my daughter" and continues to do so, convincingly, until the last two lines, in which he confesses that he has no daughter after all, and doesn't want one either. For most of the poem, Kees's imagination tries on the idea of having a daughter. Then he rejects the idea because of all the possible heartache that might come of it. We believe him all the way through, then he pulls the rug out from under us. But since he makes his confession within the poem, we do not feel deceived.

Why are some of our poets recreating their lives? Can it be that they are merely trying to make their material more exciting? Is the country so in need of new confessional poems that it is necessary to construct them around events that never happened? Is this phenomenon caused by the "publish or perish" pressure on writers who are affiliated with universities, or is it indicative of some bigger ethical or moral problem?

The poet and critic Jonathan Holden has said, in a letter, ". . . much of the problem stems from the general blurring of genres in this post-modern ambience, such that the distinction between History and Fiction is no longer as clear cut as we had thought (hoped) it was." No doubt that's true. But though poets may have bought into postmodern theory, have their *readers* been prepared for this?

Since we know there are ways of writing about fictional situations—the dramatic poem, for example—the fact that some poets are not identifying their work as dramatic suggests that, in fact, they are up to no good. I credit my friend, the poet Bob King, with coming up with a pretty good test as to where the line should be drawn: does the poet get some extraliterary credit or sympathy from the lie? If the answer is no, the invented detail, the lie, is not bad.

All lyric poets, of course, alter details to some degree. On the other hand, I once knew a poet who carried fealty to the truth to an extreme. He wrote a poem about a cleaning woman he and his wife had once employed and from whom they had suffered painful indignities. When he showed it to me in manuscript he'd included a line: "The cans of pop I bought her." I said, "If you'd change that 'cans' to 'bottles,' you'd have a more interesting sound to that line," and he said, "But I can't do that; they were cans."

It seems acceptable to me to change a pop can to a pop bottle, but I would have felt deceived if I'd learned the poet had fabricated the story of his family's suffering at the hands of this woman. It is despicable to exploit the trust a reader has in the truth of lyric poetry in order to gather undeserved sympathy to one's self. Why do we permit this kind of behavior in poetry when we would shrink from it in any other social situation?

Carol Frost

Self-Pity

I.

I dream I am riding a unicycle with an angel who has tin wings, the two of us balanced on the seat. I am dying. Soon I will be covered with tubes. I am happy.

The next night a wounded deer is being chased by black dogs. I remove the arrow from his shoulder so that he can run more swiftly, but he falls. His chest turns to breast plate. His one powerful arm is covered with pagan signs. As he dies, I wake, sheets soaked, heart fluttering, weeping.

My dreams seem to come true when I am diagnosed as having breast cancer a few weeks later, and I must negotiate the distances between tears and joy, futility and the everyday. What suppleness of imagination or intuition made me aware of bodily danger before the doctors knew anything? I wonder. Will I be able to haul myself out of my fears, open the door and walk outside, observing the greater power of the elements? Will the suspension of time, as in dreaming, still occur when I sit in my studio to write, hours passing in minutes? How will things change?

The trouble with most answers is that they don't last—they don't make a permanent bridge between sense and feeling. Our belief and disbelief change with our experience and swing with our moods. Poetry acknowledges this, the words instigating in the reader an echo of a sense and feeling the poem presents, the author more like the idiot referred to in *Macbeth*—"Life is a tale / Told by an idiot"—than a philosopher or moralist. I think I write poetry because it doesn't say *all* that it means. There are surely other reasons, too, but my sense that poetry is based on an imaginative (and partial) perception of essentials is at the heart.

I returned to my desk to find out what I believed at the moment. For several years I had been writing poems in a form of my own devising:

eleven-line lyrics. I was interested in the different ways to fill that meta-phoric room, what doors or windows to leave open or shut to influence the quality of light, and the speed and slowness of the air currents. I took pleasure in the plastic qualities of the sentence, made small rhyth-mic phrases and placed them against others, tried new ways of making metaphors, and, ultimately, worked each poem to define an abstraction. I rarely wrote in the first person. Now I knew how to write this kind of poem, and I wanted to write something different.

There are two reasons I have avoided the first-person pronoun. First, readers encountering the "I" may substitute an interest in the affairs and concerns of a presumably real person for the experience of the poem. Second, I may be unable to finesse the language, the image, and the line to clarify the emotion and experience with sufficient variety and force to move the poem toward the universal and memorable. The problem in-volves sentimentality, which can come upon any of us under all manner of odd circumstances. Fatigue, illness, the swelling chords of violins— these and many other circumstances can make our emotions too facile. Farewells, reunions, landscapes of a certain quality, sunsets, the rich smell of lilacs—we could blush for our inappropriate responses. Most remark-able of all, perhaps, are the effects of self-regard. I reluctantly recall that the last time I rummaged through a trunk filled with childhood memen-tos, my very stupid journal entries from four months in Paris filled my eyes with tears. There was no pain, no image, no wording or recollec-tion, no thought, no sadness or displaced joy that could explain my secret response. Something was distorted. When the sentimentality di-rected toward oneself is too vague to fully articulate—perhaps involving tendencies to think and feel certain things and to behave certain ways as complement to the self—there are dangers. One danger seems clear: to substitute for the rich experience inherent in a poem the stock thoughts and feelings (nowadays, more apt to be shocking than tender) of a strangely honored "I."

Pronouns, like all words, have their own little aromas. While *kitten* and *tiger* have in common their feline nature, they induce very different associations and responses—tigers don't play with string. The same holds true for *he* and *she.* Two different sets of cultural attitudes waft into our thinking and feeling at the mention of the two genders and become part of any reader's understanding of, and reaction to, the events in a poem. A poem that ignores our underlying attitudes and stock associations, failing to assimilate them into the poem's total context, risks being misread. The point is not that when we read or write a poem that we assume the behaviors appropriate to gender—or the accepted behavior of cats—will be dramatized. The point would be that those attitudes and basic values that are *external* to the poem, but held by readers, are made to work for the particular experience that a poem is. Indeed, the clash between external attitudes and those in the poem may be sharp, as in these lines from Emily Dickinson: "She dealt her pretty words like blades / How brilliantly they shone." The effect of the lines is no doubt enhanced by the surprising juxtaposition of the feminine pronoun with knives other than cutlery. Even if this is tableware, the element of danger implied by the word "brilliantly" and the agency of the woman who deals them (who speaks so sharply and ironically), and is in control, clashes with our expectations of womanly behavior, especially in the nineteenth century. Our cultural attitudes are called into question and an excitement ensues.

Several years ago, while writing a poem about a group of people saving a sea creature washed up on the beach, I discovered that the poem reads differently if a woman, instead of a man, throws the creature back into the Atlantic. All kinds of notions, mythical and unwanted, arise; and the gesture of rescue, cupping hands underneath the torn flesh, seems sentimental if the woman does it, but unexpectedly tender coming from a man. I suspect this is more the case because the poet is a woman, and the quality of the image and statement would alter slightly, at least in the reader's mind, if the poet were a man. Perhaps then a woman could be the rescuer, the male poet having made a woman a hero, not of his own gender or who was implicitly himself. Here are the last lines:

> Then he puts his hands under the terrible flesh and heaves it
> as far as he can into the Atlantic, as if it were the mirror
> of a lost estate, the dawn-time of the world's first season.

As subtle as the shift in reader perspective might seem to be with a change in the pronoun, any change in response matters.

"A pronoun may seem like a small matter, but she matters, he matters, it matters, they all matter," said John Berryman, who goes on to reveal that "without this invention . . . I could not have written either of the two long poems." ["Homage to Mistress Bradstreet" and *The Dream Songs*] Berryman's poems are filled with autobiography, but the self that he presents is less *him*self than a person warring with several sides of his psyche, *our*selves shifting emotionally and intellectually in the world. We see this, and more, how the poet is simultaneously put in and left out of a poem, in *Dream Song #1*:

Huffy Henry hid   the day,
unappeasable Henry sulked.
I see his point,—a trying to put things over.
It was the thought that they thought
they could do it made Henry wicked & away.
But he should have come out and talked.

All the world like a woolen lover
once did seem on Henry's side.
Then came a departure.
Thereafter nothing fell out as it might or ought.
I don't see how Henry, pried
open for all the world to see, survived.

What he has now to say is a long
wonder the world can bear & be.
Once in a sycamore I was glad
all at the top, and I sang.
Hard on the land wears the strong sea
and empty grows every bed.

The pronouns are carefully adjusted to universalize Henry's experience of losing his sense of gladness and ease with the world after "a departure." Henry becomes uncommunicative and feels exposed, "pried open for all the world to see." The first-person speaker is familiar with Henry's story and sympathetic—"I see his point"—but if he knows who the perpetrators of Henry's anxiety are, he isn't telling. They are simply referred to as *they;* they could be anybody. The poem is really about Henry's state of mind, and again, the "I" seems to know it well. Who could that "I" be but Berryman, both the model for Henry ("Henry both is and isn't me," said Berryman in an interview) and another side of the poet, or a good, empathetic observer, perhaps a friend, who, seeing Henry's withdrawal and knowing something about Henry's life, muses about the psychological cause and effect, remembering his own early joy—"Once in a sycamore I was glad / all at the top, and I sang—" and acknowledging his own losses in the figure of the empty bed? We can identify with Henry and his loss and we can identify with the speaker who has witnessed Henry's plight and sees a similarity between himself and Henry—both are familiar. But the poem is even more richly universalized in the last two lines with its metaphor for erosion and endurance, the strong sea bearing down on the land in a world that the speaker says earlier "can bear and be," and in the phrase "every bed." *Every* implies that no one is exempt from loss—that it is natural for us all—him, me, them, and us.

Surely the poem is informed, on one level, by Berryman's father's death when Berryman was a boy, with his resulting suspicions about whether his mother, her lover, and the coroner had put something over on him by calling the suspicious death suicide. But Berryman's crafting of the poem makes this a tertiary concern, and our sympathies are not specific to the poet but to the character of Henry, so much like ourselves. Readers can think of losses other than the death of a parent, since the loss referred to in the poem is generalized—"a departure." The poem exposes us to a reality that is universal and a psychology we are familiar with on a wide spectrum; and though the poet is clearly a part of the drama of the poem, the emotions revealed are not simply expressions of the poet.

The first-person pronoun seems the trickiest of all, because of the tendency, in present tense, for a persona to be created whose utterances and behaviors seem too tenderly self-regarding. In James Wright's "A Prayer to Escape from the Market Place," we identify the person who speaks the poem, the "I," with the author of the poem, since the poem is not a dramatic monologue:

> I renounce the blindness of the magazines.
> I want to lie down under a tree.

This is the only duty that is not death.
This is everlasting happiness
Of small winds.
Suddenly,
A pheasant flutters, and I turn
Only to see him vanishing at the damp edge
Of the road.

The voice of the poet-speaker sounds, for this reader, over the top. Why, for instance, does he need to *pray* to return to the natural world? Will he never read the *New Yorker* or *Harper's Magazine* again? ("I renounce the blindness of the magazines.") Is the act of lying under a tree really death-defying? ("This is the only duty that is not death.") There is too much self-regard.

The poet asks us to imagine the passing moments as he walks in the woods, at one point turning to watch a pheasant fly away. So much depends on that figure, expressing the watcher's realization of the tenuousness of his desire to have things perfect ("This is everlasting happiness"), but one guesses that no irony is intended, only more complaint, whereas I am tempted, because of the hyperbole, to read the whole of the poem ironically. If a reader is predisposed toward the thought that nature is superior to commerce, feels as the poet/speaker does, or likes the poet, the poem may convince; but the exaggerations in the poem do not help an unconvinced reader to absorb into his own heart the poet's sadness. (Isn't the art and value of poetry to be found most surely in the heart and mind of the reader whose convictions differ from the poet's?) Since there is no other implicit or explicit motivation in Wright's poem for the lamentation, the uses of the first person—look at me *turn,* listen to what I *want*—provide one: this is the way I feel. And think. It's as if the subject of the poem is the poet's consciousness and sensitivity.

Walt Whitman's poem, "Hour Continuing Long," provides an example of universalizing the first person even as it dwells upon the poet-speaker's solitary grief:

Hours continuing long, sore and heavy hearted,
Hours of the dusk, when I withdraw to a lonesome and unfrequented
    spot, seating myself, leaning my face on my hands;

Hours sleepless, deep in the night, when I go forth, speeding swiftly
    the country roads, or through the city streets, or pacing miles and
    miles, stifling plaintive cries;
Hours discouraged, distracted—for the one I cannot content myself
    without, soon I saw him content himself without me;
Hours when I am forgotten (O weeks and months are passing, but I
    believe I am never to forget!)
Sullen and suffering hours! (I am ashamed—but it is useless—I am
    what I am;)
Hours of my torment—I wonder if other men ever have the like, out
    of the like feelings?
Is there even one other like me—distracted—his friend, his lover, lost
    to him?
Is he too as I am now? Does he still rise in the morning, dejected,
    thinking who is lost to him? and at night awaking, think who is
    lost?
Does he too harbor his friendship silent and endless? harbor his an-
    guish and passion?
Does some stray reminder, or the casual mention of a name, bring the
    fit back upon him, taciturn and deprest?
Does he see himself reflected in me? In these hours, does he see the face
    of his hours reflected?

As in the Wright poem, we are invited to think of the "I" as being the poet himself, here a lover forsaken. But the invitation is also made to identify with the speaker when the weariness and dejection that the "I" feels in lines 1–6 is widened to include those whose situation might be similar. The first part of the poem is written in statements about the poet's grief, while lines 7–12 ask questions about "other men" or "even one"—a "he" who may "still rise in the morning, dejected, thinking who is lost to him, and at night, / awaking, thinking who is lost," having suffered as the poet-speaker has. In that shift where the writer hopes to find a twin (the "even one") in grief, the poem essentially asks whether someone might see himself reflected in the poet's circumstance and feeling. In the list of questions addressed to "another," another question is implied— whether the reader can imagine and feel this experience. Even if the reader has never lost a lover or is heterosexual, the reader may well remember or imagine an "hour" when a measure of solace was found in thinking that there could be others who, at some time, felt the same as the poet. Despite all the adjectives and images of self-pity *(sore, heavy hearted, lonesome and unfrequented spot, pacing miles and miles, stifling plaintive cries, discouraged distracted, sullen, suffering, I am ashamed, it is useless, torment),* the repetitions of the noun phrase ("Hours . . .") to emphasize the lengthiness of the speaker's sorrow ("O weeks and months are passing"), and the pictures of the "I" sitting, walking the streets at night, "leaning my face on my hands," despite the exaggerations and the autobiography (Whitman's homosexuality), we can find ourselves. We have been asked to do so through the skillful adjustments of syntax and pronoun.

Beyond the betrayal by the lover ("The one I cannot content myself without, soon I saw him content himself without me") the motivation for the poem is clarified in lines 6 and 7. The poet's sense of unexplained shame (about his self-pity or, perhaps, his homosexuality) sends him out from himself and into society to look for a man, or group of men, who might understand. And in this gesture, this reaching out, the reader can find yet another way to respond to the poem. Might we not be those who could understand and not recoil, could forgive the "I" his self-regard? The poem has built in a variety of reasons for the focus on "I," so that what would in a less well-written poem sound like maundering sounds, here, perfectly apt. It is also worth noting that even as reference to the self continues into the last line ("Does he see himself reflected in me?"), the last words of the poem are about the other: "In these hours does he see the face of his hours reflected."

In the weeks since I began wishing to change my work, the dangers involved in writing in the first person—where the poet is both put in and left out—have come to be alluring. What accents and syncopations, what vocabulary, metaphoric purchase, shifts in syntax and point of view can I discover to help me give voice to the most difficult events in my life? Certainly there are models to be followed: the reticence in William Wordsworth's first-person narrative in the Lucy poems; Thomas Hardy's intent and meditative first-person voice in "Wessex Heights," shaping the images of a man haunted by his past; Robert Lowell in "Skunk Hour," who manages to say, "I hear / my ill-spirit sob in each blood cell, / as if my hand were at its throat. . . . / I myself am hell" with neither irony nor self-pity; Randall Jarrell, whose "I" in "A Man Meets a Woman on a Street" walks behind a woman (later, as it turns out, his wife) for blocks and blocks, then touches her on the nape of her neck; W. D. Snodgrass's "I," his daughter's father ("I lift you on your swing and must / shove you away") in Section 7 of "Heart's Needle"; and Frank O'Hara, whose first line in "Why I Am Not a Painter" is "I am not a painter, I am a poet"—a very tricky start.

I have sat at my desk and written two poems in the first person as a beginning:

Waking

It was dusk, the light hesitating
and a murmur in the wind, when the deer, exhausted,
turned to look at me, an arrow in its side.

Though I pity dreamers, taking a thread
and weaving it upon the loom of Self—the secret,
gaudy, wonderful new cloth—, I will tell the end of the story.

His shoulder was torn, the joint held by one sinew,
which I severed with the blade of the arrow,
so when he ran there were no impediments.

The black dogs that followed were swifter,
their barking ancient, despicable.

As he fell, his chest turned to breast plate,
his one powerful arm covered with pagan signs.

Nearly stupid in my waiting for what would happen next,
each breath propelling me and him toward dust,
I woke, the sheets soaked, heart fluttering—:

When death comes into the sleeping room as through a tiny hole,
like a rent in the Covenant, it hurts.

Thaw

Clouds brown in a puddle

to find beautiful; the fields

violet and blue-green trees

manger-rich, ah, sweet, the dirt;

gathering head

and unable to tell mercy

in this presence, this absence,

Can the flawed heart fill?

in a cold fever,

turn from winter, then turn again.

but move to and from my nature

sweet that teach me

and cold western gray—

and feathers of snow, volleys

what I thought myself to be,

that comes with this joy,

that I may have to leave this place

like the skies Job learned

chaste, yes, but faraway

on dawn's cold sleeve;

the music of melting

where blind fishes wait, cold

from fathomless grace

this cold presence.

I saw in a flash of pain,

all my Februaries

What can I do

and call those moments

to find in the drift of eastern gray

in currents, spicules

of sunlight—that I am no longer

even with the overwhelming regret

the simple assumption

sooner than I want?

II.

All poetry is autobiographical in its revelations of the motions a mind makes. The hesitancies, detours, innuendoes, spirals of lies and truths, as a person remembers or invents, are as essentially personal as the facts of that person's life. If readers look for event first, and take for granted the manner of telling, even so the texture, the syntax, the distribution of the literal and figurative, the *timing* of a writer's disclosures, false or true, are important in establishing, among other things, the authenticity of the work. We know many poems that lean too heavily upon their subject; the fact of some trouble or trial, as asserted in the poem, can be documented as having occurred to the writer, but the voicing or stance in the poem is somehow at odds with its gravity—we doubt its authenticity in much the same way we may come to doubt a person's character.

The verbal contraption Auden said a poem is can tell us as much about the writer as a chair; every turn of the lathe and every peg tells us about the woodworker, even if our main purpose is to rest there comfortably, considering our own affairs. We may ask: Is it made of burlwood or tiger maple? What rough or fine brushstrokes applied the patina of lacquer or oil? What economy, what sense of design is present? What can be learned, revealed no less in the handiwork than in the expression, is what is essential to and about the artist—the state of awareness or remembrance, feeling, intent, proclivity, reason, care, regard, trifle, judgment, and imagination, but not whether the trees grew in his backyard.

III.

I will tell the rest of the story. Six months to the day after I had a mastectomy, I had my last chemo treatment and insisted on a celebration. Secretly, I was blue, and stiff with confusions. The aches and symptoms of the healing poisons in my blood reminded me daily that I was fighting the cancer, but it seemed there was nothing more to do. Was I healing or uncured? No one could say for certain, and I would look in the mirror and see hairlessness and strain. Who was I then? I, who had always had a physical relationship with the world and built my trust on that bedrock, felt the ground shifting. I was helpless to decide whether I wanted reconstructive surgery. I wept at the drop of a hat. I was frozen. I nearly fell apart. And I could neither write nor dream—my thoughts wore a groove: *and if I die, and if I die* . . .

I wanted to be warmed again into existence, to be imagined, to be known, to be identified, but I couldn't believe in myself, nor in poetry, nor in beauty. Not for several months. Then I began to paint water-colors of my garden, of labyrinthian woods, of tumultuous skies. I think I started to paint less because I couldn't write than because I'd never made the time to try it, and I'd wanted to paint since I was a child. I'm no good. I only paint what I think I see, not what I must paint so another can see what I've seen. But that hasn't mattered. And during the summer after the cancer, I found great pleasure out-of-doors, in daylight and gloom, letting the pigment run into the petals of water outlined in pencil—flowers with beautiful Latin names. Perhaps painting wasn't the reason for my new calm. Perhaps it was only the passing of time, the mobile, evanescent mornings, the smoky evenings, one after another, until my sense of impermanence came to feel normal.

One morning I found a newly dead bird beside our country road, a beauty with speckles and a red patch at the throat. I carried it home, and placed it on my desk. It was still warm. I took out my paints, wanting, I think, to preserve that harrowing moment so close to both death and life. While I painted, a bead of liquid formed in the bird's beak and pooled on my desk, and all theory and all distance went out of me. I thought of my friend Larry Levis, the poet, who had died the year before. Such a brilliant writer—edgy and original. I thought of the weak consolation in the revelation, that his pen had been open on a pad of yellow paper where his last lines lay, scratched over, revised. After I finished the painting, I showed it to a friend who said, "Oh, a flicker." In my bird book I saw that it was true, my bird was an Eastern woodpecker with a brown back, "whitish below with black spots," and a red patch on the nape. I again felt the pleasure in expression, of resemblance, of naming, of knowing, and of powerful emotion. Because of the confluence of object, art, and feelings for another, I'd gotten over myself. I felt I could write again.

That night my dreams came back. I was crossing an enclosed bridge

much like the Bridge of Sighs, and when I couldn't get past a locked
door in the middle of the structure, I slipped out a window and into a
tea-colored river, swimming upstream to a castle where I was handed a
bowl filled with a precious liquid. I swam back, with one hand held
above the surface of the water, to preserve the contents of my metal
bowl, and as I approached a bend in the river, five or six children appeared. They had wet garlands of greeny leaf and flower on their heads,
and they swam toward me smiling. The dream was far too private and
sentimental to recount in verse, but I wasn't looking for a subject for
poetry. I think I may have been waiting for a return of equivalence,
where an image is several things, besides itself, and emotion is as universal as it is personal. If the cancer had made me too literal and too self-
absorbed for a time, it also gave me a certain insight into some necessary
qualities of imagination—motion, above all, and the ability to go on, as
if the imagination trusted or could go on without.

Flicker

Beauty is for amateurs
        —William Matthews

Chisel-billed, eye cerulean, with a crimson nuchal patch,
flicker lay on the ground, still-warm, and went on aging:
intricate, stricken watch, pear in a dessicating wind.

I brought it home and began with the box of watercolors
to wash the eye with milk for the clouds and sky it fell from,
then dragged my partly dried brush over the rough paper surface

for true textures on the wings, imagining old orchards, umber and si-
    enna,
where I'd seen the undulating flight of loose flocks. I studied
the yellow undertail, then daubed with the colored water

along the gray and dun stripes. As for my pulse, I felt for
    temperament—
for gravestone, for shadow—to affect the utter silence after a long, long
    day
of call, *whurdle, peah*, drum, and *wicka*. Then I blotted and scraped
    the throat.

I saw dusk falling like a comment on each detail
that led to it and gradually was lost and leaving.
A hint of song must be caught, a clarity of neither light nor memory,

and it must be in the physical form of the flicker
and the orchard where the wind makes a soft racket—song that breaks
    the learned heart.

I stared and stared by lamplight, stroking the white,
thinking sour-gum, dogwood, poison ivy berry, river mist, imagining
    the free side of the hills,
when a bead of liquid formed in the flicker's beak and pooled on my
    desk.

My evasions went up in smoke. With colors, tones, casements,
and stars with exact names, who could but feign the moments
once lived that will never be lived again?

Who has a home in this good world and doesn't yearn?
I do. It's mine. I do.

Stephen Dunn

Degrees of Fidelity

Several years ago in an essay, I found myself invoking Robert Frost's wonderful statement, "We shall be known by the delicacy of where we stop short." I tried to use it as a standard that would resonate into our dealings with others, especially those closest to us, and into matters of aesthetics. What we choose not to do in a poem, for example, may reveal as much about us as what we choose to do. This seems particularly true if our subject involves family.

Yet, as poets, our fidelity to people we know is always complicated by our fidelities to the poem and the language we find ourselves using, not to mention to truth itself. While in many instances, our subjects will be served by restraint, we can imagine in other instances that they might be served by extravagance, a going beyond proprieties and conventions. By the end of my essay, I found myself embracing Frost's statement and arguing for a poetry of uncommon, surpassing gestures. I don't think one necessarily excludes the other.

Nevertheless, poems—restrained or extravagant or some combination of the two—that involve or implicate family members should raise certain questions for those of us who write them. Why are we writing about this particular subject in the first place? Certainly we have the entire world of experience to draw from. Why this poem about brother, or mother? Why now? And what must such a poem do to involve strangers in what's personal to us? As the cry of its own occasion, a worthy poem ideally should suggest some answers to those questions.

My experience as both a writer and reader has convinced me that most poems about family should be put in a locked cabinet, like diaries, kept, if kept at all, as private data for our children to find after we're dead. Some family poems, of course, driven by necessity and in search of the elusive properties of their subjects, deserve the light of day. For the poems to merit this, their authors need to develop new allegiances—to texture, tone, rhythm (to name just a few)—as the poem evolves. In other words, pretty soon aesthetic matters as well as subject matter must be driving the poem. If not, there'll be Trouble with a capital T in Poetry City. Beware the poet who values content more than the handling of content, a danger especially present in our most personal poems.

If poems about family are always going to involve some degree of personal disclosure, how that disclosure is tonally delivered, not to mention paced and framed, usually will determine its success. Sylvia Plath's "Daddy" is interesting to examine in this regard. It is clearly a poem of extravagance, but not without discipline. Whatever we might think of its claims, it's clear that Plath had as much allegiance to sound pattern, rhythm, and to overall orchestration of effects as she did to indicting her father. It's an amazing, vitriolic performance. Despite her bile, she remained committed to the poem as poem, a made thing, a system of words and sounds. It's a poem, though, that never confronts self, and that always asserts rather than explores. Yet it's only because of biographical reasons that we question its tone. If we were ignorant of her biography, we would readily accept it as a poem of rage. Plath was burdened by the psychological weight of her perceived victimization, but, of course, didn't have to worry that the victimizer might see her poem. He was long dead. The poem reads like an exorcism, and she no doubt found a kind of radical freedom in its composition, a freedom achieved at high cost. Yet we can be sure that she was also liberated, paradoxically, by what was at the heart of her poem's complaint: her father's absence.

The dead free us as much as the living constrain us. But constraint, I would argue, is often a useful thing to feel. The need to suppress can be the impetus to transformation, to ingenuity, to the virtues of indirection. Think of how the dramatic structure in "Home Burial" gave Frost permission to examine and explore the alienation in a particular marriage. He must have felt that he needed such a construct (tantamount to a mask) to engage in what was personal to him. Or how Theodore Roethke's rhymes and iambic trimeter in "My Papa's Waltz" helped create a tone that lightened what otherwise might be construed as a father's violence.

Roethke's fidelity to form, we can say, kept the extravagant in check. We should consider it our good fortune that many poets have been unable or have chosen not to address their subjects directly.

I know someone who is able to write about his adulteries because, he says, his wife is not interested in reading his poems. (That fact alone might be a good reason for adultery.) Yet I'm not sure that the freedom he feels necessarily makes for better poetry. It seems like a sad, not a radical, freedom, insufficiently hard won. Most of us are cognizant that the poem we write that implicates or involves our spouses or significant others will constitute a matter of delicacy. If, at a certain time in our lives, that sort of poem insists on itself, becomes necessary subject matter, then so be it. If handled more or less directly, we'll need to seek just the right tactics that will permit us to go far enough so that we understand what stopping short might mean. But maybe we'll pretend we're a flower, like Louise Glück. Or find a strategy like Berryman's in his *Dream Songs* where competing voices and rarefied syntax blur the purely autobiographical. Artifice will not only save poems, but perhaps marriages as well. The too naked poem, one that makes dirty laundry its flag, that never gets beyond its original impulse, is a poem we have failed. We should hide it from everyone.

Is a poem ever worth the discomfort or embarrassment of, say, the family member it alludes to or discusses? Certainly many poets have thought so, especially since the advent of so-called confessional poetry in the late fifties. My loosely held rule is that if my poem has found ways to discover and explore its subject, if it has on balance become more of a fictive than a confessional act, then—regardless of its connotations—*I* will not be discomforted or embarrassed by it. But to raise the notion of the fictive is to also raise corollary questions. What, if anything, would we falsify, say about our mothers, for the sake of being interesting? Do family stories, written in the first person, make a covenant with the reader that implies a fidelity to the actual? If they were written in third person, would that covenant change? Put crudely, how many among us would sell out our grandmothers for an exquisite stanza? We know that Plath's father, for example, was not a Nazi. But no one knows for sure whether my mother, in fact, obliged me after I requested to see her breasts when I was twelve, as I claim she did in my poem "The Routine Things Around the House."

> When Mother died
> I thought: now I'll have a death poem.
> That was unforgivable
>
> yet I've since forgiven myself
> as sons are able to do
> who've been loved by their mothers.
>
> I stared into the coffin
> knowing how long she'd live,
> how many lifetimes there are
>
> in the sweet revisions of memory.
> It's hard to know exactly
> how we ease ourselves back from sadness,
>
> but I remembered when I was twelve,
> 1951, before the world
> unbuttoned its blouse.
>
> I had asked my mother (I was trembling)
> if I could see her breasts
> and she took me into her room
>
> without embarrassment or coyness
> and I stared at them,
> afraid to ask for more.
>
> Now, years later, someone tells me
> Cancers who've never had mother love
> are doomed and I, a Cancer,
>
> feel blessed again. What luck
> to have had a mother
> who showed me her breasts
>
> when girls my age were developing
> their separate countries,
> what luck

she didn't doom me
with too much or too little.
Had I asked to touch,

perhaps to suck them,
what would she have done?
Mother, dead woman

who I think permits me
to love women easily,
this poem

is dedicated to where
we stopped, to the incompleteness
that was sufficient

and to how you buttoned up,
began doing the routine things
around the house.

I tell you here that she did show me her breasts. Would I have written so if she hadn't? I don't think I would have. I think, though, there *are* details that I made up. I've lived so long with the way I mythologized that event that I can't remember which ones are which. But I do remember feeling, after much revision, that all the details, fictive or actual, contributed to the poem's emotional veracity.

The truth is that for many years the poem made me uncomfortable. To mishandle such subject matter was to descend into the vulgar. When I was finally able to get myself to include it in a book, it was because I'd discovered its hidden subject. The poem was not just a provocative personal story about a mother's grace under pressure, as I had thought, but was also about limits. The way she showed me her breasts and then buttoned up had taught me something important about when and how to stop short. When I realized that, the poem's conclusion, which had eluded me, came to me in seconds.

There are degrees of fidelity to the actual. I don't know a single poet who wouldn't hesitate at locating, say, a spousal argument in Paramus instead of Princeton if that change better served the poem's sonics. Although some family matters and memories should, I suppose, be sacrosanct, very few, even with the best of intentions, are immutable. In essence, they are emotionally incomplete without the stories that shape and subjectify them. Large events in our lives especially have a para-factual existence. When we start talking about them, we are already changing them.

We will be known by our track record. If we hold nothing dear, that will show and indict us in time. If our falsifications and embellishments, in large, served the genuine and the true, that, too, will show over time. If we were restrained when our emotional stakes were already small, we will have misused restraint. If our extravagances were more glitter than substance, we probably should have found more ways to contain and constrain. Finally, the writer's worst sin is to be uninteresting. I wouldn't kill off my grandmother for an exquisite stanza, but I'd certainly travel with her to Bolivia, where we never went, or rescue her from her inveterate silence, if setting and speech could bring her alive.

Andrew Hudgins

The Glass Anvil:
"The Lies of an Autobiographer"

> *Memory is a strange Bell—*
> *Jubilee, and Knell.*
>
> > —Emily Dickinson

Vows are dangerous. As a freshman in high school, when I read poems only for class assignments and even then reluctantly, I vowed that if I ever wrote anything as silly as a poem at least I'd never write about anything as silly as flowers. Flowers struck me as effeminate, nonutilitarian, decorative at best, and, at worst, an utter waste of time and money. As a subject for poetry they combined those shortcomings with a complete lack of serious engagement with the world and its ills. In time, I became a gardener, and as a poet I've returned again and again to the traditional subject that I so scorned, finding it fecund with meaning and rich with emotional significance. And I've enjoyed the uneasy honor of having one of my lines quoted in the Smith and Hawken gardening catalog next to a photograph of, and a paean to, a Scottish manure fork.

In college, in mild revolt against my Southern Baptist upbringing, I vowed I'd never write about religious subjects, which seemed to me artistically spent and intellectually vacant. Later, because they were all the mode in the 1960s and '70s, I vowed I wouldn't write poems about paintings. The idea of making art about art appeared to me parasitic and to place the second work of art, in this case the poem, at an extra and enfeebling remove from life. I ended up writing a book of poems, *The Never-Ending,* which has, as one of its recurring subjects, the life of Christ as portrayed in paintings.

In similar fashion I vowed, because I was tired of so-called confessional poetry with its often lurid self-revelations, not to write about myself. So, probably as a result of that vow, I wrote a childhood memoir. In poems. *The Glass Hammer: A Southern Childhood.* But when I broke my vow, finally admitting that what I'd begun *was* an autobiography, I made another vow: that I, as I alone could do, would tell the honest truth. This vow was a reiteration of a vow I'd made as a child. By age twelve I'd read dozens of childhood memoirs with sentimental portraits of a loving if harried Mama, a loving if occasionally frustrated and angry Papa, and a supportive if moralistic community. Despite some obstacles, success came so easily for the gifted child in these memoirs that it seemed inevitable—and all I could think was that those charmed lives, fascinating as they were, were nothing like mine.

A few years later, having read dozens more childhood memoirs, I began to say, "They're lying. All those writers are just lying. Life isn't that simple." But as I thought about it, I began to see that they weren't consciously lying; they just didn't remember. And I vowed then, with all the plentiful rage and gravity that a fifteen-year-old Southern boy steeped in codes of honor and manhood can bring to a vow, that if I ever wrote about my life, I'd do it while I was still angry and that my book would be brutal, ruthless, scorchingly honest. I'd blow the lid off the pot, dammit.

But as soon as I began writing in earnest, I realized that some lies—though now we literary sorts call them "fictions"—are inevitable. Others are merely convenient. Autobiography is in some ways a translation of actuality onto the page, and in other ways, a selective and imaginative recreation, a work of art—and the two roles can go to bed together and enjoy their uneasy congress only by lying to each other. But the lies are loving lies, told with hope and good intentions, and I'd like to talk about some of the ways autobiography—or at least mine—lies. I've arranged these fictions in ascending order of transgression, from misdemeanor to felony.

1. The first lie, the whitest lie, the lie that hardly troubles my conscience at all, is the lie of narrative cogency. It consists of clearing the narrative underbrush so the story, like a flowering crab apple in a lot overgrown with sumac, can be more easily seen and appreciated. Exposition, explanation, and qualification are boring. They try the reader's

patience. And with its emphasis on condensed intensity, poetry is even less tolerant of them than prose. In *The Glass Hammer*, I didn't bother to explain my family's frequent moves from one air force base to another as my father was transferred around the country. He retired in Montgomery, Alabama, where I went to high school and college, and since I long ago decided that Montgomery was my hometown, I simply set the whole book there.

And I combined characters and incidents. Here's part of a poem called "Original Sin":

> I'd watched
> hens jab the dirty silk
> of spider webs, jerk back,
> pause, flip their heads, and swallow
> live spiders. *Only a thing that's poisonous itself*
> *eats spiders,* Grandmomma said.
> And I believed her. I'd seen them
> rake each other's raw
> red flaws until they'd crippled
> or killed a bird that could
> have been themselves. Or me.
> But when Grandmomma marched
> out to the tree, I followed
> and crowed at the hens as she
> grabbed one bird by the neck
> and snapped her wrist. Waist-high,
> held out away from her,
> the dead bird walked on air
> and flapped. I ran behind,
> crowed, clucked, and flapped my arms
> triumphantly, till Grandmomma
> said, *Shush, boy,* and I shushed.

In early versions of the poem, the versions closest to actual events, the person who calls the chickens poisonous is my aunt, not my grandmother. But having three characters in the poem—aunt, grandmother, me—complicated the scene unnecessarily and left the poem diffuse and unfocused. When I merged aunt and grandmother into one character, the scene snapped into artistic and dramatic coherence, and I was able to finish the poem. It was, I believe, a good aesthetic decision, one well worth the sacrifice of literal truth.

The problem with the lie of narrative cogency is that, in life, the stories *don't* stand clear of the underbrush; the flowering crab apple is obscured by sumac. So even this white lie falsifies experience: intensification and clarity *are* misrepresentations. But I've listened to so many well-intentioned friends agonize to get pointless facts straight that I don't worry about this lie too much: "In the third grade, Miss Porter hit me with a ruler for . . . no, wait—I think it was the fourth grade because Daddy hadn't yet bought the green Plymouth. But, then, maybe I'm confusing Uncle Ralph's green Dodge with Daddy's Plymouth. He—Daddy, I mean—really loved that car. . . ." Torture by exactitude.

2. If the lie of narrative cogency contracts, condenses, tightens memory, the lie of texture expands it. Some details, of course, are welded forever into our memories: how Grandmother smelled of Vicks VapoRub, the way Mother always mispronounced "municipal" as "mu-NINCE-ipal," then mocked herself for not being able to say it properly. But most details slide out of our memories because they aren't important until we try to write about the past, and then they are essential because storytelling thrives on details that enrich the texture of bare plot. The accumulation of precise and telling details is what makes the story, scene, image, line vivid in the reader's imagination, while memory tends to drop details and preserve the emotional reaction they evoked. So, in order to capture the reality of an experience, I was, in an odd paradox, sometimes forced to invent details to make the experience more believable.

For instance: in "Funeral Parlor Fan," I wrote about a handheld fan very popular in rural, un-air-conditioned churches. On one side, the fan has a sentimental picture of Jesus and on the other, an advertisement for a local funeral home.

> I fanned
> a little more, grew bored, and jabbed
> my brother, kicked the seat in front of me
> till, casually, my mother's hand
> dipped out and popped my head, not hard,

> with Jesus praying in the garden
> or, flipped, Hobb's Funeral Home. And just
> to hear myself talk, I'd say *ouch*
> and get another dose of Jesus,
> and slightly harder too. The beat
> resumed: tick tock, tick tock, and I
> took up the worn, two-sided fan
> and tried—small hands—to keep the beat.
> Tick: Jesus. Tock: Hobb's Funeral Home.

Although the poem says *Hobb's* Funeral Home, I can't remember what funeral home actually supplied fans to the Vineyard Baptist Church. I needed a one-syllable word and, after much flipping through books looking at names, I chose Hobb. As many hours as I sat in church, reading and rereading the back of those fans, you'd think I'd remember the name emblazoned in huge letters on them. You'd think I'd remember the name of the people who buried one of my grandfathers, both grandmothers, two uncles, one cousin, and my mother. But I don't, and this particular poem would sound unconvincing and I would sound moronic if I jerked it to a halt and admitted my ignorance.

3. The lie of fictional convention. While every word of "When I Was Saved" is literally true, I can't help feeling that this poem about my being born-again and baptized into the Southern Baptist Church, because of its subject, meshes too easily with what readers anticipate when they read a book subtitled, *A Southern Childhood.* Religion, anguish, sweat, guilty sex, and physical deformity are, after all, characteristics of Southern writing that readers expect:

> I couldn't breathe at all
> when I, damp handkerchief clamped on my mouth,
> was lowered into death. I went down easy,
> stayed, panicked, struggled, and was yanked back up,
> red-faced and dripping. After that, each Sunday
> I went to preaching early so I could sit
> behind a boy whose torn right ear did not
> attach entirely to his head. Through that
> pink gap of gristle, I'd watch the preacher shout,
> croon, soothe—between that boy's head and his ear.

More sinners lumbered up the aisle. I longed
to run up and again be purged of Adam,
who was reborn each night, like Lazarus,
by my own hand, beneath the sweat-drenched sheets.

I worry that I may have traded on elements that I've come to understand are exotic to readers who did not grow up in evangelical Christian churches. One of the most disconcerting things about writing an auto-biography was seeing my life, which I'd preferred to think of as unique, take on recognizable literary conventions. The autobiographer takes his or her own life as material and, once it is material, it, for some purposes, stops being life and becomes primarily material. Then it falls into cate-gories of material, like the coming-of-age story or the Southern gro-tesque. I suddenly looked up from the page I was writing and saw myself not as myself, an individual, but as a character in a poem fathered by William Faulkner and carried to term by Flannery O'Connor.

Questions arise: Did they teach me to see what I see or did they teach me how to write about what I see? Or did we all drink from the well of common cultural experience? I prefer to believe the last possibility, but I suspect it's a combination of the three. One thing I don't point out in the poem, though, is that my conversion and baptism took place not in Alabama, but in San Bernardino, California, while my father was sta-tioned at nearby Norton Air Force Base.

4. The lie of emotional evasion. The sin of omission. The things that make us evasive and shifty in life are the things we will attempt to slide over on the page. Sex and death are the deep sources of most euphemism and avoidance—as well as other forms of emotional flinching, ducking, dodging, fudging, and sidestepping. Although we'll write about actions we were ashamed of once, but have since come to terms with, the actions and attitudes we remain ashamed of are hard to put on the page. It's dif-ficult for me to say what I'm evasive about. If I had been deliberately eva-sive about something while writing the book, I'd probably still want to sidestep it; and since many evasions are self-deceptions, how can I admit to ducking a subject I'm unaware of ducking?

If I recognized that I wanted to slide over something, I made myself go right at it. One source of evasion that's especially sensitive to a Southerner is our culture's touchiest taboo at the moment: race. It's a subject that I tried to write about for decades, but always failed. It overwhelmed anything I could say about it. It seemed to overwhelm language itself. But since I knew overlooking racism would be dishonest, I forced myself to write about it. Although I'm generally pleased with the poems that resulted, I learned that it takes a lot of energy to blast through the resistance to writing about difficult and painful subjects, and, as a consequence, the things I don't want to say are the things I say harshest and loudest. I'm afraid I may have overemphasized the anguish, unhappiness, and sorrow I felt as a child when trying to come to terms with—trying to *understand*— the past and present racism of the world around me.

I don't think I was evasive about death. I've been obsessed with death since I was a child and, if anything, I give it too much attention in the book. But I was evasive about sex, and not because I'd enjoyed such a rollicking adolescence that I didn't want to brag or that I wished to spare the reputations of my many lovers. Rather the opposite. Raised Southern Baptist, a faith I took seriously even as I was seriously troubled by it, I didn't, in fact, have sex till I was married. (Well, depending on exactly how one defines sex.) But on the few occasions I've shared that fact with friends, I've either been called a liar to my face or marveled at with polite and amused sympathy. It took many attempts before I was able to mention, quickly and in passing, that my first sexual experience took place on my wedding night, and I only put it in the book because I felt I had to.

5. Emotional evasion is merely the first step on the path that leads to the considerably more egregious lie of the recreated self. When I, as a teenager, began to write, one of my first discoveries was that I could make myself look good. This temptation is, of course, an extension of the human tendency to recount events so our motives are clear, understandable, noble, while other people's are left unexamined or put in a bad light. And in writing, with the opportunity to explain ourselves even more fully and thoughtfully, as well as to shade or shape facts, circumstances, and actions, it's easier yet to make ourselves the heroes of our own lives. For about six months after this discovery, I was enthralled by how I could be so much wittier, shrewder, kinder, more sensitive, and more knowledgeable on the page than I am in life. I could be the me I'd

always wanted to be—and without doing the hard work of attaining the virtues I claimed for myself. But it was sleazy, this self-ennobling, and I knew it was sleazy. Soon I reacted against it, and vowed I wouldn't do it anymore. Maybe because I was once so in love with how I could present the reader with a new and improved version of myself, I react with almost physical revulsion when I suspect a writer is gilding his blemishes. My wife says I now take a perverse delight in putting unnecessarily ugly constructions on my own motives. Perhaps she's right. The truth is, being wrong, flawed, crude, ungracious, and incomplete is pretty much the story of my life. But it's also true that presenting myself on the page as such packs an emotional kick for both writer and reader.

Consider how I come across in "The Colonel":

My father lifts the crippled airman's body
and jokes about how light he is and how
we need some rain. He holds him while the man's
young wife strips off the yellowed linen, cracks
white sheets above the bed and lets them drift
across the mattress. She smooths them, tucks the corner.
My father lays the shriveled Christian down.
Three times one week, four times the next. A job
he shares with someone from another church.
He comes home ashen. And every single time,
before he leaves the house he turns to me,
false casually, "You want to come along?"
"Do you need help?" I ask, and he says no.
He leaves. I watch teevee. I'm sixteen, shit!
And I don't want to be a soldier yet.

In the poem I refuse to assist my father in a disagreeable but noble task, though I do imply that if he'd said my help was necessary, I'd have obliged. But I did prettify my actions. As I wrote about this incident, it seemed to me to show the sullen refusal of an adolescent to embrace cheerfully the responsibilities of adulthood and the obligation to serve others, so I changed my age in the poem to sixteen. Actually, I was in my late twenties, living briefly with my father after my first marriage had failed and I was between jobs. Even when making ourselves look bad we can still find a way to make ourselves look good. "Gilding our blemishes," I called it a few paragraphs ago, when I was scorning others for doing the same.

6. Lies of extended consciousness. This mystical-sounding category covers two kinds of lies. One is the outright appropriation of other people's experiences. Theft. But it's not really theft, the thief protests. The story was just lying around and John Reese wasn't using it. He's in the air force now. What's he going to do with his story? Besides, I need it more than he does. I can put it to use. And in "The Benedictine Hand," I put to use my friend's story about his high-school biology teacher who, while showing the class how to insert a glass tube into a rubber stopper, slipped and jabbed the tube into her palm:

> "Now that's what you are not supposed to do,"
> she said. She held two frozen fingers up,
> as if to bless us. "I've cut the median nerve.
> This is what's called the Benedictine Hand.
> It's paralyzed." She flexed her thumb and last
> two fingers. The blessing fingers stayed erect.
> Then, pale, she wrapped her red hand in a wad
> of towels, left the room—quick, angry steps.

As I say, I didn't see this happen. My friend John Reese saw it, a boy who was enough like me, I'm tempted to argue, that it makes little difference that he saw it and I didn't. Not only could I have easily been the boy who saw his teacher ram a jagged glass tube into her palm, I know exactly which one of my own teachers would have done it and how she would have reacted. Since the day in the Huntingdon College dining room when John told me the story, my teacher has so many times in my imagination driven that tube into her palm and stood before the class with blood trickling down her left wrist and forearm, that I can only with great difficulty, remember that it's not a memory.

After *The Glass Hammer* was published, I called John and apologized for stealing his story. He didn't know what I was talking about. He'd forgotten. Which only proves that the story was more important to me than it was to him and thus rightly mine because I realized its true value. Is it really stealing, the thief asks, if the victim doesn't miss it when it's taken?

A more subtle, less clearly transgressive form of the lie of extended consciousness occurs when the writer applies knowledge he or she has as an adult to a childhood experience. That's what I do in "Fireflies After Twilight," in which I reflect on being a boy on a screened-in porch, watching fireflies till I fell asleep:

> Rarely more
> than one light quavered at a time,
> flicking its diminishing sexual light
> against the crowded pines. Eros
> and Thanatos I'll call it now
> but then I simply called it fear.
> If I'm still frightened—and I am—
> it's complicated with yearnings
> toward doubleness and indecision:
> how during sunlight I block light,
> which warms my back and loosens me,
> while after dark I stand out, white
> against the black pines, usually
> but not always at odds with nature,
> God and the gods. . . .

I am almost as different from that child I once was as I am from John Reese. Just as I stole John's story, I am, in this poem, stealing a story from my young self and using it for my adult reflections—reflections that would baffle and annoy the ten- or twelve-year-old boy who lived the experience. Ten or twelve? See? I don't even know him well enough to know how old he is. The adult interprets that boy's life in ways the boy would not comprehend and would probably reject out-of-hand as making a big deal out of nothing.

And now we have already moved deeply into the next lie.

7. The lie of interpretation. The essential lie. When I was about three-quarters of the way through *The Glass Hammer,* I sent what I'd written to my editor, Peter Davison, a writer with a clear eye for writing and the ability to make himself excruciatingly clear even to those who have ears and cannot hear.

"The book doesn't go anywhere," he said.

"Yeah, I know. I don't want it to. If the book ended with a forced sense of reconciliation, it'd be a lie."

"I didn't say it should have a forced sense of reconciliation. I said it didn't go anywhere."

"Life doesn't go anywhere. That's the point."

"It's unsatisfying to read a book that just stops. As it is now, your manuscript just drops off the table. Think about how you'd feel if you were reading it."

And finally, what friends had been trying to tell me for almost a year became crystal clear. My vow to write while I was still angry had brought me this far but it was now making it impossible for me to end the book. "I was pissed off then and I'm still pissed off now, but at least I can laugh about it" isn't much in the way of making one's life comprehensible to a reader. That's a truth I normally have a firm grasp on but had let slip from my hands while grappling with the psychological complexities that got churned up when I tried to turn my personal life into literary material. Grudgingly, I went back to work, trying to make sense out of material—my life!—that I had resisted making sense out of because first I'd have to understand it, and that understanding could be tentative, provisional, and painful. Then I'd have to forgive it, which is painful. Then I'd have to ask for forgiveness, which is even more painful. Then I'd have to write it all down, through many drafts, which would mean going through the whole ordeal over and over again. Aesthetics and psychology are uncomfortably interwoven, but in autobiography, the warp and woof is pulled even tighter than in most fiction because the writer's own emotional, spiritual, and intellectual progress becomes the aesthetic progress of the book.

But was I wrong to resist meaning, resolution, closure? Interpretation is the lie of tendentiousness. We live our lives, most of us, ambivalently, full of unresolved emotions and guilts, unsure of where we're going and where we've been, and, more unnervingly, unsure of why we're where we are. But all that suspended feeling and thought, if it remains suspended, makes for an unsatisfying aesthetic experience. The problem boils down to this: life has no intrinsic meaning while art has to have it. Or at least significance. Or, if not significance, shape. The biographer is given a natural closure for his or her book—death. But the autobiographer, being alive, has to choose where to end. That act of choice, an aesthetic decision, then echoes throughout the rest of the book, modifying and shedding light and dark on all that has come before, more like the end of a novel than the end of a biography, more like the closing of a fictional world than the end of one life in the continuing flow of history.

The greatest poem about childhood is Wordsworth's *The Prelude,* a poem I hated from the moment I began reading it. I hated it, not as a poem. As a poem, it's magnificent. I hated it as a romantic and romanticized view of childhood. Stephen Gill, in his fine biography of Wordsworth, returns time after time to Wordsworth's poetic account of his own childhood, pointing out where the poet is being interpretative— where he violates chronology, where he is evasive, and where it's impossible to discern if he's being literally accurate, as he shapes his story to demonstrate how nature was the dominant force in his childhood. Almost everything that does not support this thesis is swept away or suppressed.

After reading Gill on Wordsworth and *The Prelude,* I finally understood I didn't hate the poem; I simply hated Wordsworth's interpretation of childhood, and was not yet willing to grant him his interpretation of his own childhood. My temperament is not romantic, and if I hated many Southern memoirs, no matter how well written, for their soft-focus sentimentality toward childhood, happy families, and the fair sex, I loved Maxim Gorky's *Childhood* and *Adolescence* for their harsh, gritty view of those same things. But Gorky lied, too. Interpreted. His grittiness is often in the service of his Marxism, as is Richard Wright's in *Black Boy.* Not that Gorky's, Wright's, or Wordsworth's interpretations are necessarily wrong. It's just that they are interpretations, and thus, like most interpretations, exclusive. Like St. Augustine's interpretation of his life, Jonathan Edwards's of his, Jean-Jacques Rousseau's of his, and Benjamin Franklin's of his. And once we've posited a reading of our lives, we tend to look back and see how all roads could only have led us to the truth because it is the truth, and all roads could only have led us to where we are because we are here. A formulated interpretation tends to drive out other possibly valid interpretations and suppress ambivalence, ambiguity, and chance. But if having an interpretation presents aesthetic difficulties, not having one, as I finally came to see, presents more. Even worse than the overdetermined, moralizing story is the story with no reflections, no point, no sense of progress—emotionally, intellectually, or spiritually. If we are listening to a story, there has to be a reason the story is being told and a reason we're listening.

My vow to stay angry was, of course, an interpretation too, but the premature interpretation of a fifteen-year-old boy, and as I thought about it, I began to see why the memoirists that I'd been angry with, and contemptuous of, had striven so hard—often too hard—to forgive and be forgiven. The rage of a sullen and oversensitive boy is unattractive but appropriate at fifteen; from the mouth of a forty-two-year-old man, it's the immature product of a stunted personality. And I would have deprived my book of any forward movement at all if, out of fidelity to the vow of a fifteen-year-old boy, I had omitted the understanding I'd struggled to acquire over the intervening twenty-seven years. Still, I'm satisfied that some—enough—of my adolescent anger, confusion, and unhappiness came through in the finished book anyway. *The Glass Hammer* was recently included on the Young Adult Library Services Association's "list of recommended books for young readers" because it was "identified as having high appeal for teens, ages 12–18, who, for whatever reasons, do not like to read"—an honor I'm still mulling over, pleasure wrestling with bafflement for the upper hand.

8. While interpretation lies by saying, "It means this," impressionism lies by saying, "It feels like this." Reading my own book, I was surprised at how my childhood came across as very rural, very country. Because my father was a career military man, I lived in Texas, New Mexico, England, Ohio, North Carolina, California, and France before he was stationed in Montgomery, Alabama, where, as I mentioned, he retired and where I attended high school and college. But both my parents grew up in Griffin, Georgia, and when they could, they took me and my brothers back there to spend time in the country with my grandmother, aunts, and uncles, as well as first, second, and third cousins arrayed in gradations of kinship that I could never comprehend. Even more important than our visiting Griffin, though, is the way my parents carried rural Georgia with them wherever they went, and from them I absorbed country expressions, speech patterns, attitudes, beliefs, and habits of thought without even knowing I was absorbing them. The

book may give an impression of a more rural childhood than the one I actually lived, but it does give a true reflection of how large those visits to Georgia loomed in my memory and imagination.

I'm always astonished at how falsely I remember things, astonished at how plastic memory is. And even when I know a memory is incorrect, part of my brain cleaves to the wrong, imagined memory, and now I hold two images in my head, two memories—and the false one is more vivid and more emotionally significant to me than the actual one. Which, then, is the truest memory? It's convenient when the actual events adequately convey the emotional experience, but sometimes they don't and the writer has to choose. I acknowledge the dilemma in a poem about my grandfather's funeral:

> A week from now I'd start
> to wonder where Da-daddy was. I'd ask.
> Momma would hug me, moan, try to explain.
> But in the hot car, now, her bright red lips
> churned wordlessly until they caught. She screamed.
> My father, cousins, kin all say I'm wrong.
> But that's how I remember it: she screamed.

> ("In a Car Outside the Vineyard Baptist Church")

While I wouldn't be so disingenuous as to argue that a false memory is valid simply because it is vivid, I would argue that there must be some subjective truth to it, some emotional truth—and that one reads an autobiography to see how the writer experienced and evaluates his or her life and a biography to find a more objective view. The lie of impressionism is the biggest lie, the least defensible logically, ethically, or morally; and it's inescapable for a writer attempting to create an artistically coherent work. Even appropriated memories, like the one about the teacher who stuck the glass tube through her hand, have an emotional force for the person who needed to appropriate them, and if that force is strong enough, it's almost as misleading to omit them as it is to include them.

My argument grows strained and my tone shrill because I'm unhappy with the illogical, unethical, and immoral position that practical experience has led me to. But the trust I bring to reading an autobiography is a reader's trust in a convincingly told tale, not the trust I bring to reading the *New York Times* or a history of Assyria, in which aesthetics are secondary to accuracy. The autobiography dances on the shifting middle ground between fact and fiction, reportage and imagination, actuality and art; and different writers will draw their lines on that ground in different places. As an artist, a poet, I drew my line considerably further to the side of impressionism than a reporter or historian might have, or than I had meant to when I began the book.

Although the lies of interpretation and impressionism bother me, they are essential. We read memoirs precisely to find out what one writer thinks his life means and how that life felt to the one who lived it. As I look back over *The Glass Hammer*, I say, yes, that is what my childhood means, and, yes, that is how it felt. And, to make those two affirmations, I accept, however uneasily, the lies I had to tell.

Brendan Galvin

The Contemporary Poet and
the Natural World

I.

In the last line of his poem "Eye and Tooth" (*For The Union Dead*, 1964), Robert Lowell concluded, "I am tired. Everyone's tired of my turmoil." Ostensibly about the complications of a toothache, the poem reaches through that to various events from the speaker's life— the "turmoil" of a personality that would become the centerpiece of the confessional movement which has come to dominate American poetry over the last thirty years. One might think that such a statement as bald as Lowell's would have signaled the beginning of the end for his group. Still, we are only now witnessing the decline of the confessional strategy, in poems that appear to be baring the author's troubled psyche but which are so intangible that the reader often can't decipher the problem.

In the work of Lowell and other confessional poets, the twentieth-century persona (exemplified by Eliot's Prufrock, for instance) is replaced by a speaker who more closely represents the author, and the poem's circumstances can usually be verified as more or less the author's own. Lately, however, the confession is often contextless, with little of the who, what, when, where, and why that might give the reader some sense of character, setting, or incident—a few clues to keep him interested. This new kind of poem supposes that the reader will take the time to work its meaning out; such presumption arises from the contemporary workshop, where students have to read one another's work in order to participate. But art is not school, and the reader who believes that details are a form of evidence, a proof of the poet's argument, can refuse to play the game without feeling like a philistine.

Michael Burkard's "Untitled" is an extreme example of the poem without context and indicates how far the confessional strategy has been pushed:

> I wanted to love those
> I wanted to love, often
> I did not want those
> who loved me; it was
>
> a disagreement with myself
> as if myself was myself,
> like trees which are so laden
> with night they are night trees,
>
> which they are not. Sometimes
> the end is a contradiction
> of the tale: the end is simply
> not the end, the contradiction
>
> of wanting the end and
> not wanting it. I want you.
> I no longer want. I wanted
> To love those I wanted.[1]

"A poem a day / Keeps Geraldo away," some optimist said, but "Untitled" seems dangerously close to the content of "infotainment." Burkard clearly doesn't believe in details, and not much can be certified about his speaker except that he has trouble making up his mind; even less can be said about the "you" addressed only in the final stanza. In Lowell's "Eye and Tooth," by contrast, we are able to judge the speaker's predicament because the poet provides us with sensory details. We don't have to suspend judgment and grant him his sincerity merely because he's a poet. A remark like, "Nothing can dislodge / the house with my first tooth / noosed in a knot to the doorknob," provides more information than all of Burkard's sixteen lines.

Another variant of the newer kind of confessional poem is one in which the directive to "make it strange" has pushed the sides of the envelope so far that whatever was enclosed seems to have fallen out somewhere in transit. Note, for instance, the empty confession and contextless images in these stanzas from John Ash's "Methodical Sonatas," with their mix of tired postmodern tropes:

As if encarmined tulips opened
with a sudden pop like that of a toy pistol
morning surprises you again,
and the new griefs already seem the old griefs
and they must move over, shift seats
in this mismanaged theatre of a life
so that the fresh pain may be installed
like a blade of glass next to wrists.

The page no longer lies flat, it blinks and rises.
The words assume green or yellow vestments,
and officiously obstruct the way forward
like secretaries in some bland outer-office,
refusing to remember your name:
you are invisible again
as if standing at a bar in England.[2]

Where are we? Are the transitions between the various similes and metaphors enough to allow the reader to follow the poem's unfolding? Or is he or she left thinking, "Modern life is fragmented, but not *this* fragmented," or even wondering, "Is this the plot summary for a new *Star Trek* episode?" If this seems flippant, consider that the reader has been exposed to such possibilities by the author, who hasn't provided enough evidence to put anyone else on the right track. Poems like "Untitled" and "Methodical Sonatas" are closed systems and can't be verified by outside experience, external reality, the natural world, or whatever one wishes to call it. There is no sense in either poem of a life lived beyond its margins.

This is not to say that everything in contemporary American poetry resembles these poems, but that works like these are common and are usually ratified by enrolling the author under the banner of Wallace Stevens. (Note the title of Burkard's book, *Fictions from the Self*, for instance.) Even recent Poet Laureate Mark Strand, relating how he tried to defend his choice of poetry as a vocation by reading "The Idea of Order at Key West" to his mother, goes on to say that

the context of a poem is likely to be only the poet's voice: a voice speaking to no one in particular and unsupported by a situation or character,
as in a work of fiction. A sense of itself is what the poem sponsors, and
not a sense of the world. It invents itself. Its necessity or urgency, its
tone, its mixture of meaning and sound are in the poet's voice. In such
isolation the poem engenders its authority.

A novel, if it is to be convincing, must share characteristics with
the world we live in. Its people must act in ways we recognize as
human, and do so in places and with objects that seem believable. We
are better prepared for reading fiction because most of what it tells us
is already known. In a poem most of what is said is neither known nor
unknown. The world of things or the world of experience that may
have given rise to the poem usually fades into the background. It is as
if the poem were replacing that world as a way of establishing its own
primacy, oddly asserting itself over the world.[3]

Strand never explains how a poem can "engender" its authority in isolation. Over whom or what? Likewise, he doesn't elaborate on categories
other than the "known or unknown," though he seems to believe in such
categories. Nor does he indicate how a poem might establish "its own primacy . . . over the world," or why it should want to. Coming from a
Stevens aficionado, such statements neglect the fact that, in Stevens, one
repeatedly comes across utterances like "reality is the central reference for
poetry," and "the real is only the base, but it is the base," and "in poetry at
least the imagination must not detach itself from reality," and "all of our
ideas come from the natural world: trees = umbrellas."[4]

II.

Mention "the natural world" in some poetry circles today and there's
likely to be a lot of wincing and scraping of chairs and running for cover.
"Forget the crocuses coming up," "the spectacular ocean undulating /
without us," and "those flamingoes standing like symbols / on their solitary, pink legs," Stephen Dunn advises a student in a poem called
"Poetry." It has to be about "women and men, men and women."[5] And
although by the last line Dunn has changed his mind, telling the begin-
ner to violate his advice, we feel he's only mollifying readers who see

beyond his clichéd crocuses, ocean, and flamingoes a genuine hostility toward bougainvillea, the Sargasso Sea, and semipalmated plovers as subjects and objects for poems.

My own anecdotal evidence for this attitude also confirms its pervasiveness. After a reading a few years ago, the young professor who had served as my host told me he couldn't get excited about my subject matter, since he'd grown up in New York City. Apparently he found the natural world esoteric; imagine how *I* felt when I later bought his first book and discovered that many of the poems were about Italian opera. A recent generous review of my work contains a sentence beginning, "If you yawn at the thought of reading a collection that opens with poems about owls and fall warblers. . . ."[6] But why should owls and fall warblers be more boring than, say, yet another poem about a poet's divorce or sex life? A former student of mine, who used to hike in the Wasatch Mountains, reports that one of his acquaintances in an M.F.A. creative writing program once phoned and said, "Phil, I need a two-syllable name of a bird that lives up there. Quick!" And recently, the editor of a glossy magazine rejected a submission of mine because he understood from marketing surveys that his audience would know nothing about growing or crossbreeding varieties of apples, the poem's subject.

Whatever happened to the idea that one of the uses of literature is to help educate both author and reader? Or the notion that part of the poet's work is to nudge us into seeing things newly and differently, into opening our eyes and minds to what is insufficiently noticed? "Poets are legislators of the unacknowledged universe," said George Oppen, putting a spin on Shelley's axiom.[7] Jacquetta Hawkes, although she is an archeologist by profession, has no qualms about writing about birds.

> Perfectly formed while men were still brutal, they now represent the continued presence of the past. Once birds sang and flirted among the leaves while men, more helpless and less accomplished, skulked between the trunks below them. Now they linger in the few trees that man has left standing, or fit themselves into the chinks of the human world, into its church towers, lamp-posts and gutters. It is quite illogical that this emotion should be concentrated on birds; insects, for example, look, and are, more ancient. Perhaps it is evoked by the

singing, whistling, and calling that fell into millions of ancestral ears and there left images that we all inherit. The verses of Medieval poets are full of birds as though in them these stored memories had risen to the surface. Once in the spring I stood at the edge of some Norfolk ploughland listening to the mating calls of the plover that were rambling ecstatically above the fields. The delicious effusions of turtle doves bubbled from a coppice at my back. It seemed to me that I had my ear to a great spiral shell and that these sounds rose from it. The shell was the vortex of time, and as the birds themselves took shape, species after species, so their distinctive songs were formed within them and had been spiralling up ever since. Now, at the very lip of the shell, they reached my present ear.[8]

This is part of a prose paragraph, but if one takes into account the rhythm of its sentences, the intriguing metaphor of the spiral shell, and the way Hawkes calls our attention to how humans and birds have over time swapped places in the biological schema—something most of us would never think about—the poetic possibilities seem evident.

Because 85 percent of Americans now live in urban areas and know very little about the natural environment, one of the aims of the poet might be to bring it to them, to make them aware of what's to be found in the vast spaces between the cities. (I will wager, for instance, that every reader of this page knows someone who believes cuckoos exist only in clocks!) Yet one rarely encounters someone like Anne Winters, who in her work about New York manages to incorporate *both* the urban and the natural with beauty and power, as in the opening stanzas of "The Billboard Man":

> At sunup at the foot of Broadway
> the Mohawk builders of cities pause
> crossing the blue flaw. They see the whole
> island carved by one glacier (a drop of vapor
> still rising and falling far out on the back of the ocean).
> They see the sunlight stream softly
> on sheetmetal, thousands aloft in the rigging, tailor birds
> stitching the sails and aqueducts of the city.
>
> In midtown, billboards and marquees light and cloud
> Broadway. Cleopatra unrolled once more

from her carpet, ape armies, interstellar wars
. . . the White Nile lets a feather fall.
Over the lobby, two billpaper profiles eye
each other, glazed and dumb as fish.
Below, in the dark, in the whir and bloom
of the orchestra, stamen stirs against pistil.[9]

If Adam, as he named the animals, became the first poet, what does it say that now some poets seem fearful, even outraged, that animals exist—and thereby may distract the writer from contemplating his or her inner life? And if poets, who are supposed to be the psychic advance guard, the lightning rods of the race, don't know anything about the environment around them, how can we hope to preserve it?

III.

What C. P. Snow noted about literary people in his essay "The Two Cultures" (1959) is at least as true today:

> They are impoverished too—perhaps more seriously, because they are vainer about it. They still like to pretend that the traditional culture is the whole of "culture," as though the natural order didn't exist. As though the exploration of the natural order was of no interest either in its own value or its consequences. As though the scientific edifice of the physical world was not, in its intellectual depth, complexity and articulation, the most beautiful and wonderful collective work of the mind of man. . . . It is rather as though, over an immense range of intellectual experience, a whole group was tone deaf.[10]

I am not suggesting that a poet has to have a Ph.D. in paleobotany, but when Gerald Stern claims to have been awakened by "two or three daws" in West Virginia,[11] and Larry Levis writes about linnets as though they were American birds,[12] I wonder how far their insights can be trusted, and I'm tempted to question their grasp of the facts, their assumption that no one will know the difference, and (at the very least) their Anglophilia in matters ornithological. Such writers put themselves in much the same predicament as the male model in a Ralph Lauren ad of a few years ago, who was fishing in the surf with a spinning reel attached to his boat rod, a freshwater fly tied to the end of his line—without benefit of a leader—and a foot or so of monofilament dangling from the knot. To carry home whatever he would catch with this rig, he had a freshwater creel about the size of a loaf of Pepperidge Farm bread over his shoulder. "Fact is not truth, but a poet who willfully defies fact cannot achieve truth," Robert Graves admonished in *The White Goddess*.[13]

Why is the biosphere an unpopular or forbidden source for some writers? Because too much bad verse about crocuses and the "spectacular ocean" has been written? This is hardly an adequate excuse, since there has been just as much bad verse about love or the end of it, about war and being against it, and about the self with its "desires" and "gestures." It is the poet's success with his approach that counts, not the general branch of experience he mines. There are no forbidden topics, only ineffectual ways of dealing with them.

The attractiveness of egocentric cerebrations is that they require no internship, no time-consuming outside reading, no looking closely at objects, and no research; you can tap into your inner life right away and get with the program. To write about the natural world with any success, however, you actually have to know something about it because what you say can be verified by an attentive reader. An overwrought "natural" trope, this one by Charles Wright for example, doesn't hold up very well when set beside the touchstone of an external reality available to everyone:

> The past is never the past:
> > it lies like a long tongue
> We walk down into the moist mouth of the future, where new teeth
> Nod like new stars around us,
> And winds that itch us, and plague our ears,
> > sound curiously like the old songs.[14]

I have never been made itchy by a wind, nor have I heard any old songs in one. (I wouldn't deny the latter possibility, but I can think of lots of golden oldies no wind could sing.) What is a wind doing in a mouth, anyway, and aren't teeth that nod loose? When coupled with stars, they too quickly recall the ancient grade-school joke: "Your teeth are like the stars. They come out every night."

Similarly, the ocean in these lines by Chase Twichell is inaccurately spectacular:

I remember the sound of the sea
stealing back its souvenirs,

its hissing aphasia,
its spume and meringue,

all the defensive petals
loosening and falling away,
exposing the sound at its very center,

the one syllable, the *no.*[15]

Unless this ocean is meant to be a repository for after-dinner leavings, "meringue" and "petals" are wrong for the context, and what is a "defensive petal," anyway? And although aphasics are capable of saying "no," they don't hiss, they try to make language sounds.[16]

Often such writing merely provides contemporary examples of over-extended pathetic fallacy, as in Roger Weingarten's "Sometimes, at Thirty-Six":

I look up at the stained

fingers of my old friend yellow birch,
who had a fatal yen for gossip, heights,
and exported blends, and imagine
the two of us pacing that nun's cap

of a hill looking east at the soft-bellied
mountains, or heaving the bone-weary
branches high over the dark
brown water, and sharing smoke, an apple

gone soft in my pocket.[17]

Such wrenchings are nearly always in the service of illness, nihilism, or some portentous frisson; each in its own way demonstrates what can happen when the emphasis is too strongly placed on the speaker rather than on the reality of what he or she is speaking about. But when the ratio of inner life to outer life is reversed, as in these lines from John Updike's

"Crab Crack," it's possible to introduce scissors, lipstick red, old men, and even pancakes to talk about blue crabs—without losing sight of the fact that the crabs and not the speaker are the poem's emphasis:

> We can feel
> at the pole's other end their fearful
> wide-legged kicking, like the fury of scissors
> if scissors had muscle. Blue and a multitude
> of colors less easily named (scum green,
> old ivory, odd ovals of lipstick red
> where the blue-glazed limbs are hinged)
> they rest in the buckets, gripping one another
> feebly, like old men fumbling in their laps,
> numb with puzzlement, their brains
> a few threads, their faces mere notches
> on the brittle, bloated pancake of each carapace.[18]

Like other people, poets seem to fear associating themselves too closely with the world "out there" for other reasons as well. Although at this late date, we probably wouldn't deny we're part of that order—originated in it, developed there, depend on it, and continue in our various annual observances to mark the salient points in its cycles—we find it hard to contemplate that under the tyranny of necessity, we are all, man and beast alike, capable of becoming ogres. "Blood is the belly of logic," as Ted Hughes has put it.[19] Still, there's another side of this, the one we usually fail to think about in the face of such arguments. Listen to Gary Snyder's version:

> But how could we *be* were it not for this planet that provided our very
> shape? Two conditions—gravity and a livable temperature range be-
> tween freezing and boiling—have given us fluids and flesh. The trees
> we climb and the ground we walk on have given us five fingers and toes.
> The "place" ... gave us far-seeing eyes, the streams and breezes gave us
> versatile tongues and whorly ears. The land gave us a stride, and the lake
> a dive. The amazement gave us our kind of mind. We should be thank-
> ful for that, and take nature's stricter lessons with some grace.[20]

Most of all, though, I believe that more than a few contemporary American poets, males in particular, have bought into the bourgeois stereotype that anyone who writes about the environment also presses lilies in books, and looks and behaves like Ernie Kovacs's unforgettable, but unfair, Percy Dovetonsils: the poet as arch-nerd, lisping and peering from the television set through lenses that magnify his eyeballs. I believe this caricature is as strong today as in the past, and it's worth noting, apropos of it, that the high-school sitcom always portrays the student scientist as a nerd, too, so, at least in that respect, the popular media *do* couple science and poetry for the public mind. It's simply not macho to write about flora and fauna or to study science, even though curiosity about the nature of things has always been one of the strongest human qualities.

Tom Lux might feel that his prose poem of the 1970s, "Green Prose," is juvenilia now, but its attitude is telling:

> I'm writing this with green ink so you'll believe me when I tell you I'm a nature poet. I'm a nature poet. You know, the ones close to the earth—the green water, blood, and breath of it all. . . . Don't move!: there's a grasshopper on my shoulder and I think he's about to nuzzle my ear!—Surely you're getting tired of this nature bunk by now. Nature is bunk! In the dry cave of every nature poet's mind there is a desire to torture chipmunks, those most detestable of small rodents, to stomp Lady Slippers, etc. And who hasn't dreamed of strangling a deer with his bare hands, of tearing out the liver and devouring it? Let's get this straight once and for all: green is the symbol of death and mourning, it's the official color of lamentation. Everyone but me has lied to you: *there is no green*—unless it comes from gashes, from far inside the blackest lung, *no green*, don't think about it or you'll die.[21]

When a poem about natural things is done well, it can provide its author with a rich source of imagery and language and its reader with an experience unavailable anywhere else. Still, the contemporary poet too often seems content with a textureless exercise in line breaks. No such problem befalls the scientist, however, so when one of them brings metaphor and simile together, as did the nineteenth-century French entomologist J. Henri Fabre to describe the Thomisus spider, it can make us wish our poets read more natural history:

> After all, this cutter of Bees' throats is a pretty, a very pretty creature, despite her unwieldy paunch fashioned like a squat pyramid and

embossed on the base, on either side, with a pimple shaped like a camel's hump. The skin, more pleasing to the eye than any satin, is milk-white in some, in others lemon-yellow. There are fine ladies among them who adorn their legs with a number of pink bracelets and their back with carmine arabesques. A narrow pale-green ribbon sometimes edges the right and left of the breast.[22]

I find it ironic in the extreme that "The Homer of the Insects," as Victor Hugo called Fabre, could employ the poet's tools of metaphor and simile to elucidate both the look and character of the spider, while many poets have narrowed their views so exclusively to the egocentric that they appear to be blind to the whole natural order. Why should this vast subject be almost solely the domain of contemporary naturalists writing in prose? You would think more poets would want to take it on, particularly when we consider a successful work like Nancy Willard's "The Insects" that challenges both Fabre's Homeric laurels and Snow's thesis on the separation of the literary and the scientific:

> They pass like a warning of snow,
>   the dragonfly, mother of millions,
> the scarab, the shepherd spider,
>   the bee. Our boundaries break
> on their jeweled eyes,
>   blind as reflectors.
> The black beetle
>   under the microscope wears the
> blue of Chartres. The armored
>   mantis, a tank in clover,
> folds its wings like a flawless
>   inlay of wood, over and over.
>
> "There is something about insects
>   that does not belong to the habits
> of our globe," said Maeterlinck,
>   touching the slick
> upholstery of the spider,
>   the watchspring and cunning
> tongue of the butterfly, blown out
>   like a paper bugle. Their humming

warns us of sickness, their silence
    of honey and frost. Asleep
in clapboards and rafters,
    their bodies keep
the cost of our apples and wool.
    A hand smashes their wings,
tearing the veined
    landscape of winter trees.
In the slow oozing of our days
    who can avoid remembering

their silken tents on the air,
    the spiders wearing their eggs
like pearls, born on muscles
    of silk, the pulse of a rose, baiting
the fly that lives for three hours,
    lives only for mating?

Under a burning glass, the creature
    we understand disappears. The dragonfly
is a hawk, the roach
    cocks his enormous legs at your acre,
eyes like turrets piercing
    eons of chitin and shale. Drummers
under the earth, the cicadas
    have waited for seventeen summers
to break their shell,
    shape of your oldest fear
of a first world
    of monsters. We are not here.[23]

Nancy Willard made "The Insects" at that intersection of the imagination and observation which includes the author's reading, even perhaps, her research. In its understated way, the final brief sentence, "We are not here," snaps the poem into a dimension it would lack without those four simple words. It's good that we are not there in the same way that it is good in D. H. Lawrence's "Humming-bird," where he depicts that diminutive creature as a terrifying giant in some primeval era: "We look at him through the wrong end of the telescope of Time / Luckily for us." And at least one other echo comes from "We are not here": the

final line of Edwin Muir's "The Animals"—"On the sixth day we came"—
with its suggestion of humankind as a creature apart from the others because of its lateness, its awareness of time and change, and its ability to
name everything. "We are not here" quietly connects "The Insects" to a
tradition, whereas the Burkard and Ash poems quoted above remain
self-referential.

IV.

I am not asking for another wave of the ecologically correct "green propaganda" that appeared everywhere after the first Earth Day, and that I was
as guilty as anyone else of writing: "Avoid the midnight light of gas sta-
tions," I advised, and, "where the sludge of engines is poured nothing
can grow"—sentiments that now seem perfectly obvious.[24] I hope, too,
that I am as aware as any other writer, of how art serves its maker before
it serves any idea or any other person, and that to play with techniques is
an enduring private pleasure. But although poetry has to deal with the
life of the mind and body, it also needs to deal with what's outside the
mind and body. Just as voice can't be considered an adequate context,
so knowledge can't be divorced from the natural world that brought it
forth. Poetry has to stop playing word games with itself "as a way of establishing its own primacy . . . over the world" and begin to recapture the
regard it used to have for nature as the central focus of experience. Like
the rest of humankind, poets have to recognize nature as the common
ground that for too long now has put up with our excesses.

Poetry's function and use, said Robert Graves in his foreword to *The
White Goddess*,

> was once a warning to man that he must keep in harmony with the
> family of living creatures among which he was born . . . ; it is now a re-
> minder that he has disregarded the warning, turned the house upside
> down by capricious experiments in philosophy, science, and industry,
> and brought ruin on himself and his family. "Nowadays" is a civiliza-
> tion in which the prime emblems of poetry are dishonored. In which
> serpent, lion, and eagle belong to the circus tent; ox, salmon, and boar
> to the cannery; racehorse and greyhound to the betting ring; and the
> sacred grove to the sawmill.

Written almost fifty years ago, perhaps this now seems only faintly pro-phetic, as well as out-of-date. We are not all that worried about the fate of the boar and the sacred grove. But if we substitute "gray whale" for the first, and "tropical rain forest" for the second, we are closer to home, and closer to where commitment to a poem that attempts to reconcile the human personality and the natural world becomes a political act. As much as any victimized human group, that world is now extensively threatened by organized forces which governments can—if they will—control. If they can't, or won't, the planet will take our race down with it.

The escapists under these conditions aren't the "nature poets," who may still find themselves pigeonholed as quaint local colorists fighting a rear-guard action for nostalgia, but those who believe they have the choice of running away from outer life to their own egos, and who say glib, hip, insupportable things like, "No one believes in his own life any-more" and multiply their own nightfalls by weeping over having had the bad luck to be born.[25] One wants to offer them a couple of bracing para-graphs from the late Edward Abbey:

> How strange and wonderful is our home, our earth, with its swirling
> vaporous atmosphere, its flowing and frozen liquids, its trembling
> plants, its creeping, crawling, climbing creatures, the croaking things
> with wings that hang on rocks and soar through fog, the furry grass,
> the scaly seas. To see our world as a space traveler might see it for the
> first time, through Venusian eyes or Martian antennae, how utterly
> rich and wild it would seem, how far beyond the power of the craziest,
> spaced-out, acid-headed imagination, even a god's, to conjure up from
> nothing.
>
> Yet some among us have the nerve, the insolence, the brass, the gall
> to whine about the limitations of our earthbound fate and yearn for
> some more perfect world beyond the sky. We are none of us good
> enough for the world we have and yet we dream of heaven.[26]

Perhaps it is impossible for poems to "bring the soul of man to God" (Yeats's phrase), and maybe it is beyond the reach of most poets to cap-ture what Richard Wilbur has called "the splendor of mere being." At the very least, however, all poets ought to acknowledge the Cape Cod carpenter's rule of thumb: "Mother Nature bats last."

Notes

1. Michael Burkard, *Fictions from the Self* (New York: W. W. Norton & Company, Inc., 1989), p. 112.

2. John Ash, "Methodical Sonatas," *Paris Review,* 107 (1988), p. 116.

3. Mark Strand, *The New York Times Book Review,* 15 September 1991, p. 36.

4. See "Three Academic Pieces," p. 71, in *The Necessary Angel* (New York: Vintage Books, 1951), and "Adagia," pp. 157–80 *passim,* in *Opus Posthumous* (New York: Alfred A. Knopf, 1957).

5. Stephen Dunn, "Poetry," *Poetry,* February 1987, p. 293.

6. X. J. Kennedy, "Discoveries and Willpower," *Shenandoah,* Winter 1991, p. 115.

7. George Oppen, *What Is a Poet?* ed. Hank Lazer (Tuscaloosa: University of Alabama Press, 1987), p. 185. ("Poets are the unacknowledged legislators of the world."—P. B. Shelley)

8. Jacquetta Hawkes, *A Land* (Boston: Beacon Press, 1991), p. 6.

9. Anne Winters, "The Billboard Man," *Key to the City* (Chicago: University of Chicago Press, 1986), p. 8.

10. C. P. Snow, *The Two Cultures: And a Second Look* (New York: New American Library, 1963), p. 37.

11. Gerald Stern, *The Gettysburg Review,* Spring 1992, p. 211.

12. Larry Levis, *The Longman Anthology of Contemporary American Poetry 1950–1980,* eds. Stuart Friebert and David Young (New York: Longman, 1983) pp. 548–55.

13. Robert Graves, *The White Goddess* (New York: Noonday Press, 1966), p. 224.

14. Charles Wright, "Yard Journal." *Zone Journals* (New York: Farrar, Straus & Giroux, 1988), p. 3.

15. Chase Twichell, "The Cut," *Perdido* (New York: Farrar, Straus & Giroux, 1991), pp. 38–39.

16. See, for instance, Barbara S. Koppel and Nancy S. Foldi, "Physician's Guide to the Evaluation of Aphasia," *Hospital Physician,* September 1986, pp. 36–50.

17. Roger Weingarten, "Sometimes, at Thirty-Six," in *New American Poets of the Eighties,* eds. Jack Myers and Roger Weingarten (Green Harbor: Wampeter Press, 1984), p.379.

18. John Updike, "Crab Crack," *Harper's,* July 1981, p. 80.

19. Ted Hughes, "An Otter," *New Selected Poems* (New York: Harper and Row, 1982), p. 43.

20. Gary Snyder, *The Practice of the Wild* (San Francisco: North Point Press, 1990), p. 29.

21. Tom Lux, "Green Prose," *The Ardis Anthology of New American Poetry,* eds. David Rigsbee and Ellendea Proffer (Ann Arbor: Ardis, 1977), p. 311.

22. *The Insect World of J. Henri Fabre* (Boston: Beacon Press, 1991), p. 291.

23. *The Longman Anthology, op. cit.,* pp. 493–94.

24. Brendan Galvin, "Proposals Made in the Name of Reason," *The Hudson Review,* 23 (Summer 1971), p. 268.

25. Charles Wright, "Stone Canyon Nocturne," *The Longman Anthology, op. cit.,* p. 513.

26. *The Best of Edward Abbey* (San Francisco: Sierra Club Books, 1984), p. 91.

Kimiko Hahn

Blunt Instrument: A *Zuihitsu*

11.30

Scratch the surface, uncover rage. A new emotion, not unlike a toy though not always a pleasure. I feel differently in control. Rather than a candied comment, I hear myself saying *ohfuckoff* and am amazed. I once saved this stuff for metaphor. For a volatile tension in each line. How exquisite it feels to read aloud those poems about cutting him off at the knees. At once dismembering the man—*and* safeguarding the children's father.

/ / /

> Where does desire recede
> when the wave pulls back into the sea—
> does the far shore heighten
> or the center depths deepen
> and where should you then place your hands.
>
> (from "Infrared," Earshot)

www.anthro.veracity.org
And at least one version must come from an old woman.

TO: johnw@queens.edu
Anthologizers suggest I include a definition and I found the one I created for a talk at Poets House—let me know if it does not make sense: *zuihitsu,* "left up to the brush," is a poetic text usually in prose that utilizes disorder as its general strategy by employing such tactics as fragmentation, juxtaposition, contradiction, variety of topics, variety of forms, variety of lengths.

Notes for ENG 395 (Comp Lit): For lecture on Japanese lit—*zuihitsu* [miscellany] and *nikki* [poetic diary]—emphasize that veracity is not as essential as the effect. Integrate quotes. From *Japanese Poetic Diaries*, Earl Miner: "Bashō is shown to have fictionalized, altered, and later revised *[The Narrow Road to the North]*." Also, "[in Japanese diary literature] there is an artistic reconstitution of fact participating in or paralleling fiction" (p. 8). And on my favorite *nikki*: "the Japanese transition from fact to art is of course in the diary rather than the letter, and it is made very explicitly in the first sentence of *The Tosa Diary* [by Ki no Tsurayuki] . . . because the author is a man using the narrative point of view of a woman."

"This pose [as a woman] was remarkably prescient [because of the coming domination by women in literature]." (ibid.)

*   *   *

I recall a sparkling blue morning. The children at day camp.

I recall a cool dark morning—the mist rolling up the beach. The children still asleep.

I recall a rainy afternoon. The children overdosing on TV.

It was a Sunday—I circled classified ads in the real estate section— imagined leaving his shit for good.

*   *   *

12.1

Even though I am the one who left the marriage, now that he is seeing someone (a housewife with a half-dozen children they can both hide behind!) I am furious with resentment. Why did I stay all those years! If I could beat him to a bloody mass I would gladly collect blunt instruments.

. . . collect anything sharp.

. . . collect household poisons.

v.
I tell him, Remember how
the wind blew spray
off the crests of waves? How
some nights our footprints
were phosphorescent?
And he says, What?

    (from "Jam," *Mosquito and Ant*)

You need to kill him for closure.

I need to kill him for closure.

                          ′ ′ ′

Perhaps your husband tired of you
before the marriage.

      (from "Infrared," *Earshot*)

                          ′ ′ ′

TO: harolds@mindset.com
I've been invited to write a piece on autobiography in poetry. To tell
you the truth I'm not clear why this issue has emerged—I've always assumed poetic license. But I am intrigued by what happens to the t/Truth
in revision—what happens to material that's set as an actual event. A
student told me about a comment on my work from an Internet chat
room—something like *Hahn fuses elements of Modernist verse and confessional narrative.* I like that.

Bush Wins!
    New York Post, 11.8.00

Too Close to Call!
    Daily News, 11.8.00

FM: harolds@mindset.com
What about that comment in a book review that criticized your politics, saying you were becoming more "conservative?" ["One wishes she would tell us more about this [motherhood] experience, so many other writers have elevated the beauty of pregnancy and giving birth. Hahn's work is just a bit too domestic—it reminds one of dust under a table or too many cat hairs on a rug."]
REPLY:
Yeah—a man reviewing how a woman should write about birth! It's messy and it hurts. And suggesting that the domestic cannot be political. Furthermore, it wasn't a review.

╱ ╱ ╱

Notes for ENG 304: if that student again protests a particular reading of her work with the remark, "But this is what really happened," tell her there is the *truth* of that event and the *Truth* of the experience as craftily expressed in the poem. That the class, in class, does not care about which body part was removed; if a tooth is more essential to the reading experience than an appendix, alter the fact.

For you read I.

(from "Infrared," *Earshot*)

The student insists on telling the truth, even boring truth.

www.anthro.veracity.org
And at least one version must come from an old woman.

You want his want, the whorls on his fingers.

(from "Infrared," *Earshot*)

xi.
X and I finally remind one another
of what is not available
and what is: hedges, rose, pine

  (from "Zinc," *Mosquito and Ant*)

❧ ❧ ❧

My students mistake blurting something out for poetry. Nerve replaces craft. (Though I do long for most of them to strike a nerve. Maybe if they lied, or exaggerated—or wrote a persona piece.) One did have the nerve to ask if I've published any books—unbelievable. As for nerve— obviously none have seen the poem on premature burial. None have read poems on dissecting a live body—naming the stunning internal organs.

FM: harolds@mindset.com
Was it Hemingway who said, "Art is a lie that tells the truth"? I think so but better look it up if you're going to use it.

FM: johnw@queens.edu
Who suggested that lyric poetry is somehow truer than narrative? I can't recall where I read that—the *Kenyon Review*?

❧ ❧ ❧

12.3
I find I use any excuse—like getting advice on children's curfews—to lay into him. Last night I said that more than his constant withdrawing, I really hate how he found pleasure in hurting me with that withdrawing. That I would weep on my side of the bed; go sit on the toilet in the dark. I thought he was asleep but he was awake. *He knew.*

12.3

The diction from a vivisection is so pure. I'm reading an antique hand-book on autopsy I gave to H on his birthday. (We both use the presents to each other!)

[What his best friend told me he said]
She thinks I found pleasure but I was doing the best I could. I was as present as I was able.

> The soldiers draped tarpaulin and nets
> over the artillery
> until the tarmac resembled a summer cottage
> in winter.
>
> (from "Infrared," *Earshot*)

> Where does the sea lap the hold?
> The tire stall in mud?
>
> (from "Infrared," *Earshot*)

> Still, desire has no intelligence.
> It is plant and planet,
> willful or spinning.
> If he falls asleep before you
> where can you place your hands.
> If the morning . . .
>
> (from "Infrared," *Earshot*)

⁄ ⁄ ⁄

> You're angry I've actually said
> how the ordinary censors us.
> You grip the wheel more, become quiet
> again. I know I should have lied,
> as usual kept despair
> to myself.
>
> (from "Errands," *Volatile*)

⁄ ⁄ ⁄

12.4

They're two rich kids living off postures of entitlement though I know he would never admit it. They must feel self-righteous for voting Democrat. Meanwhile she's a trust-fund housewife who wants to push his ambitions instead of having her own and he's still trying to be ambitious. In our relationship he knew from day one how rejection hurt me—but had little ambition there either. He knew he recalled my mother's rejection.

Like his mother.

Like my mother.

Yours.

www.anthro.veracity.org
From an old woman, preferably one with silver hair.

✦ ✦ ✦

Q: How autobiographical is *Mosquito and Ant?*
A: I never admit to sexual intercourse with X.

TO: johnw@queens.edu
The poems stay illicit although in revision I struck out references to fucking. Because of my daughters. It's wrong. Or at least cowardly. Or maybe *implying* is more artistic? I could think that and feel self-righteous.
REPLY:
You did what you had to. Getting back to your essay—include some quotes. Your poetry is the bomb.

Notes for ENG 395 (Comp Lit): "But if Issa's intention [in *Oraga Haru*] is not purely autobiographical, and we find that his account of what purports to be a 'historical' year is actually an artistic deception, and that he has woven into the fabric suggestions and experiences which come from other years and other areas of his life and mind—if indeed some of them be not pure fiction. He has, with the instinct of the real artist, shaped this year so that it may more fitly reveal the truth of him as a man than any one year, historically considered, could possibly do."

(*The Year of My Life: A Translation of Issa's Oraga Haru*
by Nobuyuki Yuasa)

Cuttings, The Hemisphere, Possession, Blindsided, The Downpour, Sewing without Mother, Morning Light, Reflections Off White, Pulse and Impulse

TO: johnw@queens.edu
I've been looking over my own *zuihitsu* and find they possess a single organizing principle: theme. Is this Western? (Like *Paterson*?) Or perhaps because mine are written as a whole—unlike Sei Shōnagon collecting them after a time then artfully arranging them. I "compile" as I compose.

TO: johnw@queens.edu
I find myself dumbing-down (in the sense of mute) my material instead of holding onto a detail that hits a nerve. To protect my daughters. And then I feel incredibly annoyed. (Do men do the same?) Sometimes I feel I need two separate writing lives: one that is risky but edited—the published version; the other, one to be kept in that proverbial secret chamber. Maybe to be published, maybe not. In fact I do have a secret sheaf I keep in my desk at school. I feel nauseous admitting this.
REPLY:
Save the rough drafts.

✦ ✦ ✦

I lean close to X, over his shoulder
into an anthology of the Beats,
to notice the pierced ear
he no longer adorns.
How would it look with
a purple ridge of teeth marks?

(from "Croissant," *Mosquito and Ant*)

/ / /

TO: johnw@queens.edu
And what about his penchant for the Other—how only one of his seven
girlfriends was a WASP—was like his mother. Though this one looks
like family and is wealthy but is still Other.
REPLY:
You're suggesting?
REPLY:
That he was raised to view the body as something not to be soiled; so
he chooses the Other over Mother because it's all right to soil the Other.
His interest for me was crossing the color line. The Orient—a location
off center.
REPLY:
Interesting how he can cross the color line but a person "of color" cannot.

/ / /

[What his best friend told me he said]
I fell in love with her because she made herself so vulnerable.

[Flaubert] liked to fart under a cover then plunge under to smell the
gas. I laughed but it wasn't really funny. Moreover I do not assume all
French relish that activity.

(from "The Hemisphere: Kuchuk Hanem,"
The Unbearable Heart)

Flaubert's encounter with an Egyptian courtesan produced a widely influential model of the Oriental woman. . . . He spoke for and represented her.

> (Edward Said, *Orientalism*)

We both use our mouths, professionally.

> (from "The Hemisphere: Kuchuk Hanem,"
> *The Unbearable Heart*)

He's half my age—and that
in itself makes the nerves sweat.
He's half covered in tattoos of insects
and reptiles and I've asked him
to add me to them. To his skin.
Instead he eats me
until there is nothing left. No mother
for my children. No wife for
that man already asleep I'm sure.

> (from first-draft notes for *Mosquito and Ant*)

✒ ✒ ✒

She suggested a good old-fashioned lead pipe.

She suggested rat poison.

She suggested anything from the kitchen.

Q: Does it really matter?
A: Because no one reads poetry?

The student typed *farther* instead of *father*. Another, *pubic* instead of *public*.

jesuschristsowhat

✒ ✒ ✒

[I tell my best friend what I said to him]
Quit telling my father about your sex life with your loser girlfriend because I end up hearing about it— and the fact is it's pathetic. The fact is, in our marriage, you barely scratched the surface of my sexuality— it was my responsibility to say something? I did. You couldn't hear me, you were so busy licking your psychic wounds. You fuck.

[What his best friend told me he said]
I've told that bitch a million times I did the best I could. I did NOT find pleasure in hurting her— I DID feel good shutting her up in that argument towards the end when she was provoking me— suggesting we try to be as intimate when off our one vacation as we can be on it. It felt good to shout— to be in control.

fuckinbitch

゛゛゛

[Edwin Lord Weeks' paintings'] fabricated nature is betrayed by the standard-bearer, whose gesture and position are inconsistent with the basic rituals of Islam. Holding a flag aloft in the shelter of the [prayer niche] while people are engaged in prayer, this figure distorts the faith by suggesting that devout believers make obeisance to a human being. Such a scene conjures up demagoguery rather than the true Muslim submission to God.

(Holly Edwards, *Noble Dreams, Wicked Pleasures: Orientalism in America, 1870–1930*)

He's such a fuckinbitch.

゛゛゛

For Freud the first question—the unconscious question—is, What do I want? and then, What fantasies of truth do I need to legitimate it?

(Adam Phillips, *On Kissing, Tickling and Being Bored*)

Beat him unconscious.

the unconscious

✎ ✎ ✎

TO: johnw@queens.edu
I include too much reflection on the form itself. Like in "Sewing": "Miner
defines a *zuihitsu* as *stray notes, expressing random thoughts in a casual
manner . . . [Though some] do show a semblance of logical structure.*" I am
attracted to this semblance. "Pulse and Impulse" is mostly commentary
on the form. But I am also tired of this oh-so-postmodern self-reflection.
REPLY:
Write more. Publish more.

✎ ✎ ✎

A: The truth, even in the elegies, is fueled by rage.

Beat, thrash, flog, pummel, lash, club—

Blow, stroke, hit, knock, rap, pound, whack, punch, dash, sock—

Kick, jab, ram, strike, hammer, batter, slap, club, boot, stamp—

12.5
I bought a hammer when I moved into this apartment—a small one. I
noticed it's labeled a *woman's hammer.*

    (Anywhere else
    girls of mixed marriages would be prostitutes or courtesans.)
                (from "Revolutions," *Earshot*)

✎ ✎ ✎

www.anthro.veracity.org
Among three distinct equatorial peoples, in the case of village crimes, a
secret society is formed where three versions of the incident are reported.
There must be three. If only two are available, the complaint is either ignored or an unbiased party composes a story from hearing the date of
birth of those involved. Moreover, at least one version must come from
an old woman. Punishments include exile or in the case of a male lying
about a female relative, public flaying is probable. Anthropologists esti-
mate from drawings on ceremonial pottery that this practice has lasted
approximately 700 years.

. . . I trespass the boundaries of fiction and nonfiction.

(from "The Hemisphere: Kuchuk Hanem," *The Unbearable Heart*)

✦ ✦ ✦

12.5
Read an entry from my 40th birthday. That I was locked into a relationship with a narcissistic man—*men* who couldn't function without a female holding a mirror up for them—and none to hold one for the
female. I didn't know. I didn't know I would put up with his pushing me
off his lap, saying, *don't crowd the driver.* Put up with his embarrassment
to kiss me on the beach.

TO: harolds@mindset.com
I feel at home with you. I feel desirable. Thank you. Thank you for
holding me like a ship. A hold.

TO: harolds@mindset.com
If the authority figure (i.e., father/mother) is symbol for truth, for the
child or adult-child, then is to bludgeon or lie finally to subvert and then
create for one's own? To own the truth?

Mornings while the husband showers
I lie on my back and come
and come
furiously thinking of a hotel bed
instead of my desk cleared of drafts.
Imagine
a mattress and mirror.

    (from first-draft notes for *Mosquito and Ant*)

12.6

Is it true the anthologizers thought of *Mosquito and Ant?* Were they attracted to it because I try to tear open the seams/seems of my marriage? That child-rearing unit. He fell asleep on our first date. He was unhappy doing art and unhappy when not. My 20-20 hindsight now. I don't feel I have enough time to let this material settle.

✐ ✐ ✐

12.7

Is this *zuihitsu* less truthful because it doesn't work a single thesis through in an expository manner (ex. How does post-confessional poetry figure into a post-Florida-recount deconstructionist text?)? More female? More connected to the body (and mind) because female and not solely devoted to the mind, as separate from the dirty flesh? [I type *deity* instead of *dirty.*]

✐ ✐ ✐

[John would never say *the bomb*—that was that sweet Derek.]

✐ ✐ ✐

Slay, exterminate, eradicate, dispose of, destroy, slaughter, butcher, strangle, decimate—

✐ ✐ ✐

. . . but to tell you the truth: I just
don't want to call the sitter, go out and sit
in a tureen of silence any longer.

(From "Errands," *Volatile*)

TO: johnw@queens.edu
Really "Errands" is not a good poem. But what do you think of my
using it anyway because it makes a point?
REPLY: What is more interesting to me is how all your complaining
about your ex—how all the supposed-confessional stuff—really goes from
complaining to becoming *his* biography. It is really not about you. He's
done it again—become the subject. Or you've let the man do it to you.

A mother of five, worn down by the age of 30 from caring for her husband and his first wife and cut off from the outside world, hanged herself in the family barn. Her 65-year-old husband later shrugged and
told a psychologist, "It was her time to go to God."

("Turkish Women Who See Death as a Way Out,"
The New York Times, 11.3.00)

＊＊＊

12.7

Vivisection is not practical. I am not interested in the careful slice. The
tender attention. What I want is gore. All over. Punish the one who was
so gladly punishing. For years. That's what I want. And adrenaline.

12.8

I completely despise remarks about poetry being therapeutic. So is kick-
ing in a door. Therapy in print—that's for journal entries. Though ultimately any new material is a chronicle of my rage.

What is my stake in this?

(from "The Hemisphere: Kuchuk Hanem,"
The Unbearable Heart)

✐ ✐ ✐

Who said?

Brooklyn
November 11, 2000

IV

Codes of Silence:
Women & Autobiography

Pamela Gemin

Bless Me, Sisters

Bless me, Father, for I have sinned: *I wanted that Nestlé Crunch bar so bad I was scared I was going to steal it.* Even then it seemed silly, an eight-year-old girl on scabby knees at the local St. Joseph's confessing an almost-covet as real tyrants cast their massive nets of sin across continents. But when the priest leaned forward and whispered the charm for penance, a hint of his pine-scented after-shave floating through the screen as his swift cross of absolution unsettled the confessional booth's stale air, I imagined my soul—the apple-sized circle of halo in my chest, infested with sin's black check marks—bleached shining clean. For the scuff tracks and waxy yellow buildup, for all the spaghetti stains of childhood, confession was the white tornado.

"You can always trust the priest," my mother would say, "because he's heard everything. You name the commandment, he's heard the commandment-breaker, and he's sworn not to tell anyone." Now I can only imagine how bored the priest must have been when his customers were children. When I formally expressed my dissatisfaction with the Church and announced my plans to stop attending Mass, my mother suggested confession as a last-ditch hope, and I obliged more for my own sake than hers. What I told the priest in the last confession I made, in 1970, was less about my sins and more about my sorrow about letting him, and my mother, down. The Church, I knew, would get over it.

Even by my late teens, despite a healthy vanity and a quick rash of coveting from department stores, I hadn't committed that many *actual* sins, though the ones I'd imagined committing would have reserved me a toasty seat in the basement of Southern Purgatory. The truth was that now, instead of telling the priest what a wretch I was, I told my girlfriends. And because they were heaven-sent girlfriends—they still are—

they listened eagerly, with appropriate horror or bliss, and inserted their own confessions along the way until we were all forgiven, sometimes four or five at a time, downstairs in somebody's basement stacking albums, playing euchre; sharing a pack of cigarettes, a giant bag of corn chips, passing the wine around.

I've read some essays in which the association of confessional poetry with the Catholic ritual of confession is discouraged, but having been raised in the Catholic tradition, I cannot consider the term "confession" unaccompanied by its triple halos of redemption, deliverance, and what I now understand to be a rare kind of peace. While my secular confessions have not always inspired these gifts—girlfriends, unlike priests, are not sworn to silence, after all—I have continued to seek them in literature, as all good English majors do, and, since the late 1970s, I have sought them almost exclusively from the work of women poets. This tendency is a direct result of having been virtually deprived of women poets in my university study, and having been discouraged from taking any of my university's wacky "new women's lib-lit courses" by well-meaning male professors, one of whom earnestly took me aside and explained, "The trouble with taking women's lit, Pamela, is that there just *isn't* any women's lit!"

But by that time I'd discovered the poems of Marge Piercy, and there was no turning back. I ripped into each of Piercy's books with the kind of enthusiasm I'd formerly reserved for Joni Mitchell albums. In no time my copies of *Hard Loving* and *Breaking Camp,* like my copies of *Court and Spark* and *Hejira,* were tattered and stained. Piercy's poems simply took my breath away. It's no exaggeration to say that I felt them deep in my body—specifically, inside the lining of my lungs—or that my eyes "blazed like the Pentecost" as I read them aloud to another male professor who encouraged my own clumsy beginnings as a poet:

Open your eyes and your belly. Let the sun rise into your chest and burn
    your throat,
stretch out your hands and tear the gauzy rain
that your world can be born from you
screaming and red.[1]

"Nobody will turn the soiled water into wine, / nobody will shout cold Lazarus alive / but you. You are your own magician,"[2] Piercy declared, and publication in the seventies of brave new anthologies like *No More Masks!* and *I Hear My Sisters Saying* gave young women of my generation their first delicious taste of women's poetry "charged with the special intensity of perception given to those occupied in that most important task of self-definition."[3] These anthologies featured work by women poets including: Gwendolyn Brooks, Rita Mae Brown, Lucille Clifton, Colette Inez, June Jordan, Faye Kicknosway, Carolyn Kizer, Maxine Kumin, Denise Levertov, Lisel Mueller, Alicia Ostriker, Marge Piercy, Adrienne Rich, Muriel Rukeyser, Sonia Sanchez, and Diane Wakoski.

Oh yes, dear professor, there *was* a women's lit, and it was thriving. The editors of *I Hear My Sisters Saying* hoped that their readers might "recognize in these poems the features of their own experience, familiar stages in their own progresses toward self-discovery," acknowledging that "[e]ach vision records some fragment of the total experience of woman . . ." Their aim was to offer poems that might "take light from one another," each poem a thread weaving into the "tapestry of women's lives. . . ."[4]

Some twenty years later, in the process of editing an anthology of coming-of-age poetry written by women of the Baby Boom generation, Paula Sergi and I noted the ways in which the confessional nature of narratives portraying women's experience, from early childhood to middle age, linked their poems, as if each woman might have told the story of them all, as if the personal nature of "telling" had created a kind of collective, confessional consciousness and, ultimately, a collective redemption. And unlike the very private nature of the sacrament, the "generational-confessional" uses its own catalog of common experience as a public accounting.

The best coming-of-age poetry tends naturally to incorporate the most familiar features of confessional poetry, "articulating moments of primary existence" and using real-life material to reveal "psychic moments from which truths—hilarious, grave, desperate, terrifying, fraudulent—are spoken."[5] Although each generation's—and each woman's—"sins" are

uniquely human, the reflective nature of coming-of-age poetry allows
readers a unique opportunity to reinsert themselves into the collective
scheme of shared history. For women writers especially, the generational-
confessional provides a vital space for discussions that might never have
been possible in real time, and unites poet and audience using a common
cultural code. Thus, some experiences considered personal and private,
dangerous, and even sacred—sexual and body-centered experience, for example—reemerge in richly textured poetry about virginity, pregnancy,
sexual discovery, and sexual violence, as experienced both individually
and collectively by women of the same generation.

Paula and I discovered Marie Howe's *What the Living Do* in the final
weeks of our anthology project, and though we could not include Howe's
"Sixth Grade," we admired the poet-speaker's narration of an early adolescent experience that transformed her neighborhood's dynamics in the
age before "sexual harassment" was a household word: "[t]he afternoon
the neighborhood boys tied [her] and Mary Lou Mahar / to Donny
Ralph's father's garage doors, spread-eagled . . .":

> A gang of boys. They pulled the heavy garage doors down,
> and tied us to them with clothesline,
> and Donny got the deer's leg severed from the buck his dad had killed,
>
> the year before, dried up and still fur-covered, and sort of
> poked it at us, dancing around the blacktop in his sneakers, laughing.
> Then somebody took it from Donny and did it.
>
> And then somebody else, and somebody after him.
> Then Donny pulled up Mary Lou's dress and held it up,
> and she began to cry, and I became a boy again, and shouted Stop . . .[6]

The speaker's becoming "a boy again" indicates how recently this border
between the boys and the girls has been drawn, how it thickens and thins
in the heat of a sixth-grade summer, when the boys leap off their bi-
cycles to jump the girls, "lie on top of [them], / then get up and walk
away." Until the garage incident, the boys' harassment has been typical,
ritualistic, just short of innocent. But now, when the boys ignore the
speaker's order to stop tormenting Mary Lou, she transforms again, this
time into a "girl-boy," pleading for a boy named Charlie to stop them:

. . . And he wouldn't.
And then more softly, and looking directly at him, I said, Charlie.

And he said Stop. And they said What? And he said Stop it.
And they did, quickly untying the ropes, weirdly quiet,
Mary Lou still weeping. And Charlie? Already gone.[7]

In "Sixth Grade," Howe depicts a political as well as a personal initiation, more effectively than a poem with a preset political agenda might, confiding her girl terror and exposing Charlie's boy vulnerability. As editors, Paula and I favored narrative poems with strong confessional overtones, poems in which women speakers took the winding, scenic route to their discoveries, over those with prescribed political agendas or reader directives. We responded most strongly to poems that bore evidence of a sort of grassroots feminism, a state of awakening and "consciousness raising" by which women all over the country—in their girlfriends' basements, in the corner booths at their favorite beer joints, on the two-lane out of town in rusty beaters, radios blaring—were slowly changing their ideas of what it meant to be female. "Why don't you girls get that straggly hair out of your face and hold up your heads! Look *up*, girls!" my friend Joanie's mother would implore as we slumped out the door in identical oversized "barracuda" jackets on our way to Friday night, seventeen. Mrs. Davidson was too busy raising her brood of seven and working with Joanie's dad at the Metro Detroit liquor store they owned to ponder *The Feminine Mystique*, but her message was no less political.

"The first time I stood in the charged air / of female rage, I didn't know that night / would always have something to do with it . . . ,"[8] writes Leslie Adrienne Miller in "Lawn Ornaments," a poem so true and immediate that it could have been written with my girl gang in mind. To avenge the jilting of one of their tribe, a gang of seven girls piles into "someone's father's finned Buick," raiding the neighborhood lawns of the pink flamingoes and "terribly grinning elves" destined for a pile on heartbreaker's lawn. "When you're a girl, rage and shame / have the same sinister, too bright smile," the speaker tells us:

and that perfectly shaved blue hill
is the body of all the men who will

make you feel it. You'll have to run
across that moonless expanse in secret
and at night; you'll have to be armed
with laughter, and girls who'll help you
make that yard crazy with cuteness,
girls who'll fill the smashed grin
of the garden dwarf with someone's tube
of Poppy Pink and jam him upside down
in a bed of plastic roses.[9]

In taking her "sisterhood is powerful" message to the streets, Miller breathes life into the bumper-sticker/textbook slogan, expanding its influence beyond the college classrooms in which many of us might not have been lucky enough to own a seat.

But there are other, sometimes less celebratory elements to explore in women's confessional poetry featuring the themes of self-discovery and identity established by women poets of the seventies. The process of attaining self-knowledge can be lonely and painful. Some of the best women poets writing today—Denise Duhamel, Allison Joseph, Laura Kasischke, Diane Seuss-Brakeman, Betsy Sholl, and Belle Waring, to name just a few—often tackle the tough subjects of sexuality, love and self-worth, family history, and cultural and political identity with fresh, ironic humor or smart, jazzy riffs of narrative infused with the poets' love of language. Others, like Kim Addonizio, Jan Beatty, Jane Mead, Sapphire, and the late Lynda Hull, cut closer to the bone in sparer, more declarative, more directly confessional tones; but for the most part their work is ultimately hopeful.

Mead, in her soulful collection *The Lord and the General Din of the World*, gives readers what Philip Levine calls, "a taste of loss, grief, and madness" as we "eavesdrop on a passionate internalized debate that is . . . no more and no less the question of whether or not we should live and . . . how we might go about it."[10] "Jesus, I am cruelly lonely,"[11] the first line of Mead's opening poem, "Concerning That Prayer I Cannot Make," *is* a prayer, and it's not the feathery talk of "soul" or the solid landscape of "river" and "bridge" and "cloud" that pull this poem along, but its immediate, directly confessional statements: "I am not equal to my longing./ Somewhere there should be a place / the exact shape of my emptiness . . ."[12] In the end, this poem/prayer honors the landscape in which it is grounded and comes back to the speaker as a kind of blessing:

Listen—
all you bare trees
burrs
brambles
pile of twigs
red and green lights flashing
muddy bottle shards
shoe half buried—listen

listen, I am holy.[13]

In declaring herself "holy" from the start, Mead's speaker establishes her poetic voice and identity, assuring that even though a woman is lonely and empty, she can also be holy and blessed at the same time, as most humans are.

Referring to Mead's "After Detox," Levine says that her poems' "moments of redemption are so charged and significant" because their subject matter is often so bleak.[14] In a reclaimed life "as clean as a bed," the mystery of faith presents itself in the simple acts of washing clothes ("The warm / machines rattle and hum, and the warm soap splashes / behind glass.") or dressing ("My socks will match. My hair will shine."[15]). And if ever there was a hopeful poem, it's Mead's "Passing a Truck Full of Chickens at Night on Highway Eighty," in which the speaker makes spiritual contact with a creature on its way to being processed, a chicken who, despite her certain doom, looks past the confines of her crate, "strain[ing]/ to see what happen[s] beyond." "*That* is the chicken I want to be,"[15] Mead's speaker finally proclaims.

Laura Kasischke's poems to the elements—"Dear Air," "Dear Earth," "Dear Fire," and "Dear Water"—take the same deliberately personal path, offering praise to the natural world in exchange for its healing powers. In "Dear Earth," for example, the speaker not only personifies the planet, but also imagines merging with it, in a physical as well as a spiritual sense:

> . . . I want
> to fall all over you like a farm, to bless
>
> your fields with weeping, fists
> of hail, black
> feathers in a frenzy
>
> out of their wrecked nests—simple
>
> gracious rain on your white grapes, or
>
> a holy blizzard of pain: My
>
> tornadoes tearing up your prairies. My
>
> red wind licking its initials in the dust.[17]

In "Dear Air," the love affair continues: "I saw you in the laundromat—my love, my voice, my empty / dove. / . . . My / *honeycomb, my fate, brief / virgin I once was.*"[18]). And in "Dear Water," the speaker declares to her subject: "I am your lost daughter and, as always, you / are listening and fish."[19] The speaker's father is the subject of "Dear Fire," but this poem is no less personal in its address, and certainly no less direct: "Every night my father dreams he golfs in Hell / with you."[20] And Kasischke's "Prayer" recalls Mead's "Concerning That Prayer I Cannot Make," in its crisis of faith:

> Dear God, I've stood
> in my own path
> and passed myself as I passed, and caught
>
> a glimpse of my own face catching a glimpse of me . . .[21]

While its critics lament the tendency toward self-centeredness in confessional poetry—the emphasis on personal rather than political issues in "an implied unity of consequence that is not to be trusted" or "an artless retelling of personal material capped off with a tidy epiphany"[22]—the guiding principle of our foremothers, that the personal *is* political, redeems the poetry of women for whom the pursuit of self-knowledge has been a revolutionary act. "[A]mong young poets, for whom the life of a woman is a public matter, such distinctions between public and private fall away,"[23] wrote Florence Howe in her introduction to *No More Masks!*

Poet Betsy Sholl vividly remembers the day, thirty-odd years ago, that she accidentally picked up a copy of Sylvia Plath's *Ariel,* took it home, drew a bath, eased into the tub, and began to read. "I was afraid I would be electrocuted,"[24] said Sholl. "There was all this *current.* I had never heard metaphors, similes, *language* buzzing like that." Now I know better than to read Kasischke in the tub. She and Sholl and the other fine women poets writing today are every bit as generous and open, every bit as bold and brave and inclusive in their work as the women who first inspired them to make poems. Reading their work, I'm back with my girls in the basement, laughing and weeping, dissing and dishing, and hearing my own voice looping back again, picking up layers of richness, strength, and volume above the music. This variation on the theme of sacrament, this holy communion of women, girlfriends and poets alike, provides the "direct God-hit" that Dianne Seuss-Brakeman craves in her poem "Hit,"[25] and the welcome homecoming she longs for in "Viceroy":

> Do you see, God, how I do not want to have to die
> To get to come home? Being your child,
> I want to be so alive that you gasp when I arrive.
> You acknowledge the grape juice on my lips.
> You light your Viceroy on the sparks of my hair.[26]

"It Blows You Hollow," the title poem of Seuss-Brakeman's first book, articulates the ineffable, supremely personal "It" that drives her poetry: "Your heart's a tilt-a-whirl, / throwing off steam into the frigid night, / spinning *heartsick, heartbreak . . .*"

> And all you want to do is revive it. You'll write
> circles around it, half-assed parables halfway told,
> with bandaged hands, with all the bones
> in your face showing, by god,
> you'll make a religion of it.[27]

Bless me, sisters, for I have sinned. I have cast my pearls before swine. I have stuffed and starved and polluted the wobbly little temple of my body. I have cheated, lied, stolen, resented, called in the middle of night and hung up the phone, willed myself crazy with anger. And you have delivered me always, your books dog-eared on the nightstand, your good words lighting my steady way, amen.

Notes

1. Marge Piercy, "The Butt of Winter," *Circles on the Water: Selected Poems of Marge Piercy* (New York: Alfred A. Knopf, 1982), p. 54.

2. Ibid., p. 6.

3. Carol Konek and Dorothy Walters, Introduction, *I Hear My Sisters Saying: Poems by Twentieth Century Women* (New York: The Thomas Y. Crowell Company, 1976), pp. v–vi.

4. Ibid., p. vi.

5. Regan Good, "Confessional Poetry: My Eyes Have Seen What My Hand Did," *Fence Magazine,* Internet. Available: <http://fencemag.com/v1n2/work/regan.good.html>.

6. Marie Howe, "Sixth Grade," *What the Living Do* (New York: W. W. Norton & Company, Inc., 1998), p. 16.

7. Ibid., p. 17.

8. Leslie Adrienne Miller, "Lawn Ornaments," *Yesterday Had a Man in It* (Pittsburgh: Carnegie Mellon University Press, 1998), p. 32.

9. Ibid., 32–33.

10. Philip Levine, Foreword, *The Lord and the General Din of the World* by Jane Mead (Louisville, Kentucky: Sarabande Books, 1996), p. xi.

11. Jane Mead, "Concerning That Prayer I Cannot Make," *The Lord and the General Din of the World* (Louisville, Kentucky: Sarabande Books, 1996), p. 1.

12. Ibid., p. 2.

13. Ibid., pp. 2–3.

14. Levine, *op. cit.,* p. xi.

15. Mead, *op. cit.,* "After Detox," p. 23.

16. Ibid., "Passing a Truck Full of Chickens at Night on Highway Eighty," p. 78.

17. Laura Kasischke, "Dear Earth," *Fire and Flower* (Farmington, Maine: alicejamesbooks, 1999), p. 14.

18. Ibid., "Dear Air," p. 26.

19. Ibid., "Dear Water," p. 63.

20. Ibid., "Dear Fire," p. 38.

21. Ibid., "Prayer," pp. 42–43.

22. Good, *op. cit.*

23. Florence Howe, Introduction, *No More Masks!* (Garden City, NY: Anchor Books, 1973), p. 3.

24. Betsy Sholl, Personal Correspondence, October 27, 2000.

25. Dianne Seuss-Brakeman, "Hit," *It Blows You Hollow* (Chelsea, MI: New Issues Press, 1999), p. 26.

26. Ibid., "Viceroy," p. 24.

27. Ibid., "It Blows You Hollow," pp. 42–43.

Louise Glück

The Forbidden

In the myth of the Garden, the forbidden exerts over the susceptible human mind irresistible allure. The force of this allure is absolute, final; the fact of it shapes, ever afterward, human character and the human vision of human destiny. The myth's potency derives from the fact that there is no going back: exile and contamination occur once, the explicit descent which is the lovers' punishment becomes a permanent burden or affliction. Which is to say: the myth is tragic.

It is a great theme—it can turn a good poet into a great poet. Its grandeur and utility explain, in part, its magnetism. But the charm doesn't always work, and many fine writers, in the grip of the narrative if not the theme, are beguiled into impassioned production of disappointing art. Moreover, material of this kind creates, for the writer, a dangerous insulation, since all negative criticism can be viewed as timidity and conservatism, terror in the presence of dark truth. But dark truth has become unnervingly popular, a literary convention which seems oddly incompatible with its experiential precursors: anguish, isolation, and shame. In actual human experience, these stigmas persist: the child who involuntarily inhabits a taboo is marked by that fact. I don't think our society's addiction to exhibitionism and obsession with progress (a narrow myth for triumph) completely explain the ease with which survivors have begun to show their wounds, making a kind of caste of isolation, competing in the previously unpermitted arena of personal shame. And the fact remains that authentic examples of transmuted suffering make plain what is missing from so many accounts.

In what would seem an impossible maneuver, any number of poets have managed to dissociate the forbidden from all tragic implication while continuing to claim for their efforts the prestige of tragedy. The proof they offer of their authenticity is biographical accuracy. We cannot, as readers, dispute what must have been genuine suffering. The question is: Why are we involved at all? What response is solicited when the documenting voice requires that we note, at all moments, its survival (even, in many cases, its survival as a soul improved by this encounter with evil)? These voices specify rage and contamination and shame; what they demand, however, is admiration for unprecedented bravery, as the speaker looks back and speaks the truth. But truth of this kind will not permit itself simply to be looked back on; it makes, when it is summoned, a kind of erosion, undermining the present with the past, substituting for the shifts and approximations and variety of anecdote the immutable fixity of fate, and for curiosity regarding an unfolding future, absolute knowledge of that future. Such truth is experienced as the inescapable place and condition, not the single experience but the defining experience endlessly recreated. When the force and misery of compulsion are missing, when the scar is missing, the ambivalence which seeks, in the self, responsibility—the collusive, initiating desire which must have been present for punishment to occur, the sense that it is better, in a way, that the self be at fault than that the world be evil—when ambivalence toward the self is missing, the written recreation, no matter how artful, forfeits emotional authority.

The test for emotional authority is emotional impact, and the great flaw in Linda McCarriston's *Eva-Mary* is that, cumulatively, it isn't moving. And it is meant to be read this way, as a whole, as it is most certainly intended to move, to shock, to break the heart. One feels in these poems the delight of the ambitious artist at discovering terrain this promising: how could anything as powerful as incest fail to make devastating art?

But *Eva-Mary* is, despite its content, despite its grounding in the forbidden, despite the many wonderful individual poems, less myth than fairy tale, designed to name, localize, master, and distance anxiety. I suppose if we could feel, as readers, the poignant inadequacy of the strategy, deeper response would be possible. But there seems no such signal here, no sense that this version of the past will not hold. Rather, the poems present themselves as the authentic telling of that past long suppressed, with all guilt absorbed by agents of suppression and all nobility divided among the helpless victims. It is an overt homage to the mother, and, as such, seems protected against charges of narcissistic self-display. But the true object of love here is the suffering child, and the problem for artists dealing with this material is to not write from pity for the child one was but to devise a language or point of view that reinhabits anguish. *Eva-Mary* uses narrative, but its attitudes are fixed. The voice speaking suffers no dilemma toward the past, never falters in its judgments; this is a poetry, for all its artfulness, of functional simplification, and the speaker's recurring move is corrective, to be certain that, as readers, we know as clearly as she does who the heroes and villains are.

I found myself, reading this book, thinking of Carolyn Forché's riveting *The Country Between Us,* which also arises out of protest, but moves deeply because it churns with self-doubt as well as rage: the poems question the self's motives, expose its vanities. Unlike McCarriston's, Forché's speaker is suspect; the poems' extraordinary drama derives equally from rage at injustice (and the poems contain the additional drama of initiation into a reality of brutal unreason) and the recurring question of complicity, since it is to the poet's distinct advantage that this reality continue. Forché's willingness to sabotage the self's stature confers on the enemy an eerie humanity: Can I trust what I see, the best poems suggest, given my preference to see it? When Forché falters, as she rarely does, she does so because self-doubt and self-scrutiny give way.

If I am harsh with *Eva-Mary* it is because McCarriston's obvious talent creates expectations the book fails to meet. A real gift is constantly apparent here, undermined by a narrowing agenda. What alarms is the sense of self-flattering choice, presumably the brave choice of risk and darkness, presumably the choice of the harrowingly real over the decorous artful but, in my view, the choice of the schematic over the ambivalent, complex, and truly dangerous. The poems of *Eva-Mary* resemble the pronouncements of that male judge they invoke and correct who, because he does not see, can speak in verdicts.

Forché travels to El Salvador a young girl; the power of the poems has its source in her hunger to be changed, whatever the cost, to be relieved of ignorance. The self she aspires to be, the Josephine-self, is worldly, informed, brutal, direct, marked by suffering, impatient; in Forché's hierarchy of values, beauty is surpassed by wisdom; ignorance, like virginity, is something to be shed as quickly as possible, not for the novelty of the experience but because divestment—preferably scourging divestment—is the only means by which adult perspective can be achieved.

Such perspective would seem, for poets, a universal ambition, which makes recognition of its absence difficult. Sharon Olds is a poet of considerable achievement and a wholesome distaste for that most depressing of strategies, the obligatory elevation of the quotidian via mythic analogy. Olds's technique, her fascination with the extreme physical, the unsayable reality, makes a case for her presence here, and *The Father* seems, atmospherically, to draw on or suggest taboos it doesn't actually investigate. Olds has an astonishing gift for that part of the act of writing which corresponds to the hunting/gathering phase, or, to put it another way, that part which is generative: many of the poems in *The Father* read as improvisations around a single word or cluster of words, and their resourcefulness, Olds's sustained scrutiny and fastidious notation of detail, amazes. This method, which characterizes nearly every individual poem in the collection, characterizes the book as well, as though William Carlos Williams's dictum regarding things had been adapted to an emotional agenda. If the book fails, as it does for me, it does so in part because the poems grow tedious: William Carlos Williams's scrutiny was democratic, or perhaps, more properly, an application of the scientific method: it was a point of honor to have no bias regarding outcome. This is Williams's vitality. But Olds uses her genius for observation to make, repeatedly, the same points, to reach the same epiphanies; the energy and diversity of detail play out as stasis. The principal figures here, the speaker and her dying father, change very little; the scenes between them change very little. While we might not expect change of a dying man (his service, to the book, might be a fixity which would permit the speaker greater range in attitude and gesture as well as feeling, since response is no longer an issue), we do expect some fluidity within the speaker. What we find instead is a recalcitrant girlishness; the voice is, here, as fixed as the father, pinned to a pre-adolescent and faintly coy obsession. To some extent the drama here, father and daughter, would seem to dictate this, and the poems do recognize the problem, though their solution is not to abandon the format but to strain it: periodically, the speaker envisions the father as her child, as a fetus inside her, and so on. What the poems do not do is move either forward or backward, backward to an earlier phase of childhood, the perspectives of which might illuminate the current confrontation, or (convincingly) forward.

These issues present themselves now for two reasons. I had the good fortune to read an unpublished collection by Martha Rhodes which treats these materials (like *The Father* and *Eva-Mary*) in a book-length collection. It is difficult to give, here, adequate sense of a collection whose distinction rests in structure: Rhodes cleaves to no fixed perspective— this is a single speaker, eccentric, various, rather than a spokesperson. This fluidity persuades because it mimics the dilemma, imitates and preserves the child's helplessly reactive mind as it survives into, and is masked by, adulthood. These short poems, by turns savage, wry, mordantly witty, tender, stern, deluded, sane, read like a series of fragments, bits of mosaic; they duplicate on the page the sense of a past's being, piece by piece, recovered; they convey, devastatingly, the moment of a pattern's emerging: the little scenes and vignettes, the suspect tools of memory, cohere heart-stoppingly and absolutely into a narrative which fuses the damaged body to the divided heart. The results of the forbidden saturate these poems; reading them we are in the presence of harm (as we never really are in the books discussed earlier) and, simultaneously, a wild, stubborn, unkillable life. A few lines will give, perhaps, some sense of Rhodes's sad sardonic voice, and the ease with which, here, past and present blur:

> She pretends to be dead
> and unless you creep up and pinch her someplace tender
> you think she really is dead.
>
> Then she gets up
> refreshed now, pink-cheeked,
> her hair a little sweaty.
>   ("For Her Children")

> Why do I always let you die,
> not lifting you from bed, just watching you
> lie breathless as your spirit

dangles from our bedroom wall
till it gives up and it's dead too.
Poof, I dream, no more you.

   ("Our Bedroom Wall")

I hate to be touched, he said,
and this was news to me

You love to be touched, I said. . .

   ("For Once")

Back home, I'd rather not tell you where I've been.
Quietly, I take off my coat.
I open a screen, lean out and wave.
Does anyone drive slowly down our street
to stare up at our lace-lit windows?

I'm waving at parked cars, a grocery stand, the bus stop.
Here we are. Who out there
wants to be us?

    ("Neither of Us")

He finds the dusty gin,
pours a double, straight,
then another. Lunch will be fast.
He'll sleep after, there,
on the sofa, I'll watch him.

It's mostly my mouth that's his,
and my hair, thinning,
pushing back from my brow, exposing
me, like him.

Oh, I've known since I was seven,
since then I've known I was him,
his.

   ("His")

 Secondly, I have been, for the last years, increasingly drawn to the work of Frank Bidart, whose territory this is. The importance of Bidart's work is difficult to overestimate; certainly he is one of the crucial figures of our time and, very likely, a major poet—we can't, I think, absolutely make such determinations regarding our contemporaries. His art, like the story of the Garden, creates narratives designed to account for what would otherwise be inexplicable suffering. Sometimes, in a kind of desperate backwards reasoning, his speakers commit crimes, to explain or justify conditions which already exist, to force the outward, in other words, to mirror the inward. More fiercely, more obsessively, more profoundly than any poet since John Berryman (whom he in no other way resembles) Bidart explores individual guilt, the insoluble dilemma. If Olds—at least the Olds of *The Father*—is unintentionally static, Bidart explodes the stasis of obsession into drama, and does so almost entirely through the resources of voice. Anguish permeates these poems, the sense, sometimes vague, sometimes explicit, of the illicit, the criminal, and with this, the corollary issue of responsibility. Using intelligence, the single means available, these speakers struggle to trace to its source their conviction of culpability: the frantic isolation of these voices and their profound shame manifest a conviction that they are themselves reason enough for exile, whether they have acted or been acted upon. In either scenario, they are trapped. If I am responsible for evil, the poems reason, I am criminal; if I am not responsible, I am a victim and maimed. But the categories will not, in any case, stay still.

Bidart's speakers are not anomalies, strange examples of life on the edge, but a means by which the issues which absorb the poet can be most richly explored. Or perhaps less issues than conditions, the givens of human life, if human life is thought through and not merely moved through. Likewise, the evolving typographical innovations function to show multiple aspects of voice: sometimes a statement is enforced to dramatize or embody the lesson that will not stay learned, sometimes such statement seems to contain debate, as though the true force of statement were question: not "I did it" but "Did I? Did I?", a disguised plea for corroboration, the testing of a statement's truth by way of its sound. But corroboration, except of a particular kind I'll discuss shortly, is impossible, in part because these speakers' failure to resolve fundamental questions regarding themselves paralyzes their capacity to judge, or trust, the outside world (in other words, they cannot trust their impressions because they have not identified their purposes) and partly because compulsive conviction of the self's guilt tends to diminish the reality of an outside world which does not, in sufficient intensity, acknowledge that guilt. What Bidart's speakers share is a terminal dependence on intelligence, and minimal relief of accuracy: ". . . insight like ashes: clung / to; useless; hated." Nothing, in these poems, is simple.

Nor is there any plausible relief. Love and passion are rare here; when they occur, they show their secret, their clandestine aspect. The only invitation eros can imagine, the only absolute available to humanity, is the creation of a non-thing, an erasure, a wound, the inflicting of damage that will not heal:

> You said
> that the dead
>
> rule and confuse our steps—
>
> that if I helped you cut your skin
> deeply enough
>
> that, at least, was IRREPARABLE . . .

The ambition of passion is to replicate the drama of Eden. Or, that drama was invented to explain the drive of two beings toward an animal pact of shared isolation, the drive to make of the body a souvenir or proof of the event.

Virtually any poem in Bidart's *In the Western Night* can stand as a paradigm; virtually any poem shocks in a way that McCarriston and Olds never do. In "Confessional" particularly, the power of the forbidden to take two hostages shows in a sustained bravura feat of disclosure. This is passion at work, with passion's drive toward the irreparable:

> she began to simplify her life, denied
> herself, and said that she and I must struggle
>
> "to divest ourselves
> of the love of CREATED BEINGS,"—
>
> and to help me to do that,
> one day
>
> > she hanged my cat.

The poem, like many of Bidart's, begins and ends in bondage, the smaller bondage of individual life contained within the larger bondage of the species, the first (apparently) caused by, cemented by, the cat's death, the second the *reason* for that death. The voice that speaks in "Confessional" is the child, the done-unto, the passive watcher, the victim; he is haunted by his mother's act because it represents his own culpability; he participates with his mother in its creation. The space in which the speaker lives with his mother is a sealed space, characterized by exclusion, intimacy, that quality of deadlock which exactly renders the condition of victimization, its conviction of its own agency, its will toward responsibility. And the guilt which gives "Confessional" its title and situation is the guilt of collusion which arises out of or creates the forbidden: not that the act of violence is specifically sought or arranged by the victim, but that its enactment binds victim to perpetrator in a pact of silence. It is the silence that is collusive, that becomes for the victim the emblem of his or her deepest relation, since only with the one who damaged him are there no secrets. And the progressive effect of such conspiracy is the gradual diminishment of all other possibility, the retreat of other voices, until, in this instance, mother and son are entirely and absolutely alone, entirely enmeshed, dependent on one another for authentication:

how can I talk about

the way in which, when I was young,

we seemed to be engaged in an ENTERPRISE
together,—

        the enterprise of "figuring out the world,"
figuring out her life, my life,—

THE MAKING OF HER SOUL,

                which somehow, in our "enterprise"
together, was the making of my soul,—

"Confessional" searches wildly for historical analogy because insight affords insufficient possibility of change. But change, for Bidart, is specious; it gives lie to the overwhelming seriousness of, the reality of, his perception. These poems do not triumph over damage and shame, they find no cure, no respite, but, in the manner of the great tragedies, Bidart's voices protest (as Edmond White has observed). And the gravity of our dilemma, in being so profoundly experienced, in being given durable form, is dignified.

There are other modes than the tragic; plainly neither McCarriston nor Olds intended to sound exactly this note. And one of the revelations of art is the discovery of a tone or perspective at once wholly un-expected and wholly true to a set of materials. The problem in both *Eva-Mary* and *The Father* isn't the refusal of the tragic vision but the failure of both authors to find alternative visions. *Eva-Mary* is limited by McCar-riston's managerial interventions, her insistence on a single rigid inter-pretation; limited, in a sense, by excess will. Whereas *The Father* suffers from an insufficiency of will or direction; the poems are nearly all better in their parts than as wholes, as is the collection. The aimlessness of the book itself suggests the single disadvantage of Olds's impressive facility: these poems read as great talent with, at the moment, nowhere to go. Neither of these conditions need determine these poets' futures. But I find myself concerned that, in their different ways, McCarriston and Olds are constrained by a like mechanism, the felt obligation of the woman writer to give encouraging voice to the life force (for want of a better term).

Because the character of the voice, in each case, is intended to be ex-pansive, nonjudgmental, rooted in the physical, intended to be the heroic voice of the survivor, one doesn't automatically associate its pro-duction with constriction. But to the poet, all obligation of this kind is constriction, and ought to be questioned or fought.

Judith Harris

Breaking the Code of Silence: Ideology and Women's Confessional Poetry

In recent years, critics have given the term "confessionalism" negative connotations. Poets who have found their way by the constellation of Sylvia Plath, Anne Sexton, John Berryman, and Robert Lowell—to name but a few of the original representatives of the confessional school— have been belittled for writing poems deemed as private, exhibitionistic, self-indulgent, narcissistic, or melodramatic.

A surfeit of confessions in poetry and on television talk shows, ex- posés, and radio have spurred these attitudes, but if we examine the works of the best confessional poets, we can clarify their shared thematic concerns, and we can rescue the term "confessionalism" from becoming just another word for sensationalism. Confessionalism has its own mode of motive and configuration, as does any literary movement. It is a poetry of ideas, or acute political consciousness, that demonstrates, through testimony, an individual's relationship to a community.

In a recent book review, entitled "The Forbidden," in the *Three- penny Review* (Summer 1993), Louise Glück applies the descriptive tags of "narcissistic," "constricted," and "tedious" to confessional works by Sharon Olds and Linda McCarriston.[1] Glück's complaints are represen- tative of many criticisms of confessional poetry. To examine how con- fessionalism seeks to break the silences that encode, censure, and censor private and public truths, we can open the discussion by responding to Glück's provocative points.

Glück finds fault with the means through which Olds and McCarriston arrive at the thresholds of speech. She suggests that a per- sonal and political agenda overdetermines these poems in a way that is "mechanistic," that weighs down the creative process and hinders discovery. Glück believes the poems strain "to give encouraging voice to the life force," and to demonstrate personal triumph over adversities.[2] She questions the immediate conjunction of private guilt, and the outside world's acknowledgment of what guilt is and how to receive it. While she would concede that these works commit themselves to social responsibility, she seems to dismiss the significance of these goals and how Olds and McCarriston's energies embrace a whole spectrum of religious and political problems that bear down on the individual and connect him or her to the collective.

Both poets achieve their powerful artistry through dissenting voice and agency rather than silence or passive resignation. If these poems struggle to affirm the life force, they do so because it is the survivor's arduous task to persevere rather than surrender. Conservation, concentration of will, self-reflection, consideration of the divisions of good and evil comprise directions of a compass for those who must daily explore new ways to live. This turn toward social responsibility is far more complex than Glück's critique suggests, for only through the personal experience of pain does pain become "disinterested" and indicative of a universal context. Confessionalism presses toward outrage and blame, *not guilt,* and this is the first integral sign of social responsibility and moral maturity.

Only through writing can the confessional poet address the collective human order by submerging the individual's evil in the deeper more impermeable causes of universal evil and its implication. In her ideological view, the crime was not individual but collective—with roots in power structures that so often invert good to evil in its own name. The past or former self (so often a child) can't do this and that is why the child is so often the ironical speaker within these poems—the child points out the corruption of the adult world in contrast to the child's purity. By revivifying the child, the confessional poet may rescue the afflicted adult. And like Wordsworth's benign child-within, the child continues to accumulate associations—former self, former heart, former soul. In *The Prelude,* Wordsworth confesses that, in later years, he lacked the spiritual confidence that the inner child naturally possessed. The restoration of the child as the inner morality and truth not yet

spoken may be analogous to the confessional process, because the child
within the poet is permitted to resurface. The poem is an opportunity
for the child to reveal and counter the tyranny she lived under when she
was unable to "speak" or disobey.

The mature poet summons the child in a variety of ways to witness,
to demonstrate the reality of victimization; to enforce justice in response
to abuse; and to liberate the adult poet from pain. This displacement of
adult perception into the child—who can feel but only partially comprehend the events that surround him or her—is a strategy for endowing the
child with conscious reflection. Contrition is available only to the mature poet, for not acting now to forestall the evil she recognizes *through
the past,* within the family or within the broader social world. Here is the
power of the expansive processes of Olds's and McCarriston's so-called
"giving encouraging voice to the life force." Their poems are imperatives
for rising from the depths, like Lazarus's need to warn and disclose, to
use the incendiary coal of language to speak, and to illuminate the broken innocence of children and their shame.

In the best poems of Olds's and McCarriston's works, private suffering is connected with collective suffering, and the poems relate our
contemporary concerns more profoundly than the poems of some reac-
tionary movements that subordinate content to the execution of form.
Plath, Olds, and McCarriston all grapple with the issues of the morality,
cruelty, and virtues of the human spirit faced with the "unbearable." In
doing so, they confront us with personal confessions of survival in art
that parallel historical chronicles of survival in extreme circumstances of
deprivation or atrocity. The survivor's irreducible presence compels us all
to be witnesses, to hear the story of martyrdom and shame, and sometimes forgiveness. Confessionalism contains the positive belief in expression as liberation from the powers who would disarm the truth.

The concentration camps provide many witnesses and confessions. In
a television interview, Elie Wiesel narrates his experience of liberation
from a concentration camp where he was a child. He recalls that children
in the camps already had the wisdom of old people because they had
been exposed to the extremes of human savagery. When the liberation
came, Wiesel recalls, an African American sergeant was confronted with

the stench, and the corpses, and emaciated forms of what were once living men and women. The sergeant cursed and cursed. He screamed and cursed all of humanity, as well as the perpetrators, for tolerating the savagery there. Wiesel said that the children wanted to thank the sergeant, to lift the man up on their shoulders in a hero's fashion, but they were far too weak, and kept falling back to the ground. The sergeant did not give up, however, and tossed himself in their arms, *trying to be light.* Wiesel recalls the man's frolic in the midst of the tumbling children; he wanted to levitate *himself for them,* he wanted to do what a savior would do: *to fly.* Wiesel's testimony is beautifully symbolic: the liberating angel opens and attempts to revitalize the children again, both physically and spiritually to restore their strength.

This confession or testimony shares "truth" that cannot be ignored, although some would try to fend it off. In *The Survivor,* Terrence Des Pres explains the hesitation of the outsider coming to the testimony of Holocaust survivors.[3] The desire to hear the truth is countered by the need to *ignore* (to cast out) and undermine the survivor by somehow pointing to his guilt. This tendency to transfer guilt to the victims themselves distorts the truth and is predicated on the outsider's need to protect himself against *what he does not wish to know,* against that which will disturb him, making his own pain seem trivial.

Burdened by the gravity of history and its succession of endless atrocities, it is inevitable that the female confessional poet, seeking a symbol to express the deepest tragedy of her own sense of victimization, would choose a constructed identity of the political martyr, the victim those in power must censor or silence for her views, beliefs, or genetic origins, which can only be extinguished along with personhood. Olds and McCarriston include in their books historical and political victims because they engage the literary reader. At the same time, these poets deconstruct the very idea of confessionals by restoring voices to the survivors, who testify that their supposed guilt was innocence, and that the judges of old are really to blame.

Linda McCarriston's poem, "Le Coursier de Jeanne d'Arc," demonstrates how martyrdom can represent the human dilemma of how to "speak" truthfully even when violence and pain seem to distort

---

everything.[4] In the poem, Jeanne d'Arc is not the central victim, at least *not yet*. Instead, her dramatic demise is displaced by the horse they burned in front of her eyes—both as a foreshadowing of the punishment she was about to receive and as an impetus for her to repent. The horse is a substitute for the children Jeanne never had: "she had no sons to burn" in a "world not of her making." Of course, mothers populate the world but have no power to provide their children with a safe world in which they might thrive.

The victims here are both the saint and her horse, whose slow agony accompanies a submerged yet articulate "voice": "the long mad godlike trumpet of his terror, / his crashing in the wood, the groan of stakes that held, the liverblack hide, the pricked ears catching first / like dryest bark, and the eyes." First "the pricked ears" and then the recording "eyes" burn at the decrees of "Men of God" who are more interested in the spectacle of a burning animal or woman than in demands of justice and truth. Jeanne d'Arc's voice and vision are threatened by their corruption, by "the cruelty that can make / . . . of what a woman hears a silence, that can make of what a woman sees / a lie." They pressure her to "confess" that what she sees and hears are *not* what she saw and not what she heard, that she is deluded by evil and blinded to good. And yet, what she confronts in the poem is tantamount to the Devil's Hell. Like Hester Prynne, Jeanne is threatening to the "Wise Men" because of self-dependence—her capacity to find God without their aid or control, and without their lies.

What McCarriston emphasizes in the poem is *not* the victimization of woman at the stake, or the "ecstasy of her agony" ("This is yet one of their lies"), but the flesh-and-blood figure of a martyr forced to watch her masculine double similarly sacrificed to the fire of purification. The horse's "chest with perfect plates of muscle," her mate, perishes before her as if it might be the last shred of her will to resist or rebel. She wrestles with the possibility of recanting, in order to avoid "the narrow corral that would not / burn until flesh had . . ." but then realizes to do so would be to surrender more than her religious beliefs, but morality. She will not "put on their truth," their mendacity, at whatever cost because it would sacrifice her own spirit, which only God, not she, can do. Deadly

fires transform hue from "yellow-green" to" blackening red" as they are
fed animal or human flesh; and in the same way, McCarriston suggests,
that the perpetrators are tainted by their own sins, forever guilty as the
blaze itself becomes the color of the charred body. Thus, this is not
simply about the martyrdom of one woman, but the *ideology of the
truth*: what is human and what is not, and what is bestial and what is
not. The body of the horse is allowed to burn "untended" as if it were
game—and here, "game" is intended to carry its cavalier meaning. This
is a savage, criminal game of torture and power and affliction. It has its
historical linkage to other forms of mass persecution and atrocity, such
as the Holocaust.

In strong poets like McCarriston or Olds, confession is a personal
outcry that seeks to address a community's consciousness by conflating
the inner domestic realm with broader, historical realities. Olds may
do so by trying to transcend her own—or the family's pain—through a
knowledge of the suffering all around her. McCarriston refutes the
derogation of the term "confessional" by insisting on her work's cool
logic, and therefore, by ironically maintaining the traditional expectations of masculine discourse, while telling stories that reveal their deceptions. Both poets wish to call our attention to how injustices imprison
victims in visible or invisible cells; yet it is the cells that unite us as one
living world. Such poetry finds its analogy in religious poetry, demon-
strating how the shocking truth of human suffering can reveal the need
for a community to support the private pains and the healing of others.

Still, readers may question the relevance (if not the morality) of a
poetry that is seemingly so private and resistant to temperance, and un-
apologetic about making anguish (personal or historically dramatic) the
centripetal force of a poem. But these suspicions may arise from traditional and stifling poetics; a poem should not be grim or offend our
sense of "good taste"; it should not be self-indulgent; it should please
rather than threaten, shock, or disgust. Yet, the poem cannot be severed
from its maker: it is asking too much from the poet to permit the reader
to exclude certain material on the basis of its taboo or shocking subjects.
When we begin to do that, we join the "conspiracy of silence." The
poems of Olds and McCarriston do not end with passive submission, or

with the internalization of death, which is also the death of speech, but with a reason to speak and hope, and with the power to change.

The word "confess" is a verb, meaning: (1) to acknowledge or disclose one's guilt, and (2) to disclose one's sins in search of absolution. Unlike the child, the mature poet has acquired the power of articulation to amend or confess the past. But sin and suffering may also be accompanied by blame. Where does guilt end and suffering begin? The poems of Sharon Olds and Linda McCarriston confront this very difficult moral and psychological problem. For when the child is the confesser of a sin in which she was forced to participate, the problem is how to speak about shameful experience in the face of propriety and censorship. When the reader rejects possibilities of where art can take a reader, the reader breaks an implicit bond of human trust that, in this context, is analogous to the priest's role as listener.

The background of confessionalism is one of a convergence of anxieties shared by an entire population shaken by World War II, and by the individual's dissociation from some of the values—religious, social, and moral—he or she once relied upon for personal stability. Civilization itself was suffering a nervous breakdown as intellectuals examined the problem of evil in its grossest form, a systematic destruction of European Jewry and the worldwide destruction to which all warring nations contributed. In the Nuremberg trials, the war criminals were interrogated to force them to disclose that each one was aware of the aberrant crimes he had committed against humanity. Without awareness, there can be no logical accountability. Awareness was proved through action, and deliberate evil was shown by deed—cover-up and secrecy.[5] Those who knew what was happening to Jews, but did not raise their voice to halt it, whose civility would not permit the possibility of human brutality, much less the fact—they were, in some ways, as guilty as the Nazis themselves.

Like the revelations of history, confession serves as an antidote to the extreme harm that civilized silence can do. The female poet working through the complexity of her own victimization may arrive at a symbology of action and submission, silence and speech, in order to overturn the scales of power and powerlessness. Thus, Plath, for example, takes on the roles of the Jew and biblical or mythological figures who have suffered and survived in order to express her own sense of degradation and justifiable outrage at her "torturers." Identification with the Jew in "Daddy" expresses a deep sense of being despised and powerless to fight the forces of brutality. Yet "Daddy" is sometimes faulted for being an artful but exhibitionist work of indulgent rage and bitterness directed at a neglectful and verbally abusive father. His abandonment of her—to death and silence—may have influenced her idiosyncratic "art of dying" in which art itself became the intangible but seductive realm into which dying seemed pleasurable. She "did it again and again," trying to perfect her art and her death simultaneously. In her work, pain and anguish serve to bind reader and poet as the one confessing, and the one hearing the confession, are bound by mutual recognition.

In "Daddy," the child's shame is supplanted by the power of her utterance when she can speak against those forces that censor her: the father, female propriety, the world of oppositions such as hate and love, torturer and tortured. We are moved by the nakedness of the confession as a testimony of the underprotected child who is violated until the perpetrator is himself silenced by death or absence. "Daddy" is about learning to speak: and this is evident by the child's primitive babbling and by the many references to silence or the failure to articulate:

> I never could talk to you.
> The tongue stuck in my jaw.
>
> It stuck in a barb wire snare . . .
> Ich, ich, ich, I could hardly speak . . .
>
> the black telephone's off at the root,
> the voices just can't worm through . . .[6]

At the end of "Daddy" the reader knows that the shame of the confesser is bound up with her utterance, which is a belated response to her silent victimization. Her identification with the Jew persecuted by the Nazi is an allusion (and also an evasion) of the conflictual terms of the poem. The Jew's guilt is untenable because the Jew is absolute victim, despised not for his or her self, but for what is less tangible, his or her *genus*. For the Nazis willed the destruction of the Jews not only from one country to another, but from the existence of the world itself. If they had succeeded, the descendants of those who survived the Holocaust would not *be*. In "Daddy," the role of the Nazi torturer is not simply predicated on hurting the child, *but in willing her out of existence*. Hence, there is a half-hidden wish to extirpate her father and herself in order to regain some primal level of communication with him in a realm beyond death. Her father's unwillingness to see her as a person, rather than being a specimen in a collective genus (i.e., female), accompanies her worst fear that, so classified, she is an abomination to him. Her femaleness brings on more self-destruction through masochistic relationships with men. But the masochist is only the flip side of the sadist, and, in some ways, needs him in order to perpetuate her agony and wrath.

While exploring the extremity of human virtue and human depravity, both Olds and McCarriston illustrate the divisions of human good and human evil. The comprehensibility of hurt and blame may divert itself back to the mature and analytical poet, or back again to the incarnation of the poet *within* the child. But the harboring of the child within the protection of the mature consciousness may not be, as some have charged, outright displays of narcissism, but moments of needed self-awareness.

In an early poem, "That Year," Olds, like Plath before her, compares herself with the Jewish captives in Auschwitz, whose fate she recalls having learned about in Social Studies "that year." The poem begins with this initial idea, "that was the year I started to bleed / crossing over the border in the night . . ."[7] That year she experienced brutality in her own private sphere: a girl discovered murdered, her father's abuse of the family, and other, more obtuse events such as getting her period, "the mask of blood," which she was unprepared for, and which she interpreted as a sign of the pain already inflicted upon her. She recognized the cause of that pain " like my father's face, the face of the guard / turning away or worse yet / turning towards me." The mature poet remembers her own sense of guilt as a child, as victim of her father's abuse, an abuse that perversely fosters within the child identical shame for being reprehensible to the parent and therefore deserving of punishment. But what if the punishment is *undeserved? Undeserved punishment is the underlying link-*

age between private confession and symbolic representation of the Jew in Auschwitz. And that is also the definition of parental force or abuse. And the association of menstruation adds to the idea that she may be rejected or hated for her difference as a female, leading to more masochistic assaults on herself (that bring "blood").

Yet the speaker then realizes that she is not to be counted among the Jews ("a word for us"), but that she was a survivor ("there was another word for me / and for many others / I was: a survivor.") The survivor rises above the shame, and rebels by sustaining her humanity—her ideological defense. Although she was not the cause of the cruelty inflicted upon her by others, she can't extricate herself from its happening; it happened *to* her and not *because* of her. She realizes that she has survived the father's threat to her autonomy and not relinquished the process of her own individuation. Even so, she knows that survivors never do forget or escape their personal guilt for surviving when others did not.

And in surviving, Olds uses her testimony to give the past meaning, even if meaning is the conflation of many emotions. In the poem "Tricks," redemption only comes through confession, speech, or writing. The mother uses her body, and not her speech, to make things happen, or conversely, to make nothing happen: "She pulls scarves out of her ears . . . / My mother the naked magician / stands on the white stage / and pulls tricks."[8] The mother is deceptive in her magician's guise: "She closes her hand / and when she opens it, nothing." Emotionally starved, the daughter counters her mother with her own *visibility and voice* as a poet-performer: "All this / I have pulled out of my mouth / right in front of your eyes." The mouth is a substitute for the mother's sexual parts from which the infant was "pulled out" like another prop in an intangible magic show. This is the power of confession—giving birth to one's self. The mother's guilt is sealed by the daughter's accusation through "the mouth" of the poem that confesses its anger while beseeching the reader's "eyes" as judge.

McCarriston, too, pushes past the limits of the silence that was once imposed upon her; and she *does* judge, blame, and try to forgive. Writing about monstrous things that happen in the private contexts of the family, she shows how the terror of the underprotected child is not easily

264 ~ JUDITH HARRIS

recalled or refined into such a lucid art of reconstruction, recollection, and tonal irony. The violent acts of the parent are resurrected in the self-witnessing representations of the victim *herself,* who cannot call herself a victim until she recognizes what the victor took from her. The survivor stays initially frozen in the past, and only later fights the impositions of her own shame—her silence, not wanting to bring the inside out. The deepest truth is the confesser's confrontation: *"Here I am, you can't wish me away."* McCarriston shows admirable discipline in maintaining a fixed eye on the brutality and does not seek a higher authority to reason with it. In her work, the child-within is a spectral figure, a beacon or lighthouse, whose beam of light is so direct and concentrated that it may cause the reader to want to blink, or look away.

What is exceptional about McCarriston is how confession becomes a trope that is deliberately inverted in order to show its signifying "difference" from itself. This poetry dramatizes innocence that is corrupted by the parent, along with the interpenetration of opposing feelings of love and hatred, anger and penance, *blaming and punishment.* Hence, confession is the refusal to be guilty under the pressures of the other who hopes to contain the victim within that guilt. In order for the daughter to use language as a belated weapon against a mother's neglect or denial or a father's sadism, she must first banish from memory the flawed representations of the betraying parent. Power generates from the extremity of a child's release into the fluid authority of language that will, due to its own limits, never tell the whole story, but can partially expel the isolation of a child taught not only to take what is handed to her, but also to privatize her pain.

Shame, horror, and self-disfigurement are compelling effects of the psychically bruised child who has accepted the bad and evil and ugly as her own flesh. Although she was innocent, the fall into corruption is not so much a complicity with the arbiter of the transgression, or their mutual punishment, but a solitary drop into groundlessness.

In McCarriston's poem, "Billy," the poet recovers a scene of horror as the abusive father is seen beating her brother:

and even our father
who stood beating you with his fists

where he'd stuck you into
a barrel, as a mountaineer might plant
a banner in a peak to keep your
skinny thirteen-year-old self erect
till he was finished—the whole
rest emanates and fades.
It was winter. You had driven
your homemade go-cart into a door
that he was saving for something . . .
I see his upper body
plunging up and down like one
of those wind-driven lawn ornaments . . .
The barrel reaches your bottom.
Your body sounds different than
a mattress. The noises he makes
are the noises of a man trying
to lift a Buick off the body
of a loved child, whose face he can
see, upturned just above the wheel
that rests on her chest, her eyes right
on his eyes, as yours were on mine.[9]

The father has raped her mother, or even her. That fact is revealed
through the metaphor of a man "trying to lift a Buick off the body of a
loved child." The sister has associated the beating with the act of rape,
and they are one. The "eyes" are autonomous, as the "eyes" of God's judgment watching the father's beating, then his raping, watching the victims
look at him with deathly horror and then to witness with the same look,
that is not guilt but the knowledge of who is to blame. The victims are
speechless, but the poet recounts the experience with extraordinary objectivity. This is by no means "a narcissistic indulgence" or "manipulation" of a reader's readiness to be shocked. This poem terrifies because it
goes beyond the horror of the act and seizes us with the truth of our own
capacity to look on and do nothing while people commit heinous crimes.
The particular complication within the poem is the mirroring of brother
and sister who corroborate the event for each other. Because they are figu-
ratively "one flesh," they serve as each other's priests, for their unspoken
confessions. And also, because they are assailed by feelings of their own

incipient evil or worthlessness derived from the father's sins, they are somehow implicated in his guilt. Do the eyes connote helplessness, guilt, or shame? What is the poet confessing if not the complexity of all three? And yet there is also anger and blame in which the reader participates, conceding that this is humanity in its most complex, incestuous light: love and hatred, abuser and abused, suffering and transcendence. If there is no room for forgiveness in the poem, there is room for understanding. A violent tableau, the memory of the terror of the child who is already locked in the "confessional / coffin" springs forth through the savagery of what has occupied and finds its justification in articulation.

In "To Judge Faolain, Dead Long Enough: A Summons" the mature poet blames, without reservation and without ambiguity, the judge who allowed her abusive father proximity to his wife, Eva-Mary, and their children. The judge's reliance on "justice" and "law" is in ironic juxtaposition to the reality of what is happening in the family. The judge's failure was in his incapacity to identify with the people he stood above as a "symbol" of authoritative justice. "Let your name be Eva-Mary. Let your birth be dawn. / Let your life be long and common, and your flesh endure."[10] The bitter and satiric irony of the last line emphasizes that the flesh, like the outer shell of beaten daughter and mother is only temporary; what does endure is the evocation of the experience and poet's right not only to talk back, to refute and correct the error of judgment, but to blame the perpetrator of that error—the judge.

The child speaks for the injustice done against her mother and turns the poem from the private confessional into an allegory about the subjugation of all dependent women who are vulnerable to the physical, spiritual, or judicial authority of men who regard women as inferior, as body, rather than "light." The mother's flesh will *not* endure; ultimately, it is the book her father has already effaced, an accounting of his sins, upon which the writer has now left her own voice, her own text of liberation. Here, womanhood, Eva-Mary, combines with the social class she represents in the courtroom. Both woman and the poor signify powerlessness before the judge's bench, a powerlessness that is *childlike* because it must go without appeal, and cannot find reality in the judge's official but artificial rhetoric. Indeed, there is someone to blame here.

My point is that *the fact of blaming does not minimize* the power of the confession as a moment of vital communion and identification of writer and reader.

The poet stands here as both witness and defense for her mother against all the violence and "unforgivable ignorance" of the men who did not see her for what she was. The title "Eva-Mary" is a suggestion that poetry (Mother, Eve) in this mode seeks to resurrect the past, to mother again, and to bear the child as a deliverer of language that seeks not to mollify, but opens up the possibilities of saying what is most difficult to confess.

Works of the confessional mode, or the "personal," offsprings of introspection and dissidence, often provoke the question among readers: *Why should we care? Why should we care about the private suffering of others?* To that position I would respond with: *Why should we not?* We read them not because they are brave, or scandalous, or masochistically enthralling. We read them not because we are, or they are, voyeurs or missionaries. We read them because they impart truth about cruelty, about the need to unify aspects of the self, and because they show the inscriptions of collective pain as a language that can be uttered, received, and transcended. We read them because they plummet through the surface, break the code of silence, and yield wisdom. These poets touch irresistible pain, pain that unites us or tears us apart. They recognize the gravity of human history that is a succession of atrocities as well as a progression of accomplishments. And we should come to recognize ourselves in them, our own vulnerabilities, in the human truth they speak, or even, as the African American sergeant did—curse, liberate, and *fly.*

Notes

1. Louise Glück, "The Forbidden," in *The Threepenny Review,* Summer 1993.

2. Ibid.

3. Terrence Des Pres, *The Survivor* (Oxford; New York: Oxford University Press, 1976), p.43.

4. Linda McCarriston, *Eva-Mary* (Triquarterly Press, 1994), pp. 69–71.

. See Berel Lang's *Act and Idea in the Nazi Genocide* (University of Chicago Press, 1990). Lang provides a rich and fascinating discussion of the motivations and beliefs underlying the idea of genocide in the psychology of Nazism, as well as the difficulty philosophical inquiry posed for him as a second-generation Jew, writing about the comprehensibility (on any rational scale) of such irrational barbarianism.

6. Sylvia Plath, *Collected Poems,* ed. Ted Hughes (New York: Harper and Row, 1981; Harper Perennial, 1992), p. 223.

7. Ibid., p. 6.

8. Ibid., p. 14.

9. McCarriston, *op. cit.,* pp. 14–15.

10. Ibid., p. 13.

Kimberly Blaeser

The Voices We Carry

> *My being is defined in ancestral voices.*
> —N. Scott Momaday, *In the Presence of the Sun*

We travel to our place in the world by the grace of others' words. The shape of every experience known only by its nestling in among the soft folds of our history. And so we write with an ink formed of our Auntie's laugh, that old plum tree's fruit. Claiming or believing in an individual voice, we delude ourselves. No voice arises from one person. I know I write out of a place, a center, that is greater than what I alone am or could be. My work is filled with the voices of other people.

A Native woman living in the twenty-first century, I am but the tiniest bud on an ancient oak tree. My lips open in the liquid language of poems because the root system of my family tree draws deeply from the dark soil of history. What I speak and write comes to me dank and tangled among the years and lives I carry. I write not only out of a knowledge of the past, but within a chamber of voices from that past.

Harold Bloom has written of the "anxiety of influence." I read the poetries of the American Indian nations as celebrations of influence. They arise chanting. Holding solidarity with the original languages of Native peoples, repeating the rhythms, echoing the dream songs, the deer songs, the night chants. They carry the ceremonial voices, the oral stories. They repeat, revive, restate. They burst, full with the spoken words of Indian people—words of relatives, tribal activists, clan leaders. Words from the land itself. Native poets and poetics *celebrate* the voices they carry.

I. Living by Your Words

On the most pragmatic level, we all absorb and return sound to create language. We hear and recognize vibration and voices while we are still in the womb. Those around us literally give us voice as we learn to speak by listening and imitating their engagement with language. Our first interaction with words and story comes to us from the community of speakers in which we grow up. Our vocabulary, volume, pronunciation, inflection all arise from that encounter. We become vocal first in a local context; that first context of speech informs all subsequent encounters. However we develop our vocalization or written language, it remains rooted in our past, embedded in the history of that early language community.

I remember how my husband used to mistake my voice for my mother's when I was speaking from White Earth in those old rhythms and tones. No matter how anglicized my off-reservation voice might become, it could always return to the "red" English of its origin. And it is that reservation-inflected English that inhabits many of the voices in my poems. *It's that way, child. The night things. Like how you learned to walk. Nobody can teach you.* In these lines from "Those Things That Come to You at Night," the sequence and construction of the phrases create a certain voice character. Together with the stressed pronunciation I am only beginning to learn to translate into print, they allow a reader access to the cultural *sound*-ings that carry place, nation, and sometimes, time. Although I seldom recognize the role of muse in my poetry, I am frequently aware of the voice origins of many of my poems. I "hear" inspiration. Often it speaks the rez language. Teachings, stories, dialogue lines come to me through what, for convention's sake, I will call my imagined encounter with one or another old-time speaker, as when in "Rewriting Your Life," I wrote, *The aches in our bones are memories I'm told.* There is a constant *hearing* and *telling* involved in the making of meaning for me. The clearest voices speak that first bicultural language.

We all recognize the rhythms of our sound background; we hear with an ear tuned at the pitch of that remembrance. A number of years ago, when my mother was in the last stages of a progressive cancer, I was

home with my first child for a visit. One afternoon I lay on the bed in my
old room nursing my baby while my parents were moving about in the
kitchen of our small house. The familiarity of the sounds—the cadence
and pitch of their voices rising and whispering themselves away, the creak
of their steps, my mother's dry cough, the crack of a paper bag folded
neatly along its edges—eased me out of time. I could have been nine or
fourteen or thirty. Life was one long afternoon spent listening, one ear
against the sun-warmed chenille spread, one hearing myself spoken in
the voices of parents and grandparents, aunties, uncles, and cousins.
Only the tug of Gavin at my breast returned me to the reality of a moment both soothing and melancholy. I understood how those muted
voices formed my link to the very ground of meaning. I didn't need to
hear the words. And I could not conceive of existence or identity beyond
the silencing of that conversation.

Inevitably, we carry those early groundings in sound and language
into our own speech and writing. Whether we hear another language
intermingled with English, absorb a particular style of music, or live
among certain background sounds, the influence will affect our ver-
balization. Among Native poets, of course, the use of Native language in
their work is the most apparent example. Ofelia Zepeda's poems
in *Ocean Power: Poems from the Desert* have entire stanzas in Tohono
O'odham. They also offer fine examples of poems constructed verbally
in a manner similar to ceremonial songs or chants: here involving a great
deal of repetition or a certain formality in word order. Our early language immersion may manifest itself in multiple other ways in poetry
from word choice to rhythm to line length. Whatever these manifesta-
tions, they attest to the cultural origins of "personal" voice.

Cultural experience, of course, also includes place experience. Our
poetic voice is sound affected by our physical environment. Whether we
sleep to the slap of ocean waves or wake daily to the sounds of city traffic,
we develop a landscape of sound that inevitably informs our verbaliza-
tion, our vocabulary, and our poetic vision. Tenure in place develops a
regional accent and a certain literacy: an onomatopoeic urge that can
sing a specific natural or urban voice, a poem that can speak the local
names for fish or plants or city bus lines, that can carry a sense of place

character whether that place be a hermitage, suburbia, a canyon or an oak savannah. In "Indian Song: Survival," for example, when Leslie Silko writes, "At sunrise / I heard ice on the cattails" or "Green spotted frog sings to the river," these images and sound references arise from a certain place intimacy. When I wrote in "Of Landscape and Narrative,"

> red-headed skeletons
> cranes all bone
> and histrionics
> parachute into fields
> dusk quiet slashed
> with awe and tremolooo,

I drew on the experience of having watched and listened to literally thousands of sandhill cranes.

But the effects of place go deeper than our conscious knowledge or simple recollection. Gerald Vizenor writes of "interior landscapes," as does Barry Lopez, and Lopez claims, "The shape of the individual mind is affected by land as it is by genes." We can see this embedding of place at the most basic level, for example, when we note how the natural ritual of seasons creates a certain internal rhythm, a felt knowledge of seasonal cycles. I make this claim poetically for the grazing female caribou preparing for migration in "Of Landscape and Narrative," describing her as having her *belly filled / with knowledge / of journey*; and, in the same poem, I claim an unconscious human land knowledge as well:

> through every body crevice
> earth moments seep in
> build nests
> hatch outlook
> linger in cells and soul.

The many intuitions and natural instincts inherited or created by place associations certainly contribute to our core sense of self; therefore, they contribute to our poetic voice and vision.

Still, many Native people understand their identity as yet more intricately linked to place. Paula Gunn Allen writes, "We are the land.

To the best of my understanding that is the fundamental idea embedded in Native American life and culture in the Southwest. . . . It is within this larger being that we . . . dance, hunt, run, heal, sing, chant, and write." We see these several layers of relationship reflected in poetry by Mohawk author Maurice Kenny. He claims a long-standing investment in place when he addresses the water in "Black River" and writes, "I hear the groans / of your throat . . . these many years." In "Legacy," he describes himself through natural images:

> my face is grass
> color of April rain;
> arms, legs are the limbs
> of birch, cedar;
> my thoughts are winds
> which blow."

In "They Tell Me I Am Lost," he aligns the origin of his voice with the elements of nature creating a litany that includes, "my chant is the wind, / my chant is the muskrat / my chant is the seed." Finally in the poem "Moccasin," we see the poet's move to make his place experience speak. He opens with the command to "Listen" and follows with the sounds:

> moccasin moccasin
> . . . drums drum
> pound pound
> rattles rattle
> sing sing
> wind howls like a wolf on the hill
> thunder thunders . . .

This personal grounding in surroundings also includes the mythology, history, and ceremony of place, and these multiple, layered relationships shape the puzzle pieces from which we form poetic patterns. When Acoma poet Simon Ortiz compiled *Going for the Rain,* he interpreted his own experience by means of the regional Keresan Pueblo emergence story and the familiar ceremonial entreaties for rain. These patterns gave rise to the sectional movements and overall structure for the collection. He relates his own journey in the context of place-specific cultural story.

Likewise, to a greater or lesser degree, land links "place" all poets, and inform or contribute to their sense of self.

But place accounts are not the only stories to affect our outlook. Indeed, our artistic perspective emerges from our broad narrative foundations. We are all storied people. We learn to understand the world through the tales we hear. Religious or cultural myths, nursery rhymes, fairy tales, parables, family anecdotes, historical accounts—these give us the sense of structure and vision we use to interpret our experience. *Our* story arises not just out of our individual perspective, but out of our continuance of a long epic tradition. From our earliest years we hear ourselves and the events of our lives compared to that of a litany of relatives. *You have a rooster laugh like your great grandma. Cousin Jim broke his arm, too, when he was only three. One summer your grandma taught each of us girls how to shoo skunks.* Family stories form a map of remembrance that we both trace and extend in time and scope. Ultimately family history overlaps cultural history. The story of my elder uncles' experiences at Indian boarding school, the account of their running away and returning home to the reservation, becomes a *tribal* tale of hardship, colonization, and resistance. As family story weds us to cultural history, the seeing and telling of connections creates the *mythic* vision—the imaginative power to bridge from self to other, from experience to possibility. When we write our lives we construct our frame and meaning from a familial or familiar tradition of telling.

Among the poems from my first two collections, I have several mother poems that might be read as serial autobiography. Looking at them in retrospect, I see the movement of these poems as exactly that of extending my poetic vision across the generations by means of story. "Certificate of Live Birth" sees in my mother's self-identification as "Caucasian" on my birth certificate *the history of Indian people in this country* and *the story of a people's capture.* It claims, in my own self-identification as "mixedblood," an *escape* from the *prison* of racial injustice. The poem "Living History" attests to the physical likeness of my mother and myself, and offers a playful overlapping of our identities. It also implies my position as carrier of history or her-story. In "our old lost loves" I express an understanding of her reality and our relationship out of time as I first trace the similarities of our experience:

> some lovers I know
> in stories
> some by heart
> for I stand
> just as you did
> on the same lake shore
> watching darkness come
> suns setting in unison
> casting long shadows
> one after another
> across the years.

I then erase the lines of our separateness as we become of the same piece—*old lost loves / you and I*—and time becomes *a single lake.* The next mother poems are of my own motherhood, but they become extensions of that family epic. In "Kitchen Voices," for instance, I hear my own voice as *but a simple translation / of those ageless kitchen voices,* and, in "Fetal Disposition," I recognize my child as displaying *an Antell stubbornness / I secretly cherish.* These and other poems express the sense of continuance that stands behind any sense of self. I understand my experience only in terms of my mother's; my mother's, my child's, or my own, only in light of our tribal and family history. So neither poetry nor so-called auto-biography, then, is ever truly an independent venture. Language and voice emerge within a speech circle; and we can only ever write "self" relationally, from within the very plural "we" context of family, community, cultural, national, or inter-national story.

II. Speaking Indian

Beyond these pragmatic determiners of poetic connection, for many Native American writers there is an idealism at work, a philosophical dedication to the notion of *the people* or *the nation.* There is a conscious commitment to hear and to carry the language, the story, and the voice of American Indian traditions into their personal poetry.

The Anishinaabeg people from whom I am descended were evicted from their original homelands, their stories were excluded from the "authorized" historical accounts, the lands they inhabited—and they themselves—were renamed, their language was silenced in boarding and mission schools, their ceremonies were forbidden, and their lifestyles and stories were labeled primitive and pagan. Like many colonized people throughout the world, my Anishinaabeg ancestors were not given a voice in their own destiny. It is my privilege and responsibility to reclaim their right to speak and to be heard. And so I try in my own writing to carry the stories, the language, and the beliefs, to embody in my poetry the culture and the people. Many Native people see their work as that of "speaking for the generations"—as Simon Ortiz entitles a recent collection of "Native Writers on Writing."

As a literary critic, I might recognize in the reservation-inflected English, for example, the "code-switching" that Keith Basso analyzes in Western Apache communities. But I know that verbal movement intimately and to me it has something to do with survival, defiance, and solidarity. The speakers of Ind'n English refuse to "pass" as white even though they might. They elect instead to stand with, and for, the community. Writing "red," they claim a plural identity—a place, a history, and a people within which they define themselves.

This political stance often manifests itself in Native poetry through the rewriting or retelling of lives and events. In "New Orleans," for example, Creek poet Joy Harjo reimagines DeSoto and his relationship with the Creek people. Miwok poet Wendy Rose has written numerous poems in response to what she sees as the silencing of Native voices in historical accounts. In "I expected my skin and blood to ripen," she speaks in the voice of and for those slain at the Wounded Knee massacre. In the preface to *Bone Dance*, Rose has spoken of her identification with the various voices she represents in her poems, explaining that their perspective has come upon her. She says, for example, of her representation of a Tasmanian woman, "I felt myself become . . . Truganinny begging her younger relatives not to let the British Museum stuff her body and put her on display as the 'Last Tasmanian'" (xvi).

Rose's conviction that she comes to "feel . . . like" those individuals she represents in poetic dialogue points to another complicated and mysterious element at play in understanding the engagement of Native authors in poetic autobiography or self-life-writing. Hertha Wong has alternately referred to Native American autobiography as "communo-bio-oratory (community life speaking)" and "auto-ethnography (self-culture-writing)," alluding, of course, to the communal and cultural identification inherent in ideas of the self. This plurality might be understood as the intertwined or inextricable emotional or intellectual nature of our reality with that of family, place, community, and history. It alternately or simultaneously might be understood as a transformational or spiritual connection that literally alters our very essence. Are we inhabited by the spirit of place, by the spirit of another being, whether human or plant or animal? Are we conjoined with another or codependent? Or is it more biological, a kind of human instinct? Do we build what John Dewey calls "funded experience"? Do we have, as Gerald Vizenor has written, a "story in our blood"; as N. Scott Momaday has claimed, "blood recollection" or "racial memory"? The variations in belief or experience are likely as numerous as the number of Native authors. This facet of Native understanding, however, seems key in my resistance to the idea of individual voice.

Sometimes I consciously embody the idea of continuance in my poetry. In 1994, writing about the treaty rights controversy in Wisconsin, I verbally link my reality with that of the spearfisher as my identity blurs with his and we become one in "Meeting Place":

> At the boat landings, I see you raise your leg, knee bent, stepping to
> shore. Your hair falls across my eyes. I tilt our chin and flick it back,
> then brush it away with the back of our hand because the fingers hold
> to the handle of the bucket. The hand is chapped with the cold night
> air. It smells of fish.

Later in the same poem, I attempt to underscore the true, timeless dimension of experience when I link the survival histories of the spearfishermen of the 1990s with the tribal fishermen of the Depression era as each face their oppressors:

> Shouting faces, angry twisted mouths, crowd in at the edges of the
> night. They are that frowning game warden of sixty years past. They
> are the resort owners' overgrown children, cursing, throwing stones.

The end of the poem becomes an attempt to understand and verbalize
my position and relationship with my people and our history:

> You are stepping out of the boat. Your hair falls full across your eyes.
> When you push it back, I am standing before you, a protector. You are
> my past, standing before me. I am at the landing, one foot on shore,
> one in shallow water.

Because each of us stands straddling realities, the borders of time and
place, our words come from the many territories we occupy at once.

Still, "Meeting Place" surfaces out of fairly conventional notions of
intergenerational connection. I know the stories and the people of these
eras. I see and feel their similar struggles. The two come together in my
imagination and in a poetic "we" voice on the page. Other poems of mine
have less "rationally" explicable origins, sources more ephemeral. Once,
visiting a creative writing class, I was asked about the poem, "Trailing
You," which speaks of a dream experience. Did the poem, the professor
wanted to know, come about as a result of a dream? I could have salvaged
that encounter with simple assent. After all, it worked for Coleridge.
Instead, I told the truth: the poem came from a stone. Yes, I had experienced a dream sequence whose details inspired part of the content, but I
hadn't had the idea to write the poem until one day, on a walk, I noticed
among the many stones about my path a particular stone that I was
somehow compelled to pick up, hold in my palm and finger gently.
When I did that, I had the idea, walked back home, and wrote the
poem, all the while still holding the stone. I know it could be explained
as coincidence, the poem *might* have come regardless, the inspiration
just happened to arrive at the moment I encountered the stone. But, honestly, that is not how it happened. The stone didn't speak, I'll give you
that. But it housed the poem and somehow released it into my trust. I
know this sounds like bizarre, New Age hocus-pocus. But at least half of
what we know or experience comes to us inexplicably by intuition, instinct, and biological predisposition. Do we know enough of energy to

dispute the possibility that sometimes feelings, words, voices, poetry arrive mysteriously? I have written, "The earth breathes stories," and when my faith and poetry is strongest, I mean that, literally.

Various Native American tribes, including my own, have belief systems that recognize a host of experiences dismissed by so-called rational science. This discussion is neither the place to enumerate these spiritual philosophies, nor the place to argue for their viability. However, these other worldviews work to configure an understanding of authorship that differs from that of many Western traditions. The poetic Dream Songs of the Anishinaabeg people, for example, arise from a kind of visionary experience. They might be inspired by, or actually in the voice of, other beings. The idea of *individual* authorship and the idea of *ownership* of creative production are then sometimes incompatible with this understanding of poetic origin.

In writings by contemporary Native poets, this cultural backdrop has sometimes resulted in intense intertextuality, with poets both incorporating excerpts from traditional oral songs or ceremonies, and engaging in dialogue with these and other voices. Whether the voices are mythic, imagined, contemporary, or literary, they contribute to the multivocal quality of much of American Indian poetry.

III. A Celebration of Influence

Multidimensional from inception to reception, poetry and the diverse energies of poems construct a community. Arising as they do from the whole of our experience, they are not ours to start. They come from a history we are born into, a collection of family names and accounts we have heard, a map of places we have traveled. They are sifted from music and books and dreams. Even in their writing, they seek shape from an aesthetic older than our remembrance of it. Beyond this, their written life and their speaking continues only by the grace of, and on the lips of, other lives. Three summers ago in France, while giving a reading, at the close of one poem I looked out to see someone in the audience mouth the final words with me. That poem was his as much as it was mine. Something was consummated in that moment. I was elated. I was humbled.

A number of years ago, I heard a story from a colleague about his experience teaching writing to Lakota grade-school students in South Dakota. The students were writing poetry. Each session my friend would share with the class some of the fine lines the students had written. In the ensuing days, the same lines began to appear in the poetry of the other students. At first he thought plagiarism. Then he began to understand the honor involved and the spirit of community this cross-pollination expressed. For a final project the class constructed a single poem from the many fine lines they had written together.

The poem that concludes my collection *Absentee Indians,* "Y2K Indian," comes from the spirit of that moment in France and from the spirit of that multi-authored Lakota poem, from a seeing into the larger experience of poetry, as collaboration and celebration of influence. It is a poem constructed of the many connections my writing and living has to the stories, experiences, and writings of others. It celebrates the woven story paths of Indian nations by building itself partly on the words of several Native authors. It stands symbolic of the voices we all carry and the many contributing voices that create our words on the page.

The experiences of my life have seldom seemed individual, isolated. They have been informed and sometimes determined by the strands of connection to people, place, and history. The meaning I build or extract is referential. Last summer, perched on ledge rock in the Boundary Waters Canoe Area Wilderness, I watched a birch tree, its limbs leaning over a lake. As its leaves turned in the breeze like waving hands, they flashed green, silver, white, green, shimmering, reflecting light. I could not then have told you the color of birch leaves, I could not have told you if they cast the sun's reflection on water, or if the water's reflection lighted them. Likewise, our lives mingle past, present, and future, shimmer on the verge of an unknown light. We take our groundings of reality from the relationships, the overlapping motions of existence. We take them through understanding not our individuality, but our continuance. And the words we write may come in the voice of a stone telling what she heard long ago when humans really talked.

Carol Muske-Dukes

Women and Poetry: Some Notes

The *and* in "Women and Poetry" appears to maintain a respectful distance between two protectorates. When we move the terms in tighter, next to each other, the words get nervous. *Women* becomes a qualifier, and *poetry* cringes—what is a *woman poet*?

Woman poet—on the face of it, the term might appear condescending. Nevertheless, it came to exist in the 1960s and 1970s as less a descriptive than an unconscious prescriptive: the distinction made between one version of history and another. The prototypical *woman poets* of the twentieth century are, of course, Sylvia Plath and Adrienne Rich. Their poems seem inevitably framed in that context. It is hard to read their early work without experiencing it as *anticipatory*; we know what is to come; we know that each poet is going to have it out with history, as Rich has written of Emily Dickinson, "on her own premises."

They were (along with Anne Sexton) the beginning of an era. Prior to this era the categories were set well apart. *Women* and *poets*. Of course, there was the Uber-frau-ish "poetess," a dread diminutive with an arched eyebrow over every syllable. *Woman poet* was used, but with about the same degree of gravity as *poetess*. But there were always women who wrote poetry. Some were major voices; some were not. There were also wives, mistresses, girlfriends, and secretaries—muses. Sometimes women poets got mixed up with the rest. How could one tell them apart?

There used to be a "black book" certain male poets would share with one another before out-of-town readings. Names and phone numbers of young ladies in Poughkeepsie or Duluth who were guaranteed (by previous trial and documented experimentation) to be impressed enough by a bit of offhand enjambment to morph into pulsing dithyrambs and cheerfully succumb. What if one of these black-book entries wrote poetry? How would she be classified? A red-hot footnote, or poetess, or both?

The distinction "woman poet" was meant to do more than provide an instant rejoinder-replacement to two polite epithets: poetess and phone-book muse. It was meant to *bear witness* to a truth. It was meant to complement Muriel Rukeyser's famous lines: "What would happen if one woman told the truth about her life? The world would split open." We are then bound to ask: *what truth?* These words also split the world of poetry written by women in two: those whose "self" stood as representative of various truths and those who continued to write as if the self was a fiction.

The aforementioned black book summed up the sexual politics of the 1950s: cocktails and hushed conversation after the reading and all the little poetesses in a row, a discreet phone number for later in the evening—a world that was orderly, predictable. But soon, that world did split open.

That world, split and presplit, is unintentionally documented by Carolyn Kizer, editor of *100 Great Poems by Women,* who took pains (as she makes clear in her introduction to the book) not to include any poems by women about "romance or domesticity"—*thereby removing conventional cultural expectations as to subject matters*—or the "conditioned truths" of women's lives.

These deliberate exclusions produce an unintentional "scientific" literary study (a control group) on women poets and subject matter. If "romance" and "domesticity"—the traditional preoccupations of women of all ages—are precluded, what is it that women then write about?

From the earliest poems onward, the poets wonder about the "self," a woman's self, defined as it often is as *other.* In what is believed to be Anne Boleyn's poem (perhaps a rejoinder to Sir Thomas Wyatt, whose famous poem "Whoso List to Hunt" marks her as a "possession" of the king's), the author cries out: "Say what ye list, it will not be; / Ye seek for that can not be found."

Next is the mercurial, bardic Queen Elizabeth I:

I am, and not; I freeze and yet am burned;
Since from myself, my otherself I turned!

       ("Self and the Otherself")

The question of *self*, for a woman poet (not to mention a *queen's* problems in this regard) is continually vexing. Kizer's anthology bears witness to this "dislocation" of self through five centuries of poetry by women. It is a complaint unfamiliar to us historically, duly acquainted as we are with the forbearance of the Madonna, likewise the talking whore or sibyl, not to mention the voice that sings beyond the genius of the sea.

Kizer eschews any restrictions on the voice of the other, including the restriction of approved subjects. What she has presented here is a distinct, separate expression of self within a chronological selection of women's poetry and a loneliness within the self unrelated to longing for others, a psyche unsplit by "love" ("If just one woman told the truth about her life . . ."). "Let Greeks be Greek and women what they are," cries the worthy Anne Bradstreet. And what is a woman's self? When ancient Ephelia cries, for example, "My soul is Masculine," it does not seem to me that she wishes to be male, rather that she wishes mightily to express the soul of Ephelia.

Again and again this sentiment appears as longing for the validation of a past, a tradition. And, not surprisingly, the voice is often wounded or angry. Witness Anne Killigrew, a seventeenth-century poet, in her poem "Upon the Saying That My Verses Were Made by Another":

The envious age, only to me alone,
Will not allow what I do write, my own;
But let them rage, and 'gainst a maid conspire,
so deathless numbers from my tunefull lyre
Do ever flow . . . I willingly accept Cassandra's fate
To speak the truth, although believed too late.

These poets were, of course, almost without exception, members of the upper classes, titled dames whose servants provided the time necessary for writing. Later, says Kizer, when the aristocratic ladies gave up on literature, or gave up on circulating it, writing was taken over by "spinsters,

who predominate, from the Brontës right down to Marianne Moore."
We hear Emily Dickinson aptly inquire, "I'm nobody, who are you?"

Poetess, muse, spinster; tinker, tailor, spy—one notices the difference
in emphasis. It appears that to write freely, one needs relief from exact-
ing circumstance—one needs independence and an understanding of
what exactly silence implies. One might infer, then, that in order to
write poetry a woman needs an *unmarried* self, a "spinster" self (besides a
room of one's own and a little sugar bowl).

Ann Killigrew's longing to "speak the truth" is echoed through the
centuries—though this longing is altogether distinct from the "truth and
honor" code of men. The inclination to *bear witness* seems aligned with
the missing self. By the time we arrive at Adrienne Rich and Sylvia Plath,
the woman poet's tradition remains no tradition. All those isolated par-
ticles of truth, from Aphra Behn to Emily Dickinson to H.D., have become a wave of probability.

The desire for a historical self and the desire for a "truth-telling self,"
or "real self," merge into a single drama, or a single dramatic voice. In
Rich's case the dramatic personae that began to fill her pages seemed (especially to young poets like me, reading her avidly) irrefutably, necessarily, *her*. All the way from "The Tourist and the Town" in *The Diamond
Cutters* to the Wild Child, from the mermaid in *Diving into the Wreck*
to Elvira Shateyeva, Marie Curie, or Caroline Herschel, it was Adrienne
Rich, now a fearless and furious repudiation of the polite coed (who'd
sweetly intoned in *A Change of World*: "Neither with rancor at the past /
Nor to upbraid the coming time"), whose call to arms reconstituted the
female literary self. Some male critics reviled her in intemperate prose,
while women read her passionately, changing their lives on a line from
one of her poems. I can vouch for it: the voice speaking from her poems
changed me, and gave me courage as a young poet.

When I arrived in New York City in 1971, I joined consciousness-
raising groups, but I found it impossible to express my own sense of
conflict. I eventually sought out women in prison, because their isolation and extremity reflected a dislocation I felt in my own life and writing. To anyone who would listen, I said that I believed that a civilization
was judged by the way it treated its most helpless citizens, those in its

institutional care—inmates of prisons and mental hospitals—and in particular, women. But it was also true that I wanted to be an *outlaw,* bold and uncompromised, not the split being that I seemed to myself. I felt like a fake: a feminist and would-be political activist who was too drawn to the literati, ambitious, cutthroat editors, glitzy dinner parties. I met literary friends, late at night, down in the Village. Confused, I separated from my then-husband, an activist-doctor, a wonderful man. I felt that I had no self and I thought that I lived in two irreconcilable worlds, politics and poetry. I longed to see the two come together.

It struck me that women in prison were living lives capable of providing instruction, and I went into the prisons without knowing exactly what that meant. I set up a writing program for inmates at the Women's House of Detention on Riker's Island, then expanded the program (called Art without Walls, née Free Space) to other prisons, recruited writer friends, and began to teach writing workshops. I fervently wished that from this most "silent" population, strong voices would emerge. I was twenty-five or twenty-six years old, too young to understand the source of my own sense of women as outlaws, my romantic regard for women who lived outside the laws of family, church, politics. I felt that women were natural anarchists, so I frequented a setting in which, I hoped, all abstractions about women and their behavior would become passionately, relievedly, literal. I would encounter women whose lives had been acts of defiance, women who were unafraid. In my passion for extremity I wanted the poem itself to change.

> . . . two women, eye to eye
> measuring each other's spirit, each other's
> limitless desire,
>> a whole new poetry beginning here.
>> (Rich, "Transcendental Etude")

There was a breakthrough that thrilled me: the humble job of editing a poem began to reflect the emergence of female identity. Rich comments on "The Tourist and the Town," a poem from *The Diamond Cutters*:

> The pronouns in the third part of the poem were originally
> masculine. But the tourist was a woman, myself, and I never saw her as

anything else. In 1953, when the poem was written, some notion of "universality" prevailed which made the feminine pronoun suspect, "personal." In this poem . . . . I have altered the pronouns not simply as a matter of fact but because they alter, for me, the dimensions of the poem.

An act as small, yet symbolic, as altering the pronouns in a poem restored it to that "other universality," the unrecognized referent: She. A She who was also an "I." The self in women's poetry, by that altered pronoun, had become immediate and historical. And, unlike previous centuries, its immediacy and historicism rose from ordinary women.

Yet there was a futuristic feel to this She as well. Nothing seemed to be separating who she was from a *new* past and a future—no more spinsters and spies.

> Well,
> She's long about her coming, who must be
> more merciless to herself than history.
> Her mind full to the wind, I see her plunge
> breasted and glancing through the currents,
> taking the light upon her
> at least as beautiful as any boy
> or helicopter,

(Rich, "Snapshots of a Daughter-in-Law")

That bionic image was, of course, inspired by Simone de Beauvoir's woman of a new age: "she is a helicopter and she is a bird." Rich's readers could feel her evolving self in struggle, "long about her coming," pushing out through the domestic toward some wild future ideal.

The She of *Ariel,* on the other hand—fiery, dark, death-obsessed, explosively self-destructive—was conflated with Plath's personal desperation. This was an alternative vision of a future that liberated the suffering consciousness from its painful constraints but destroyed the physical self in the process. Plath captured the collective imagination with her challenge to an unjust past. Rich also summoned history and held it to account but, simultaneously, beamed it forward in time. At that moment, Rich offered the possibility of turning, transformed, from the ruins of the past and, in true 1960s and post-Wordsworthian style, dreamed of a common language, a relocation of feminism outside the "phallo-centered, written-out" vulgate. Outside the center, Plath's vision (or the vision of *Ariel*) occurred at the bloody intersection of the personal and historical—and Plath, like a well-trained terrorist, blew herself up with the corrupt installation.

So, we have the two stances:

I am bombarded yet   I stand

I have been standing all my life in the
direct path of a battery of signals
the most accurately-transmitted most
untranslatable language in the universe.

> (Rich, "Planetarium")

And I
Am the arrow,

The dew that flies
Suicidal, at one with the drive
into the red

Eye, the cauldron of morning.

> (Plath, "Ariel")

What did these passages convey to a young woman poet? Two statements; two shapes of longing—one shape projecting its own arc like a missile and the second a tower, Mrs. Ramsay's lighthouse beacon, the longed-for horizon, unflinching. The two positions appealed to me. Rich's stood for bold, unintimidated word power, courage of conviction; Plath's for fearless harrowing insight, Houdini-like escapes from the conventional idiom. More significantly, both poets gave speech to women's silence—and Rich's language embodied women's power to *act*, women's new and unintimidated anger, and (though this can only be glimpsed over time, and I couldn't see it then) her language also revealed a fierce and uncompromising Shelleyan spirit, ultimately capable of renewal, forgiveness. Plath turned feelings of personal impotence into inverse power, destructive ecstasy, and she possessed, by nature, a manner of expression that, while infinitely transcendent, kept a grim eyeball on the transgressor. Plath was a virtuoso debt collector. Neither poet seemed to be at peace with Keats's notion of negative capability (or a poet's lack of self), although this lack of self is precisely what gives Plath's work its tension and Rich's its politics. Plath's eye roves over objects in the landscape, filling them with her fierce, disembodied will. Rich rarely extols female qualities like empathy, tender-heartedness, etc., perhaps because it happens that women may be just *too good* at negative capability, if we understand it as a kind of cultivated self-absence.

I rehearsed these two shapes, admiring, in my imagination, and cataloged them as emergent "selves" (as if there were only two choices available to the developing poetic identity: defiant resistance or lyric emotional meltdown). Apart from the compelling poetry, the implacability of each shape (syntactically and politically and, yes, as a conventional "masculine" shape now relimned) revealed something wonderful and ominous about the future. But then, I had always been seduced by an idea of fate in poetry, as in life.

I watched Rich stand firm, weathering the assault of criticism, Plath ejecting from the poem's argument like a pilot from a cockpit, catapulting headlong into her own explosion—and I was edified; I burrowed in my journal and found a couple of prophecies I now saw fulfilled:

> Yet I am now and then haunted by some semi-mystic very profound life of a woman, which shall all be told on one occasion; and time shall be utterly obliterated; future shall somehow blossom out of the past.
>
> (Virginia Woolf)

> Someday there will be girls and women whose name will no longer signify merely an opposite of masculine, but something in itself, something that makes one think, not of any complement and limit, but only of life and existence: the feminine human being.
>
> (Rainer Maria Rilke)

Certainly, Ted Hughes understood what was in the air, the emerging shapes of longing—he understood they were *projections*—and he knew what to say about this:

A real self, as we know, is a rare thing. The direct speech of a real self is rarer still. . . . When a real self finds language, and manages to speak, it is surely a dazzling event—as *Ariel* was.

But *Ariel's* self, it turned out, its direct speech, was to a significant degree an invention of editing. Hughes changed Plath's original manuscript order (by adding and dropping poems, altering sequence, thereby reinforcing certain themes) so dramatically that what remains of *Ariel* is a riveting, aggressive work: a suicide note to the world. As the critic Marjorie Perloff has previously established, this was not the book Plath had intended to publish. Melinda Patton, a graduate student at the University of Southern California, recently described Plath's original order as an "epic journey." She calls Hughes's reassembling of the book an "unauthorized autobiography"; the conclusion that Hughes's editing argues for is the inevitability of Plath's death. The last line of the book is "Fixed stars govern a life." Plath's own version ended with the visionary "bee" poems, and the last line of her book would have read, "The bees are flying. They taste the Spring." Whether her version is more life affirming is hardly the point. The point is that Plath and her suicide persona became one. Clearly, she chose to end her life. But did she intend that her book (a book she dedicated to her children) be read as evidence of self-destruction? We will not know. The "Russian roulette-playing" Plath (with, as Lowell had it, "six cartridges in the cylinder"), that reckless self cheering for its own annihilation, the desperado we all rode behind, sprang fully armed from the head of Ted Hughes.

In her momentous essay, "When We Dead Awaken," Rich refuses the traditional view of the imagination (or male appropriation of its contexts) in a chilling indictment: "to be a female human being, trying to fulfill female functions in a traditional way, is in direct conflict with the subversive function of the imagination." Ironically, Hughes saw this too. Long before, W. H. Auden had complimented Rich and the poems in *A Change of World* for their "detachment from the self and its emotions." Now it seemed the self of a woman poet could be created by sheer force of will, as Hughes created the persona of *Ariel,* editing carefully "to" the myth of the scorned woman's fury, the scorched earth of her self-destructive power. And the idea of an unvarying self-truth, once a psychological fiction, became an unassailable tenet of a redeemable, demonstrable past. *Thus women poets did not go back to discover a historical self, but went forward to create a self.*

I was in grade school in 1958, the year Plath and Rich met for the first time, on a rainy night at Radcliffe, after a Ted Hughes reading. I didn't encounter Plath until I was in graduate school in San Francisco in 1969. I remember my poetry teacher, Kathleen Fraser, reading "Daddy" aloud— and the effect of those brutal hypnotic epithets, incantatory but explosive: a poem of flung grenades. *Who* was *this woman? Where did she get the nerve to write like that?* The late-afternoon sun streaming through the window lit up Kathleen Fraser's waist-length auburn hair as she sat on a high stool in front of the classroom reading the poems. She looked (I remember) luminous, backlit, as the harsh syllables fell from her lips.

The Ariel poems—I didn't just read them, I breathed them in; they ran in my blood. I was a timid, uncertain poet, a girl bruised in the way young women in their early twenties, trying to live independently, are inevitably bruised by circumstance. They have discovered that the world is not exactly welcoming them into its "pre-race paddock," into the fraternal chambers in which the networks get woven, political contacts settled on a handshake .

A violent chord reverberated within me. If women needed to be *outlaws* of poetry, Plath and Rich filled the bill. If Plath was a literary Jeanne d'Arc, riding headstrong, burning, whipping her mount straight into the jaws of death, then Rich was Antigone, an authority above conventional law. Her famous line about Marie Curie, that "her wounds come from the same source as her power," continues to thrill me in its stark rightness. I was grateful to her; I am still grateful that she had the courage to stand up to Creon, to hurl his words back at him. I have never found her excessive. Rather, her outspoken voice told me that women were finally free to break the taboos against writing explicitly about whatever had been hidden, glossed over, buried in shame. Still, I saw her self as mythological, heroic, unattainable.

All of this was, in a sense, preparatory. There was a new shape of expression emerging. I recall that Rich was widely attacked by critics for a poem called "Rape" (1972), in which she illustrated (like a police artist sketching a suspect) the claustrophobic all-surrounding sense of threat felt by a raped woman giving testimony in a police precinct about her ordeal; giving language, in the process, to women's darkest suspicion of male authority ("There is a cop who is both prowler and father . . ."). This poem was taken by many to be an act of linguistic violence against men, a case of reverse sexism, when Rich's intent was expository, the revelation of the consciousness of a typical woman, after sexual trauma. Statistics bear out Rich's portrait of female distrust, yet this illustration was thought of as hyperbolic, malicious, exaggerated.

Rich reconfirmed the divisions in male and female assumptions about a shared reality; her revelations moved women to insight, anger, and the will to change. Yet what gradually emerged after the collective "internalization" of poems like "Rape," was a model, a shape of poetic discourse based roughly on *the act of testimony.*

In the evolution of this model, a voice testifying to mistreatment, for example, could offer itself as substitution for imaginative knowledge in a poem. This poetic approach quickly became popular as a kind of verbal emergency, the post-trauma voice repeating its harrowing experience as for a transcript. Rich's poem can be taken as an unconscious precursor of what was to come stylistically: the enactment of the voice of extremity—not simply as a literary convention, rather as a *moral event.* Whereas Rich wished to demonstrate a sensibility, the poems that followed wished to *be* that sensibility.

That a poem evolves from a popular consciousness has no special significance in and of itself; it happens all the time. Nevertheless, though it is commonplace to suggest that the attractions of unadorned, exhortative speech are many, it is only criticism, in its applications, that provides the architecture of the *interpretation* of that consciousness. (In this sense, criticism is like a funhouse mirror, reflecting and distorting at once.) Thus, a second wave, which was a combined force of expressive and critical solidarity, hit the long expanse of shore covered with the footprints of Plath and Rich.

Jeredith Merrin, in her important book *An Enabling Humility,* hints at how this reinterpretation of Plath and Rich's expansiveness occurred.

Examining *Stealing the Language* by Alicia Ostriker, Merrin points out how the critic fails to explore the range and various array (the "humanness") of women poets at hand, choosing rather to explicate poetry that "most often takes as its subjects the female body, female anger and violence, female eroticism." It is, she says, "writing that adopts as a conscious strategy what Ostriker, *echoing Rich,* calls 'revisionist mythmaking' and that aggressively engages the reader's attention, tends toward the colloquial and employs the autobiographical "I" (my emphasis). In effect, Hughes's "real self." The real self and the myth have now become one. The truth is being told—and the world is splitting open. Sort of.

Eavan Boland, the Irish poet and essayist, was eighteen (just a year older than I) and a student at Trinity College the winter that Plath killed herself at her flat on Fitzroy Road in London in 1963. Boland remembers the cold, the "frost smoking" on the windowsill of her garden flat. When she thinks of Plath, she thinks of her along with two babies under three, and she remembers the quality of that cold.

Boland also believes that women need to reconnect to a past, inhabit a self, but first she asks that some rethinking be done. She has even "created a tradition"—if we read her poem "The Journey" (in *Outside History*) as a Genesis vision. Certainly, it is a revision of Aeneas's visit to the Underworld in the sixth book of the *Aeniad.* In the poem, Sappho establishes a kind of matrilinear line of women poets, through Boland.

> there are not many of us; you are dear
>
> and stand beside me as my own daughter.
> I have brought you here so you will know forever
> the silences in which are our beginnings

When I read this, it seemed to me that Boland had done something that Rich had long discussed: she had established a connection, indeed a right of succession, to a women's past, even though the poem belied her efforts by its insistence on silence as a process of understanding. The impulse is not theoretical; Boland directs herself as a character in the poem's drama. She points to the poem's gainsaying, the poem's own subversion of Sappho's message, then lets the poem stand as its own object. It is important that the poem settle in its place "outside the story," in the margins of Book VI, for there it begins to glow with new power.

The legacy of the tradition refuses to be a history or to bear witness to any new past. As the narrator-poet begs permission to write about the suffering souls of children who died of typhus and cholera, to wave the late twentieth-century wand of witness, Sappho cautions against misrepresenting these souls in the language of possession: "what you have seen is beyond speech, / beyond song, only not beyond love." Like Rich, Boland wishes to investigate what we take for granted about women and poetry. She isolates the same crucial moments in metaphor that Rich excavates then rejects as poisoned by tradition. But whereas Rich dreams of a neo-protolanguage, Boland wants to reenter the extant language, resee it, reexamine this uncentered "drama of expression." Boland attacks the problem in a poststructuralist fervor; the subject/object relationship has to be reversed, since this oppressive pattern is at the heart of the argument about women and poetry. (In this fervor she defies most poststructuralist tradition as well, since woman becomes the real subject, not an object of regard.) Further, her intent, unlike that of the deconstructionists, is not to show us that all texts subvert their author's intentions, but rather that women poets can quite deliberately subvert the textual assumptions of the dominant tradition, reshape them, or honor the inevitable silence within them. I see her efforts as an attempt to demythologize the voice of the post-trauma self.

For my own part, I had discovered that few women had interpreted Rich as I did, that is, as Antigone. The desert crossed by Rich was now an overpopulated frontier town loud with voices, and, whereas Rich's voice opened a new shape, these other voices often seemed to make the world smaller. Instead of naming and reimagining the familiar, the familiar constituted an ongoing grievance.

"Was there really no name for my life in poetry?" Boland demands of this overtrod terrain. In her book *Object Lessons,* she sees herself caught between the "heresy of romanticism" and the "new feminist angers." For Boland subversion in language is an "act of rescue" versus a "strategy of possession." We have had, Boland feels, enough rhetoric of ownership. The spirit in which Carolyn Kizer dismisses the domestic would not elicit approval from Boland, but she would understand it. What she herself prefers is a quiet coup in the world we take for granted, the "sensory world which inflected the mortality of the body." Thus, an object reclaimed—silk, pearls, a tree—would be wrested free from the "ageless, perfect" state of traditional regard and "flawed" time:

> And the object she returns to rescue,
> with her newly-made Orphic powers and
> intelligence, would be herself: a fixed
> presence in the underworld of the traditional
> poem.
>
> (233)

The object would be herself: Boland's "act of rescue" is a technique, not a stance. It, too, wishes to alter the shape of longing but not by creating, as Michel Foucault says, "absences" that must be filled. Women would not remain preoccupied with *unnaming,* dismantling the "master narratives" (a task akin to yodelling backwards). Boland would harken to critic Page duBois's analysis of women's position in the narrative in *Sappho Burning*:

> The study of narrative structure that has been a focus of some recent literary theory often seems incapable of thinking beyond the type of text exemplified by the Homeric epic. Female characters have been described as static, fixed entities in oral literatures, and structuralists and their heirs, the semioticians, often generalize from oral texts to describe women as objects, things to be exchanged, markers of place both geographically and textually.

Women as objects. The object is herself: How to move this object, this self? By authenticating lives? Simply by retelling women's stories as history? This is the crucial choice, and Boland's desire to "subjectify" the object differs crucially from the calculated elevation of personal, circumstantial detail. The movement in the truth-telling poem is finally, antitruth; it sets up a persona and a history resident in a kind of uncriticizable hot zone surrounded by a *cordon sanitaire*. Thus restricted in the present, we find it harder to set critical standards or visit the past to dis-passionately examine the poetry there by women. Yet Boland's interpre-tations also struggle mightily (and not always successfully) to avoid the same collective mythification of the self, to avoid the same implacable ac-ceptance of the self as documentable detail. (It is finally true that diction-analysis tends toward the reductive, like biography.)

A poem is an *act* (or an action); a poem is forever moving through space. To me it is a grave misrepresentation to substitute stasis for this animation. In this inert category sits the self-referential speaker, who does not move beyond self-acknowledgment, the subject matter limiting it-self to documentable experience.

Paradoxically, a poem can be seen to embody a biographical self, when, in fact, it does not. Ted Hughes says that Plath's life is "devoid of circumstantial biographical detail," and he is correct. Rich's poems also lack ongoing personal facts. Both poets project an intimacy that is largely fictional. In Plath's case, Hughes speculates (somewhat disingenuously, given his editing of *Ariel*) that "that lack" has given rise to the "fantasies" of Plath's readers. Despite the transparency of his position, Hughes has unintentionally touched on a useful critical insight. To project autobiog-raphy is to possess the subject, to own it, to recruit it for a cause.

Since Wordsworth introduced the ego into poetry, we have labored to understand exactly what autobiography is and why it has such power to persuade us. It seems to me that autobiography is fiction like any other narrative. One apparently arguable difference from fiction is in the in-tensity of the moral discourse implicit in the stories of many lives, par-ticularly lives of suffering. Still, the power of this discourse is in no way compromised or jeopardized by the inevitable selection process that at-tends all telling; in fact, the story is often "truer" in reordering, enhancing. On the other hand, if its power to persuade is based on the insistence on a moral tautology ("all victims are innocent and good"), it manipulates the reader and provides catharsis without understanding. The difference in Rich's "story of the self" (and Plath's, for that matter) is that they are not based on parable-like narratives, and they admit that there is an ex-tenuating world.

An excerpt from Rich's poem "From a Survivor":

The pact that we made was the ordinary pact
of men & women in those days

I don't know who we thought we were
that our personalities
could resist the failures of the race

Here, testimony exists to confront a world beyond the self and the drama
of the self, even the world of silence—or the unanswerable. The movement in the poems is not toward self-justification (or self-enclosure) but,
rather, *movement out of the self.* The inescapable condition of autobiography is self-justification.

What other dangers lie in the illusion (and undeniable persuasive-
ness) of the truth-telling self? As Louise Glück observes, "But truth of
this kind will not permit itself simply to be looked back on; it makes,
when it is summoned, a kind of erosion, undermining the present with
the past, substituting for the shifts and approximations and variety of
anecdote the immutable fixity of fate and for curiosity regarding an unfolding future, absolute knowledge of that future." (*Proofs and Theories,*
Ecco Press, 1995). Again, it is time that is eroded. The assumption of this
self fixes not only a history, but the nature of anticipation and expectation. A stasis as literal as that which is imposed by tradition on women
is imposed on the imagination. Further, if the dominant tradition has
persisted in objectifying women, surely the counter-impulse, that of
oversubjectifying the self, is as grievous an error. When ambivalence toward the self is missing, as Glück says, the written recreation, no matter
how artful, forfeits emotional authority. When Sylvia Plath writes, in
"Daddy . . ."

I have always been scared of *you,*
With your Luftwaffe, your gobbledygoo.
And your neat moustache
And your Aryan eye, bright blue.
Panzer-man, panzer-man, O You——

Not God but a swastika
So black no sky could squeak through.

> Every woman adores a Fascist,
> The boot in the face, the brute
> Brute heart of a brute like you.

. . . we feel manipulated, but we are conscious of the intent to manipulate. In fact, this crudely expressed, childish intent is emphatically part of the pathos and persona of the poem. "Daddy" is a self-indulgent, hand-cranked catharsis, not even close, by my lights, to Plath's later visionary work. Yet, as obvious as its effects are, they seem refined by comparison to the following—Sharon Olds's "The Takers":

> Hitler entered Paris the way my
> sister entered my room at night,
> sat astride me, squeezed me with her knees,
> held her thumbnails to the skin of my wrists and
> peed on me, knowing Mother would
> never believe my story. It was very
> silent, her dim face above me
> gleaming in the shadows, the dark gold
> smell of her urine spreading through the room, its
> heat boiling on my legs, my small
> pelvis wet.

The difference between "Daddy" and the "The Takers" is the difference between a poem and testimony. Sharon Olds is an extremely talented poet, and, like Plath's "Daddy," this does not represent her best work. The fact that it was written, however, at another moment in history than "Daddy" is obvious in every facet of its presentation. Unlike "Daddy," Olds's poem lacks any noticeable rhythmic pattern beyond the flat conversational tone of the speaker. This is a stylistic choice, a choice that cleverly counterbalances the melodrama and shocking details of the poem's content—and its (like Plath's) uneasy appropriation of the Nazi/victim paradigm. The poem also has a journalistic feel; unlike Plath's poem, we are presented with a recounting of incontrovertible facts, as distinguished from a child's nightmarish imaginings.

How interesting, then, given the solid weight of these effects, that "Daddy" still seems the more shocking—indeed, the more intrinsically true—poem?

Jeredith Merrin reiterates that "the emphasis on female patterns of
suffering and struggle tends to highlight commonality while overlooking psychological and artistic difference." Merrin quotes Jan Montefiore,
who asks, in *Feminism and Poetry,* "the question which such assumption
of the primacy of female experience in women's poems avoids asking":
simply, "What makes a poem different from autobiography, fictionalized or otherwise?"

While "When We Dead Awaken" seems to urge women toward a
purely female and self-enclosed experience, Merrin notes that Rich provides a description of "a certain freedom of mind" required for a writer,
as opposed to literal-minded confinement:

> freedom to press on, to enter the currents of your thought like a glider
> pilot . . . if the imagination is to transcend and transform experience it
> has to question, to challenge, to conceive of alternatives, perhaps to the
> very life you are living at this moment. You have to be free to play
> around with the idea that day might be night, love might be hate;
> nothing can be too sacred for the imagination to turn into its opposite
> or call experimentally by another name.

(*On Lies, Secrets and Silence: Selected Prose, 1966–1978*)

A poem is different from autobiography and the negotiation between
these differing truths of the self is dialectical, exhilarating, and essential.
It *is* a profound act of subversion—something like Keats's negative capability. The voice of truth, like the term *woman poet,* becomes an endlessly fluid, negotiable contract with language. Language teaches us
humility *and* anarchy, and these simultaneously.

Frank Bidart, a passionately autobiographical poet, addresses some
of these questions in the interview that ends *In the Western Night.* The
notion of the poem as action, as he points out, is Aristotelian, tragedy as
the imitation of an action. "But the sense that a poem must be animated
by a unifying central action—that it both 'imitates' an action and is *itself*
an action—has been largely ignored by twentieth-century aesthetics."
Further, he describes the poem as a "journey the *shape* of which has significance" [my emphasis].

Bidart doesn't equivocate. "All art is artifice." Yet he quotes Robert
Frost's statement: "No tears in the writer, no tears in the reader"; we have

to cry those tears to make the poem convincing. But, as any actor will confirm, those tears can come from anywhere: literal, empathetic, or invented sorrow. The *emotional authority,* the emotional truth, of those tears should be recognized as the apriori condition of the poem's action—but inseparable from the poet's need to create, to fabricate, to subvert.

He describes a wonderful experiment performed by Keats: his search for "the true voice of feeling," as distinct from "the false beauty proceeding from Art." Keats set out to put an X next to the "false beauty" passages and a double line next to the true voice of feeling. The experiment failed. Keats found that he could not separate the two. "Upon my soul 'twas imagination I cannot make the distinction—Every now & then there is a Miltonic intonation—But I cannot make the division properly."

In prison, when I encouraged my students to "tell the truth about their lives," the world (or the barred cells) did not split open. Mainly, this was because there was another kind of tradition already operating in prison: the unwritten etiquette behind bars connected to one's past. Everyone came to know what everyone else's record, or rap sheet, contained, but no one talked openly about these things. In an environment in which no one admitted guilt and the crime was not discussed, the idea of telling all was novel, even slightly abhorrent. And, when they finally began, tentatively, to document biography in verse, I discovered that there was a direct relationship between gravity of offense and willingness to divulge one's history. Quite naturally, writing about how one became a shoplifter (or "booster") was a bit less painful than providing details of how a family member died at one's hand.

Then one woman, a new arrival in the workshop, broke the ice. Patricia wrote an unforgettable poem about how the prison authorities had denied her the right to attend her baby daughter's funeral. Her two-year-old girl had been hospitalized after a fall that occurred just prior to Patricia's arrest. The little girl had died during Patricia's first day in prison. Patricia wrote a savage, bitter, uncompromising poem in classic English ballad meter that called for the reader to witness this injustice, this unyielding official refusal to allow a mother to hold her dead baby in her arms one last time. ("My baby lyin' in a cold steel drawer . . .") Make no mistake, the poem's voice was extreme: she was willing to "turn the prison floor red" with "screw" (correctional officer) blood to "shoot her way to her baby's side."

Like most of the incarcerated women, Patricia was poor and black. She supported herself by whatever means were available to her. And it seems she'd been arrested as an accessory (in an overwhelming number of cases, as I'd recently discovered, women offenders were companions to men who had committed crimes of armed robbery, larceny, or breaking and entering); Patricia told us she had been at her boyfriend's side when he robbed a bar with a gun. She had been sent to prison to await sentencing, while her baby died without her. Patricia was inconsolable— and unforgiving. She read the poem aloud, weeping, then let the workshop members copy it so that it could be sent out "on the drum," passed from hand-to-hand inside the institution.

As their teacher, did I think this intemperate? Not at all. I believed the poem was its own force. After eliciting truth from these women, how could I caution them against publication of truth? Though I must admit, *my* sense of any poem's persuasive power precluded its being taken seriously behind bars, where it seemed to me that daily suffering exceeded language. I was taken aback by how many women wept at these words. And, beyond that initial shock, I never expected to see such regard duplicated in the minds of the prison authorities.

Nonetheless, the desperation of Patricia's plight moved us all, and I went to plead with the warden to allow her to visit her daughter's grave. The warden shook her head. On my next visit to the prison, a few days later, I discovered that Patricia had been thrown into the "Bing" (solitary confinement) for an attempt to incite a riot. Oddly (because civilians were rarely allowed in the punitive solitary area), I was permitted to visit Patricia in her tiny bare cell, with its dungeon-like observation slit, its single, ceiling bulb. I expected to find her distraught, but she was filled with energy; she'd been scratching poems into the wall (crisscrossed with graffiti from previous tenants) using a bent spoon. She begged me to bring her Bing contraband—paper, a pen—so that she could write more. Her eyes were bright and fierce. She told me that she'd been freed by this experience; she felt more powerful than she ever had in her life. I left that cell knowing with absolute clarity what had happened. I'd told my students to write the truth. Now one of them had, and had been censored, had suffered cruel and unusual punishment as a result of telling that truth. I remember thinking dazedly that poetry *did* make things happen.

I went straight to the warden's office and stood before her, demanding that Patricia be released. I told her that she had acted precipitously, that the institution would never succeed in censoring the truth. I asked her to allow me to bear responsibility for what had happened; I'd even be willing to go to the Bing in Patricia's place or suffer whatever penalty they deemed appropriate. If Patricia were not released, if the prison would not let me take on some of Patricia's punishment, then I would go to the press and publish an exposé of this barbarous act of repression. I remember that I said "barbarous."

The warden (a pretty, military-looking black woman in her fifties) sighed deeply, opened a desk drawer, and handed me a file. Inside the file folder were coroner's photographs of a child who had been beaten to death. She said the child was Patricia's two-year-old daughter. The warden told me that it was the district attorney's belief that Patricia's pimp had kicked and punched the baby till she died, then shoved her below the closet floorboards in Patricia's apartment, while Patricia stood by, an accessory. Aiding and abetting first-degree homicide was the crime with which she'd been charged. The warden said that Patricia had used the poem (and me) to try to gain sympathy for herself, to get me to plead for a furlough. Once released, the warden said, she'd have disappeared. I handed the file back to her. I couldn't bear to look any longer at the tiny shattered body.

But there was something else. Not even Patricia, she went on, realized how deeply the poem would affect the other women in prison, women routinely separated from their children, some destined never to see them again. (It is important to note here that the Women's Correctional Institution on Riker's Island was a detention facility, nicknamed the Women's House of Detention, as well as a prison for sentenced inmates. A majority of the women had not been convicted of any crime; they were awaiting sentencing, unable to afford bail. At that time, in the early 1970s, it was possible and legal for a detention inmate to "fall off the calendar" and end up waiting up to two years to stand trial. Since then, the laws have been changed and a detainee must appear before a judge within an allotted time. Then, as now, a woman's children—if her relatives were unable or unfit to keep them—were routinely made wards of the state at the time of her arrest, before any court appearance. A woman might finally be judged innocent and still have lost her family.)

The near riot caused by Patricia's poem had been a case of women quoting the poem to one another in the halls, cell-to-cell, shouting out lines about "screw blood" and "offing the warden" on their way to the laundry or the kitchen. Screaming the poem at the officers, louder and louder, gathering in groups to read the poem aloud—why? Because the poem said: women have no power, the state takes your children away from you, flings them into foster homes; you may never see your children again, even at death. They'd pushed up against the bars, calling out to the violators of their maternal rights. *Give them back, motherfuckers, give them back.* The emotional authority of Patricia's voice shook the foundations of the prison with more force than the planes taking off every twelve seconds from La Guardia Airport, just yards across the bay. *Give her back, motherfucker, give her back.*

I looked at the warden. She had the unthinkable photographs in front of her. But she was indeed the state, all that my Marcuse-saturated brain had learned to distrust. Yet she had proof. Whatever the truth was, I was still responsible for Patricia's time in the Bing. And I *was* responsible; the warden agreed with me on this. But she would not release Patricia from her punitive cell. Why, I asked her, if she is guilty of standing by as someone killed her daughter, why is she still writing self-exonerating poems? But I knew the answer even as I asked the question. Patricia was still following my assignment—telling the truth, as she perceived it.

The warden hoped that I had learned a lesson. My punishment was simply that I be allowed to go on teaching poetry at the Women's House—which was, of course, intolerable. I wanted to run away and never come back. But now I had to return in a different capacity: as an offender, whose offense was treating lives and life stories with the condescension that oversimplifies truth. Each day Patricia spent in the Bing (another three days, then she was arraigned and eventually sentenced and transferred) would be on my conscience, along with my unwitting promotion of a situation that allowed the prison to use freely its formidable, unappealable powers of censorship and punishment.

But what about my own version of the story? Certainly, I have heightened some aspects, dimmed others. Should I cry that I still see those merciless black-and-white morgue photos of that broken, bruised two-year-old body? I do not. In memory the images shift in the warden's hand. What she is showing me, as I recall, is her truth, her reason for maintaining institutional order. The child's abused body exists here only as the object of other narratives, including the state's. It has no subject. And the child's voice is silenced forever. Could anyone presume to speak for her? Sappho's voice cautions from Boland's poem as we beg to witness: some things are beyond speech, beyond song, not beyond love.

I know there are many ways to view this story. I was negligent and presumptuous; that's indisputable. Some people may suspect that the warden was duplicitous, offering pictures of another inmate's child. Maybe Patricia wanted to get out to locate the pimp, to kill him. I don't know. I will never know, though later I heard from an appellate lawyer that Patricia had turned state's evidence against her co-defendant, the pimp.

Dickinson again: "Tell all the truth / but tell it slant." I still believe both conflicting truths about that poem: that it was a fabrication, yet it was unassailable and accurate. To deny the importance of that poem would be to deny the significance of art, for the rhetorical power of its language moved people to tears, caused them to stand up and demand justice from their jailers. "Where are our children?" they cried. "This is a house of detention; we've not yet been convicted of a crime, and yet you rob us of our families." Patricia had unwittingly written a bigger truth. And this is why the poem of witness *must exist*—because it is necessary to refresh moral life.

On the other hand, to accept the poem's veracity as an inherent component of its art would lead only to the "immutability," the stasis of prescription Glück describes, and to self-justification, indefensible and ultimately impossible. Patricia, perhaps guilty of her daughter's death, perhaps not, chose to tell her story. Her "real self" poem was the avenue to absolution. Instead of a woman who killed her child, she became a heroine, a courageous victim. Beneath the poem's syntax was a hidden shape of longing, that shape a woman's arms make when holding a dead child—or perhaps the shape a mother's arms make when holding a child dead by her own hand. It contained the perfect ratio of truth to invention. It moved its audience, and it offered the great extenuating fact of motherhood, thus healing Patricia. What more astonishing, transformative thing can art do? The truth of art, not the truth of truth. Patricia, I saw at last, might have been the outlaw I'd been looking for, but I couldn't face the dilemma she presented.

The warden was right. I'd learned a lesson: I would never have said it at the time, but I'd come to understand something inexorable about the way a poem could be. I saw how Patricia had erected a self on a form of desire. There is indeed "fabrication" in objects; there is fabrication implicit in the self, which is, after all, an object, too. I came to believe that there is in the writerly imagination a deep ungovernable impulse to invent, fictionalize, to tell the truth, but "slant." And this desire rises from the same anarchical source as the truth-telling impulse. Each desire represents, of course, a passion for meaning, for an act that will bring order, a shape to experience.

Marilyn Chin

Translating Self: Stealing from Wang Wei, Kowtowing to Hughes, Hooking Up with Keats, Undone by Donne

I am an autobiographical poet. That is to say, what I write always begins with my life, my ideas, my experiences, my concerns, and, by extension, the poems are always about my family, my tribe, my people. My nation, my god. My, my, my, my, my. The challenge, then, is to write an autobiographical poetry that could trill on without boring myself or the reader. Although I can dress up in myriad ways and parade in front of the mirror, I love to garb myself in the varied baubles of two literary histories.

Here is a quintessential autobiographical "identity" poem. An identity poem is an American invention, born out of minority discourse. I must proclaim my identity, because the privileged majority, at best, has always misunderstood who I am and, at worst, wished to wipe me out of my existence. Therefore, I must button down my ethnic pride and assert myself with a clear, loud voice and claim my place on this land:

How I Got That Name
an essay on assimilation

I am Marilyn Mei Ling Chin.
Oh, how I love the resoluteness
of that first person singular
followed by that stalwart indicative
of "be," without the uncertain i-n-g
of "becoming." Of course,
the name had been changed
somewhere between Angel Island and the sea,

when my father the paperson
in the late 1950s
obsessed with a bombshell blonde
transliterated "Mei Ling" to "Marilyn."
And nobody dared question
his initial impulse for we all know
lust drove men to greatness,
not goodness, not decency.

My self, in this poem, is inextricably bound to my immigration history. The poem describes how the new immigrant arrived, noting Angel
Island and my naming. How one is named is, of course, an important
matter for anyone, but it was a real rite of passage in this case, as my name
was changed from a quaint Chinese Mei Ling to the name of a bombshell American icon, Marilyn Monroe. Thus far in the poem I am carrying on the identity-poem convention; it is not until my father comes in,
both reviled and lampooned in this passage (but with a light touch, in
sync with the tone of the rest of the poem), that the confessional moment arrives. Then we can truly call this a contemporary American confessional lyric, obsessed with family secrets and transgressions.

I truly believe in identity poems. At one point or another, an immigrant poet must tell the audience where she came from. But even though
"How I Got That Name" is currently my most anthologized poem, it is
the kind of poem I could only write once. I must move on to find other
vessels to tell my story, which, since I am a Chinese American woman,
is complicated. So I love to take conventions from both the Eastern and
Western side of my literary heritage and remake them into my own
image (*voilà*, the mirror, again!). The process is an ever-evolving one.
My challenge as a poet is to find interesting ways to tell my complex tale.

I love, for example, to use the Chinese lyric model. Chinese poetry is
predominantly lyrical. That is to say, short lyrics dominate over narrative and dramatic poetry. The Chinese poet uses the lyric, in a variety of
forms and hundreds of different meters, to evoke her deepest feelings
and most serious thoughts. Like the best Western lyrics, the best Chinese
lyrics are intensely personal, but can emanate from a universal context.
In the strongest poems, the poet is always aware of historical and cos-

mic forces. Whereas most Western poets since the Romantics yearn to be "original" and somehow defy the past, the Chinese have deep respect for antiquity; therefore, their work can be simultaneously personal and highly traditional. Tu Fu may write about the death of his infant daughter, but at the same time he alludes to images and lines of a famous mourning poem from the Shih Ching, incorporating that work more as homage than reckless borrowing.

As a Chinese American lyric poet, I feel that I have a lot of ammunition. For example, here is a simple Chinese-style poem, "Family Restaurant," from my forthcoming book *Rhapsody in Plain Yellow*.

Family Restaurant

Empty Lotus Room, no patrons
    Only a telephone rings and rings
Muffled by an adjoining wall
    He murmurs to a distant lover
His wife head-bent peeling shrimp
    Hums an ancient tune about magpies
His daughter wide-eyed, little fists
    Vows to never forgive him
His shadow enters the deep forest
    Blackening the shimmering moss

If one had to categorize, perhaps this would be considered as much a narrative as a personal lyric. The narration is third person. But the poem is really about the daughter and, by extension, about myself. Thus, it is in a real sense an autobiographical poem. It recounts a memory of an evening in 1966, in my uncle's restaurant in Roseburg, Oregon. Although the scene is self-explanatory, what's less apparent to a Western reader is that the poem alludes to a famous *chueh-chu* (quatrain) by Wang Wei:

Deer Park

王維　鹿柴

Empty mountain no see man
But hear man language sound
Returning shadows enter deep forest
Again shines green moss/lichen top

空山不見人
但聞人語響
返景入深林
復照青苔上

The place is in Wang Wei's country estate. Wang Wei was a wealthy, privileged court poet and very famous in his time. Westerners sometimes make the mistake of believing that his Buddhist hermit poems were written by a poor, ascetic poet. Let's just say that he was so rich that he owned a private retreat: I think of it as his own Yaddo, fraught with water holes and a forest and a few tamed Bambis.

Thus, my respectful poetic homage to Wang Wei as Chinese ancestor is immediately subverted by my contemporary American class awareness: "Empty Lotus Room, no patrons." The tranquility of Wang Wei's mountain turns into off-hours in a Chinese restaurant. The family restaurant as a busy, difficult immigrant occupation is part of a particularly American iconography. Yes, there are Chinese restaurants all over the globe. Yes, I've eaten in bad chop-suey joints in New Zealand as well as in Switzerland. But, the Chinese American Take Out restaurant is a cultural artifact seared into our American childhood memories. Every family in the United States has its favorite Chinese restaurant. Sweet and Sour, fortune cookies, fried wontons are all Chinese American, not Chinese inventions.

In Wang Wei's poem, any human voices are drowned out. Perhaps Wang Wei was "sitting" and achieving enlightenment, so there is finally only the poet's consciousness and nature. The light seeks through the forest and finds that clump of moss. He finds the moss mesmerizing in his state of sitting, of deep contemplation. This is a kind of Zennish Chinese poem that many Western poets love to imitate.

My replacement of the forest setting with an empty restaurant scene obviously subverts the high idea of the poet's contemplative moment. Wang Wei's moment of enlightenment, however profound, gives way to my telling part of my own story: this girl's father is talking to his lover while his wife is in the other room working hard for the restaurant. Thus, the theme of my father's betrayal takes over the "higher" theme of the poet's transcendent consciousness.

Reversals occur in the last two lines in my poem. Any enlightenment would be "blackened." The small child witnesses moral decay of the family, witnesses trouble, betrayal. This is an all too familiar and familial story in America. Already personal experience has tainted this child. Family secrets. Broken homes. Family problems trapped within these Chinese restaurant walls. All happy families are happy in the same way, each unhappy family is unhappy in its own way, as Tolstoy said.

And my way is Chinese American, of course, not simply Chinese. Wang Wei's "Empty Mountain" is not a lonely place, just a place where pure thought occurs, far from the troubled hubbub of humanity. In contrast, the empty off-hours rooms in "Family Restaurant" are where my truth is played out with all the dirt, the grit of human relationships. The "tune about magpies" alludes to that Chinese love story, where once a year the magpies build a bridge for the herd boy and the spinning maiden, where they meet in the cosmos in a romantic tryst. The irony in my poem is that the mother sings this tune while her husband—my father—is in the midst of betraying her. Both poems are intensely personal and autobiographical.

I have written about my father's betrayals over and over again. Obviously, it is an issue that I have not resolved to this day. As I will show later, it permeates my poetic identity.

As a Chinese American poet, I have always wanted to be in tune with both sides of my literary history. I am very aware of the history of the lyric in English, from Shakespeare to Donne to Keats to the contemporary lyrics by women poets. Early in my career, I wrote a lot of sonnets and sonnetish things with sometimes modern line breaks. For instance, I wrote a crown of postcolonial "unholy" sonnets subverting Donne:

Mother was the cross
mulish woman, who scrubbed her house bald.
Her floor, her child
must be clean, clean to impress.
Now the soap still sticks to the ceiling
of my mouth; what I say leaks out of the small apse
of my heart. They are all dead, my mother's half.
Who will marry me, the clean eyesore of spring?

Auntie Jade with the fat green face, the only one alive,
squats me in front of the mirror,
winds my hair up into a beehive,
"Be prepared to meet thy tall dark savior!"

Grandmother, tomorrow I must anoint my head
in white, the color of mourning,
white, the pallor of the dead.

The Chin matriarchy made a fine trinity, an amulet against the institution of marriage and hegemonic Christian domination. Notice the line breaks after "cross," "apse," "ceiling," and "savior" for special effect.

From American women poets I learned psychological intensity. I learned the passion and fierceness that comes out of anger, outrage, dispossession, racism, repression, inconsolable angst, and sadness. I, along with many young women poets, was influenced by the confessional, over-the-top suicidal rage of Plath as well as the "witness" and social-protest lyrics of Adrienne Rich. For me, the two influences are not contradictory. "Daddy, I have had to kill you." I can relate to that. "There is a cop who is both prowler and father." Yes, I can learn from that. Hostility can be a fine art. The autobiographer in me wants to sing about the sins of my father; the political activist in me wants to tear down the patriarchy.

I claim the entire lyric tradition as my own. Just as I have adopted and adapted the forms and styles of Wang Wei to my own purposes, I have at times taken Keats as my model, or Shakespeare, or Plath. Often, I use the shake-and-bake method of composition, creating my own hybrid lyric by sampling echoes and references from both East and West. "Reggae Renga," for instance, is a tumultuous marriage between a Martialian, moralistic epigram with an Issan haiku and a Marleyesque reggae guitar. The hair on the caterpillar references an Issa poem. "Man (pronounced mon) you are no good" is in Jamaican accent. The last line is a perverted Keats line. "White" in place of "wight" turns a personal love poem about an abusive relationship into a political anthem:

Reggae Renga

A man flat on his back can't go to the doctor.

Let him die, woman, so that he will no longer beat you.

He says, "Meet me at the hallowed temple near the Buddha's topknot."

He is dying, dying fast. In his delirium he is ever so beautiful.

I am late and reach only as far as the earlobes where I hear he has gone.

There are trees on the mountains and branches on the trees.

My anger so clear—I can see the hairs on the caterpillar and the wind on the hairs.

I can tell the paths that he has violated by the bent lay of the grasses.

Within him is a worm that loves itself and forgets whom he is loving, his mouth or his asshole.

Near the tombstone is a plum tree; a cock crows upon it, saying, "Man, you are no good!"

The people of my country are baleful; they've sent me to accuse you!

What is your ailment, wretched white, your ailment, will no birds sing?

I also believe that it is important for me to pay homage to the African American tradition. It makes sense that I, a Chinese American poet, claim African American artists as my masters. First of all, Asian Americans owe a lot to the African American civil rights movement. Martin Luther King and Malcolm X sacrificed their lives for all of us. I have always looked up to African American leaders, intellectuals, and writers for instruction and inspiration. I learned from them that the self must represent a struggle that is larger than the self. I also learned that political protest is not anathema to the lyric; and indeed, together, they make a powerful art. A poem is not a place in which we negotiate with the oppressor, it's a place where we talk back. Nowhere will we find a chorus of voices more diverse and compelling than those in the African American community. I learned from the uncompromising, in-your-face aesthetics of Amiri Baraka and June Jordan as well as from the formalized democratic anthems of Margaret Walker and Gwendolyn Brooks. Then, there are the jazzy improvs and strong rhythms of Quincy

Troupe and Yusef Komunyakaa. More recently, I've been studying the blues form, refined and codified by Langston Hughes.

I make reference to Keats, Donne, and Shakespeare every time I write a sonnet, but the blues is a homegrown form with a rich history that is equally alive to me. If I bow to Keats and Wang Wei, I must also bow to Langston Hughes. To be true to the selves that I am, I must keep my muse versatile and diverse.

Blues on Yellow

The canary died in the gold mine, her dreams got lost in the sieve.
The canary died in the gold mine, her dreams got lost in the sieve.
Her husband the crow killed under the railroad, the spokes hath shorn
    his wings.

Something's cookin' in Chin's kitchen, ten thousand yellow bellied sap
    suckers baked in a pie.
Something's cookin' in Chin's kitchen, ten thousand yellow bellied sap
    suckers baked in a pie.
Something's cookin' in Chin's kitchen, die die yellow bird, die die.

O crack an egg on the griddle, yellow will ooze into white.
O crack an egg on the griddle, yellow will ooze into white.
Run, run, sweet little Puritan, yellow will ooze into white.

If you cut my yellow wrists, I'll teach my yellow toes to write.
If you cut my yellow wrists, I'll teach my yellow toes to write.
If you cut my yellow fists, I'll teach my yellow feet to fight.

Do not be afraid to perish, my mother, Buddha's compassion is nigh.
Do not be afraid to perish, my mother, our boat will sail tonight.
Your babies will reach the promiseland, the stars will be their guide.

I am so mellow yellow, mellow yellow, Buddha sings in my veins.
I am so mellow yellow, mellow yellow, Buddha sings in my veins.
O take me to the land of the unreborn, there's no life on earth without
    pain.

This poem began as a dirge for my mother, who was very depressed in her latter years. She stopped eating and died. The blues, above all, is about pain. I'm working with this particular American convention to write about my mother's suffering and my own pain at her passing. Somewhere along the line, the dirge becomes a dark political anthem.

Just adding that drop of "yellow" blood gives the blues song a new social context: the gold mine and the railroad, a hot restaurant kitchen, and traditional Chinese coolie jobs replace cotton fields, slave ships, and coal mines. I invoke "Buddha" instead of "the lord" or "Jesus." Yes, I borrow the traditional twelve-bar, three-line structure, just as I have learned from the wailing of Lightnin' Hopkins and others. But though I have heard the sliding bottlenecks, banjos, harmonicas, and scratchy emotive singing, in my mind I mix in a lute, an erhu, a butterfly harp, gongs, Chinese drums, and the screechy background falsetto of a Chinese operatic singer.

"O crack an egg on the griddle, yellow will ooze into white" is a political conceit about miscegenation, mixbreeding, the melting pot. Yes, once again I am using a Chinese American food trope. Food marks my immigrant beginnings as a daughter of a cook-turned-restaurant-owner. I freely use a food motif in my lyrics because moogoogaipan is more familiar to me in fragrance and character than, let's say, a nosegay of spring flowers. "Crack an egg on the griddle, yellow will ooze into white" came out of real experience as I used to stand on a stool and crack eggs on a greasy griddle for those 99-cent breakfast specials. Sunnyside up, over easy (my grandmother called an egg a purse because there's a gold coin in it), or scrambled. It is good artifice to take experience and turn it into a conceit. Donne must have been bitten by many fleas before he had the idea to use one as an argument for sex.

The image of "head-bent, peeling shrimp" (from "Family Restaurant") is also from experience. I used to sit on the steps in the back of the restaurant and peel hundreds of shrimp. My uncle, the miser, only gave me a dime for four hours of peeling. One day, my fingers blew up like sausages; and my grandmother chewed my uncle out; and I was prevented from doing that chore again. I am told that restaurants now order frozen shrimp already peeled, so this experience not only speaks to my heritage but dates me to the sixties, before the advanced processing of food.

Every image in my poems seems to fill with autobiography. The challenge for a lyric poet is not just harnessing the imagination to make things up, but being able to take ordinary experience and memories and make them radiate with meaning. To make the common egg become a political conceit, as a common flea can be a metaphysical one.

Both in form and content, then, my poetry draws freely from multiple traditions. Consider the following poem, which I loosely fashioned after anonymous English ballads of high chivalry and bawdy tales. (I squeezed in a "monk" for respect.)

Song of the Giant Calabash

At the market I bought a calabash
    to make my father stew.
He spat and called it bitter,
    his sputum seeded the ground.

Out came a giant calabash
    shaped like Buddha's long head.
I baked it with honey and jujubes
    to feed my father again.

"Useless girl! I said I hate calabash!"
    He slapped his bowl to the floor.
The rains poured down from heaven,
    green mists and healing clouds blue.

Again another calabash
    Rounder than Buddha's mighty torso.
I mixed it with wild cat and agar
    and called it "A Monk's Mock Lamb."

"Dead girl! I said I hate calabash,"
    he burst into a thousand flames.
His head smashed open—well, like a calabash.
    He perished, headlong into his bowl.

Faint light into a silent altar.
    Blue, blue, the mist of spring.
The sun shone through her hardy trellis
    and danced on his empty bed.

This morning I cut my last calabash,
    carved a large bottle-gourd of dreams.
I shall float her down the river
    Into Buddha's eternal dawn.

The poem is cast in loose ballad form, and, like most ballads, is a narrative. The food trope again provides a Chinese flavor. Only a calabash is not really edible. The calabash or gourd in Chinese motif is supposed to be filled with magic. It is either filled with good luck or the elixir of eternal life. This one is also in Buddha's image and serves as protection for the girl. In fact, since a gourd is not edible, it serves as a conceit for the girl's obstinacy and endurance, which drive her to finally kill her father. In the final twist, one might say that yes, it is a magical gourd that can fulfill one's wishes. The protagonist is half situated in Portland Oregon, and half in some rural village lost in time.

Again the poem comes from autobiographical truth. One day, after work, my father was sitting at the table in his underwear. It was record-breaking heat and we were all in our underwear. My grandmother ordered me to make him coffee. So, I did. The first cup I brought to him, he said, "Stupid girl, it's too hot, it almost burn my lip off." So, I brought the coffee back into the kitchen, thinking, of course, "asshole." Nonetheless, I carefully blew on it and cooled it down. I brought it back to him, he sipped it and said, "Idiot girl, it's too weak, go brew me another cup." So, I went back to the kitchen and stuffed the pot with coffee and let it brew, again. Then, I brought it to him and he spat it out: "Dead girl, it's too bitter! Get out, get out of my sight!" (The curse "dead girl" is a common phrase in working-class homes.) My father hated his life and cursed us day and night; and I was "filial pious" and traditional enough not to talk back. But my hatred for him was already deep. Thus, in my poem, the daughter makes a pun of "to make my father stew" and continues to put weird things in his pottage in order to disguise the inedible, magic gourd; ultimately she makes him so angry that he has a heart attack and dies.

Writing poetry is about giving the powerless power, turning the tables so that the eater will be eaten, the oppressor oppressed, and the moral will have just retribution against the immoral.

My friends tell me, "Stop beating your father." Well, I can't and I won't. It's an obsession, but it feeds my poetry. And my poetry feeds into the larger historical banquet. I am writing against the patriarchy not as some feminist abstraction but as lived experience. My father's sins, my father's immoral behavior, constitutes a small flea on the larger beast that has oppressed women for centuries and has almost destroyed the world.

In "Song of the Giant Calabash," Buddha becomes whole at the very end and gives the protagonist some peace. "The sun shone through her hardy trellis / and danced on his empty bed." His death gives her salvation. This is an anti-Confucian idea of filial piety. The oppressor-father will stop his oppressive behavior only after he is dead. The more the oppressor spits on the ground, the more calabash. The "hardiness" of the gourd is, of course, metaphorical for the hardiness of this girl and, by extension, for my own willfulness.

The truth is that we all do survive childhood traumas and float down the river with a large bottle-gourd of dreams. These examples from my poems are, I believe, very different from one another. We can get to autobiographical truth in myriad ways. How memory and experience is formalized into song is both the autobiographical poet's challenge and her ecstasy.

In short, Chinese American writers who draw from two cultural histories must extract from multiple sources. Not only do we serve as cultural translators, we synthesize the form and content of the two great traditions that came before us. The result is a cross-fertilization of culture, creating new models to accurately portray Chinese American identity. No one cultural style can adequately express my experiences. I must sample and draw from East and West, modern and ancient. As a lyric poet I must infuse my art with my own personal history and passions. This autobiographical means to proclaim identity is a reversal of the current postmodern criticism which declares that stylistic innovation is dead. The signifiers are not empty but allude to referents that hold generational and personal meaning because the Chinese American poet must reclaim lost voices, simultaneously debunking and reconstructing the past to reflect her own mirror image. My task is to constantly reinvent my particular history through the truth of my experiences.

Alicia Ostriker

Beyond Confession:
The Poetics of Postmodern Witness

To the famous declaration of Theodor Adorno, that there can be no poetry after Auschwitz, a possible response is that there *must* be poetry after Auschwitz. Not to go on with poetry would be like not going on with life: a surrender to the powers of human destruction. We may understand, however, that by "Auschwitz" we mean not only the holocaust of World War II, but an ongoing concatenation of horrors scarring twentieth-century history and spilling over into the present millennium, to which we are unavoidably exposed by the excellence of our technology. Books, newsprint, radio, television, photography, film, video, and silicon chips daily convey to us the news—it is no longer news—of our violence and corruptibility as a species. Daily we are invited to despair, or to complicit apathy.

Fifty years ago the poet Muriel Rukeyser knew something about this, and rejected both despair and apathy. One of her poems begins, "I lived in the first century of world wars. / Most mornings I would be more or less insane." The poem goes on to say how the poet, along with similarly crazed friends, making her poems "for others unseen and unborn,"

> . . . would try to imagine them, try to find each other
> to construct peace, to make love, to reconcile
> waking with sleeping, ourselves with each other,
> ourselves with ourselves . . .

After a stanza pause, the poem concludes simply, "I lived in the first century of those wars." Almost a self-obituary (like Yeats's "Say that my glory was I had such friends"), this is Rukeyser's way of explaining that the struggle with the world and the struggle with the self are inextricably one. It is a way of saying that the struggle can be neither won nor abandoned. Similarly, Bertolt Brecht, in his famous "To Those Born Later," writes not only "To sleep I lay down among the murderers," but also:

Our forces were slight.
Our goal
Lay far in the distance.
It was clearly visible, though I myself
Was unlikely to reach it.

Pablo Neruda, in "Letter to Miguel Otero Silva," writes:

That is why you write your songs, so that someday the disgraced and
     wounded America
can let its butterflies tremble and collect its emeralds
without the terrifying blood of beatings, coagulated
on the hands of the executioners and the businessmen.

In the Talmudic *Ethics of the Fathers,* a line I cherish declares: "It is not incumbent on you to finish the task. Neither are you free to give it up."

Our condition, then, is not new. But for each time and place, there may be appropriately new forms of response to the illness whose two feverish sides are private life and public sphere. In its own time, confessional poetry was such a response. Although Robert Lowell and John Berryman, Sylvia Plath, and Anne Sexton have been misread as merely personal, merely self-indulgent, merely sick, what these poets in fact sing, orate, or shriek is the individual and society with choke holds on each other. One might write an essay on the poets of the fifties as seismographs registering the twin impacts of holocaust and atom bomb in the Cold War atmosphere of "containment" in which the American spirit was forcibly, as Lowell says, "tranquilized." Alcoholism, mental illness, an epidemic of suicide among his friends, prompted Berryman to growl, in one of his *Dream Songs,* "I'm cross with God who has wrecked this generation." Yet, as Lowell sadly proposes, "Why not say what happened?" Has anyone ever remarked that the self-destructiveness of a generation of poets might not be pure coincidence of private malaise, but a consequence of porousness to the disasters of history?

Let us say that as poets we want—some portion of us wants, needs—to resist surrender to what "Auschwitz" metonymically represents and, with luck, to imagine alternatives. We understand that silence is surrender. Art destroys silence, as Shostakovich says in his memoir, *Testimony,* commenting on the publication of Yevtushenko's poem "Babi Yar," which lamented the massacre of the Jews of Kiev during World War II and its subsequent cover-up. But how is resistance to be poetically organized? Obviously not by a poetics *purely* of the self. The poem must include history. It must contain the news. But a poetics that *denies* self is also useless; for without a consciousness that desires, suffers, and chooses, there is no ethical or political model for the reader.

At root, the issue is a formal one.[1] "In a bad time," Wallace Stevens remarks of the beggar, "It is not a question of captious repartee. / What has he that becomes his heart's strong core?" The beggar, he answers, "has his poverty and nothing more." But it behooves Melpomene, the muse of tragedy, to avoid the sordidness of bare boards and an unlit theater. "Speak loftier lines," he advises her. "Make sure / The audience beholds you, not your gown." Language poetry, notwithstanding the political posturing of its advocates, seems to me politically vacuous not only because of its captious repartee, and its systematic abandonment of the lyric "I," but because it denies that the morally responsible human subject is even theoretically possible. As to the other most conspicuous movement in contemporary poetry, neo-formalism, what makes so much (though not all) of this poetry morally expendable is a failure to reckon, in formal terms, with the historical cataclysms that surround and batter us.

In this essay I want to look at three instances of what I tentatively call the poetics of postmodern witness: Adrienne Rich's "Atlas of a Difficult World," Carolyn Forché's *Angel of History,* and Sharon Doubiago's *South America Mi Hija.* These are ambitiously long poems or sequences of poems, global in reach, formally experimental, each quite different from the others, but sharing certain common assumptions. Postmodern witness, as I see it in these poets, is a marriage of opposites. It employs the fragmented structures and polyglot associations originating in T. S. Eliot's *The Waste Land,* Ezra Pound's *Cantos,* and William Carlos Williams's

Paterson, those epitomes of high modernism. Like these modernist works, poems of postmodern witness reach toward the objectively ency-clopedic; reject master narratives; and refuse to pretend to coherence. But where high modernism rejects the autobiographical "I," these poets retain it. Or should I say regain it? Eliot's "extinction of personality," Pound's "persona," Williams's "Dr. Paterson" seem oddly evasive in com-parison. (When, exactly, did poets decide to deny being actual people? When did the tyranny of the impersonal persona begin? Certainly not in the time of John Donne and George Herbert, Jonathan Swift and Alex-ander Pope, William Wordsworth and John Keats; or that of The-ocritus and Sappho, for that matter.) In the poetry I am looking at here, it is crucial that the poet is *present* and *located* in the poem. The poet is not simply a phantom manipulator of words but a confused actual per-son, caught in a world of catastrophe that the poem must somehow both mirror and transcend.

Probably the best-known work in this mode is the title poem of Adrienne Rich's *An Atlas of the Difficult World* (1991). An atlas is both a book of maps, and the name of the mythic Titan who carries the world on his shoulders. Both senses apply. Rich, for nearly half a century, has charted America's mental and emotional landscapes in poetry and essays distinguished by tough intelligence, urgent feeling, vivid imagery, lan-guage as tensile as the rigging of ships. She has also been a voice of con-science and conscientiousness:

> I have to cast my lot with those
> who age after age, perversely,
>
> With no extraordinary power,
> reconstitute the world.

In the essay "When We Dead Awaken," describing the formalism and restraint of her early writing as "asbestos gloves," Rich went on to say, "In the late fifties, I was able to write, for the first time, directly about experiencing myself as a woman—until then I had tried very hard *not* to identify myself as a female poet." A generation of women poets knew precisely what that meant; the knowledge has revolutionized American poetry; and Rich has broken new ground with each new book. What does it mean, she is constantly asking—what can it mean to be a woman, a thinking woman, a feminist, a political activist, to be a lesbian, a Jew, a North American, a white person, an inhabitant of a poisoned planet? What does it mean to be a dreamer, a poet? What can we do with our rage, our despair, our love—those "necessities of life"? How are all these realities connected? What are the costs of the lives we choose, what are the risks, the possibilities? What histories lie behind us? What difference can we make to the future?

Always rooted in land and history, Rich's center of gravity moved a decade and a half ago from New England to the West Coast. The long title poem of *Atlas of a Difficult World* includes some signature landscape poetry:

> Within two miles of the Pacific rounding
> this long bay, sheening the light for miles
> inland, floating its fog through redwood rifts and over
> strawberry and artichoke fields. . . .
> —this is where I live now.

But the American landscape now also means "the desert where missiles are planted like corms . . . the breadbasket of foreclosed farms . . . the suburbs of acquiescence." Structurally the poem is a thirteen-part sequence of troubled, fragmentary meditations and memories. The opening section evokes migrant workers poisoned by Malathion, juxtaposed with a woman eating those strawberries in a clean kitchen, and anonymous voices —"a woman's voice, a man's voice," perhaps those of the poet's students, the "voice of the freeway" servicing agribusiness, interrupted, in turn, by the poet's meditation on individual violence: "I don't want to hear how he beat her after the earthquake, / tore up her writing, threw the kerosene / lantern into her face waiting / like an unbearable mirror of his own." Not wanting to hear is what we all may feel, and that is part of the poet's point. But the poet makes us, as well as herself, listen.

Another section quotes the Black Panther George Jackson's *Letters from Soledad Prison*. Yet another addresses the Gulf War. For those of us (I count myself) thrown into despair by our country's deeds, by flags blossoming on our neighbors' lawns, by media celebrations of the technological fix provided by Patriot missiles, Rich broods:

322 ~ ALICIA OSTRIKER

A patriot is not a weapon.   A patriot is one who wrestles for the soul
    of her country
as she wrestles for her own being, for the soul of his country
(gazing through the great circle of Window Rock into the sheen of the
    Viet Nam Wall)
as he wrestles for his own being.   A patriot is a citizen trying to wake
from the burnt-out dream of innocence, the nightmare
of the white general and the Black general posed in their camouflage.

Part of what divides Rich's work from the poetry of propaganda, with
which it is sometimes confused, is her insistence on a personal wrestling,
which can never ultimately stand in righteously complacent judgment
of others. When she writes that "every flag that flies today is a cry of
pain," I am forced to recall not only that Americans are confident killers,
but that the killers are themselves in pain: Isn't that what the "camouflage" of high-tech control always conceals?

The next part of Rich's strength as a poet in "Atlas" is the unobtrusive
way she gathers allusions. A list of battle sites—"Wounded Knee, Los
Alamos, Selma, the last airlift from Saigon"—leads to "states without a
cause" echoing "rebel without a cause." "Pilgrim ants pouring out from
the bronze eyes, ears, nostrils / the mouth of Liberty," are also the Puritan
founders of New England. Chinese immigrants writing poems on the
walls of Angel Island, the Pacific Rim equivalent of Ellis Island, are
paired with the influence of African design on Alabama quilts. The connection Rich makes between the disasters of war and the natural disasters
of earthquake and freezing comes to us all the way from the Bible and
The Golden Bough, and "wrestling" is what Jacob does with the angel in
the Book of Genesis. Notice, too, the inclusiveness: "all women . . . all
men" are Rich's audience and subject.

The penultimate section of "Atlas" is a love poem to Rich's partner.
The close is another litany:

I know you are reading this poem
late, before leaving your office
of the one intense yellow lamp-spot and the darkening
    window
in the lassitude of a building faded to quiet

long after rush-hour. I know you are reading this poem
standing up in a bookstore far from the ocean
on a gray day of early spring, faint flakes driven
across the plains' enormous spaces around you.
I know you are reading this poem
in a room where too much has happened for you to bear
where the bedclothes lie in stagnant coils on the bed. . . .
I know you are reading this poem as you pace beside the stove
warming milk, a crying child on your shoulder, a book in your hand
because life is short and you too are thirsty. . . .
I know you are reading this poem listening for something, torn
    between bitterness and hope
turning back once again to the task you cannot refuse.

When I last taught *Atlas of the Difficult World* in my course on poetry by women at Rutgers University, one of my favorite students raised his hand at the close of a class hour to say that he had been mistaken about Rich. He had thought she was "a lesbian separatist," but now he was astonished and moved at her inclusiveness and generosity. I consider this an important response, because it registers both the student's discomfort with an identity politics that divides, instead of joining, one community with another, and his sense of how personally engaged the poet is in trying to imagine a society of coalition. Hers, too, is the task that cannot be refused.

    One way of describing the poetics of postmodern witness is to say that it combines modernist strategies with the poetry of witness. This latter phrase, originally associated with the Polish poet and Nobel laureate Czeslaw Miłosz, is the subtitle of Carolyn Forché's anthology *Against Forgetting*, a collection of work by some 140 twentieth-century poets of "extremity"—poets of five continents who personally testify to our century's horrors, from Armenian genocide to Tiananmen Square. Forché's own second volume, *The Country Between Us,* was testimony to civil war in El Salvador; with a few exceptions, its poems were in a conventional "first-person free-verse lyric-narrative" form that Forché has now abandoned. *The Angel of History* (1994) is another matter. The book takes its title from Walter Benjamin's memorable image:

This is how one pictures the angel of history. His face is turned to-ward the past. Where we perceive a chain of events, he sees one single catastrophe which keeps piling wreckage and hurls it in front of his feet. The angel would like to stay, awaken the dead, and make whole what has been smashed. But a storm is blowing in from Paradise; it has got caught in his wings with such a violence that the angel can no longer close them. The storm irresistibly propels him into the future to which his back is turned, while the pile of debris before him grows skyward.

Both in content and structure, Forché's poems attempt to represent both "the pile of debris" that is twentieth-century history and the helpless yet indestructible impulse "to make whole what has been smashed." A barely sketched, always elliptic "I" in one fractured section after another records scraps of her own and others' memories of war, genocide, the disappeared in El Salvador, the destruction of Hiroshima, the Chernobyl disaster. The voice at times dips into French or Czech, at times quotes bits of Valéry or Heidegger or Lanzmann's *Shoah,* at times begins to record a scene that is then violently blown away. So at one moment the poet's paternal grandmother, Anna, whom the poet seems to be visiting in Prague, is stirring a trash fire from which

> sparks rise in the night along with pages of burning
> ash from the week's papers.
> one peeling away from the rest,
> an ashen page framed in brilliance.

> For a moment, the words are visible, even though fire has destroyed them, so
> transparent has the page become.
> The sparks from this fire hiss out among the stars and in thirty years appear
> as tracer rounds.

> *They didn't want you to know the past. They were hoping in this way you could escape it.*

Is the italicized line the grandmother's statement, the granddaughter's private thought? We have no way to know. Elsewhere in Eastern Europe, a wind blown from Chernobyl "brought us blue roses . . . something was wrong with the milk." Elsewhere again, the poet remarks,

> If a city, ruin, if an animal, hunger,
> If a grave, anonymous.
> If a century, this.

Forché calls the book "a gathering of utterances . . . polyphonic, broken, haunted, and in ruins, with no possibility of restoration." It is also a book of formal delicacy, precision of phrasing, and recurrent reminders of what language can and cannot do. In the opening section, which takes place in a Paris hospital where the author has just given birth to her first child, we meet a Jewish survivor of Vichy France, "tiny Ellie, at the edge of her bed, peeling her skin from her arm as if it were an opera glove." Hidden during the war, "Winter took one of her sons, and her own attempt to silence him, the other." The world is worse now than it was then, Ellie tells the author. "But when asked in what sense the world was worse, she answered, *pardon, est-ce que je vous dérange?*" It becomes a refrain, which, of course, is also addressed to the reader. *"Bonsoir, je m'appelle Ellie. Est-que je vous dérange?" Am I disturbing you?* Late in the book we walk through a Japanese garden with another woman, a survivor of Hiroshima:

> I don't like this particular red flower because
> it reminds me of a woman's brain crushed under a roof.
>
> perhaps my language is too precise, and therefore difficult to
> understand?

Not difficult to understand, but difficult to bear—and the fragmentary quality of Forché's writing registers the way consciousness cracks under the weight.

Least well-known of the books I am looking at is Sharon Doubiago's *South America Mi Hija,* originally published by Calyx in 1989, and reissued by the University of Pittsburgh Press in 1992. Doubiago, a West Coast writer of poetry, fiction, and memoir, has taken the entire range of the Americas as her scene. *South America Mi Hija* is an extraordinary account, in verse, of the poet's journey with her fifteen-year-old daughter, from California down through Colombia, Ecuador, and Peru, to Machu Picchu, the great city of the Inca—by public bus.

From the start the theme is violence. "Descent: La Violencia" is the title of the opening section:

> Out the window, Colombia, out the window
> the road beneath the window, the mountain village.
> Out the window men on white donkeys, women in a crooked door.
> Inside the window, back of the bus
> I carry our daughter down the cordilleras, the Andes.
> Out the window armed farmers
> carry marijuana to market.
>
> Out the window Bogotá, city of thieves.
> Out the window, the guns, the revolutionaries,
> the lust of the police. Inside the window
> the civil war, *you must take turns,* it is whispered,
> *to sleep. Everyone has had someone*
> *killed.*
>
> Out the window the bus descends the continent . . .
> We fly faster than last night's news warning of travel, we fly
> over deep green valleys, mist-filled.
> He sees around blind curves, he takes us over
> flowering rock walls, landslides, a five-year-old boy
> building an adobe brick house.
> We fly past women washing clothes on a rock, we fly
> above the clouds, above the road, how many days and nights . . .
> over the fog, over the coffee plants, over the jungle, the swollen rivers,
> the cows and grasses streaming down the mountain side, the dark sky
> of the East, over the grass huts perched on the abyss, over
> these people who never traverse
> to the outside. *If we go slow,*
> it is explained,
> *the bandits will stop us.*

I quote much of the poem's opening page here, to give a sense of its amplitude and tempo, and the way sensuous detail grounds the political. As the journey proceeds, views of the beauty and poverty, squalor, cruelty and mystery "out the window" alternate with "inside" meditations

on mother-daughter, mother-son, male-female love and betrayal—
biological, psychic, mythic. Sexually threatening episodes recur: a near-
rape by border guards, the ubiquity of *Penthouse* and *Hustler* pinups,
machismo hassling of mother and daughter as fair-game *gringas*. In a
park, a man with a small daughter in his lap exposes himself to the poet
and her daughter. Young thugs in Lima snatch a suitcase at high noon.
There are also moments of comedy and joy, as when the daughter successfully bargains with a moneychanger, or, as they mount the 3,000
steps to the ruins of Machu Picchu:

> we climb, *Madre de piedra, espuma de los cóndores*
> above the clouds
> that splash below us like the sea
> "Oh Mom!" she shouts back, "I want
>
> to always travel!"

Several kinds of volatile combinations crosscut the narrative line.
Doubiago intersects revisionist versions of Egyptian, Hindu, Christian,
and classic myths, in particular the Demeter-Persephone-Hades story,
with personal, colonial, and contemporary history. The sacrifice of female virgins at Machu Picchu fuses with the conquest of Inca culture by
the Spanish, of Spanish Peru by American capitalism, and of the earth
by human rapine, and there are dream-links to the poet's own complicity
in a history of conquest and betrayal by lovers and husbands, attempting
to comprehend:

> why love
> has always failed . . . I was the woman
> behind his wars. . . . Women go blank
> in their wild desperation
> for Amor . . . I was pregnant with the world like a blank
> Blanks the impotent make
> in their munitions factories.

Fear and muteness are recurrent themes: "My mother couldn't speak I
can't." At the same time, linguistically, the book's demotic English opens
itself increasingly to Spanish, then Quecha; tonally it shifts between the

meditative and the oracular, in a medley that is at once quest, lament, and prophecy:

> As the urge to the Lord is sexual
> As the Beloved is the land
> As ecstasy is identical with all existence
> as the Muse is a woman in orgasm
> As death is Love's accomplishment
> As the child is born from the child
> As my daughter is my mother

As with Rich and Forché, quotes and allusions lace the poem—Pablo Neruda (constantly) and César Vallejo, Walt Whitman, H.D., and Robert Duncan, historians and mythographers, feminist visionaries like Susan Griffin, Nor Hall, and Dorothy Dinnerstein. Dinnerstein's conviction that "the male-female conspiracy to keep history mad has become impossible to sustain" is a recurrent and agonizing motif throughout *South America Mi Hija*.

Passionately intellectual, Doubiago insists on grounding thought in body. "I touch the stone and know" is the anaphoric refrain of the book's closing meditation. What I fear for Doubiago is the condescension of a fashion-ridden critical poetic establishment that will be inclined to dismiss her conjunction of spirituality, politics, and psychic quest as a poetics rooted in the idealism of the 1960s, not sufficiently up-to-date—as if one measured poetic excellence by degree of chic disaffection rather than by beauty and power. Doubiago herself, in a lucid and forceful essay on Forché's *The Country Between Us,* which appeared in *American Poetry Review* in 1982, defended the poet against academic critics made uncomfortable by Forché's politics. Quoting Meridel Le Sueur's remark that the critic is the Puritan in North America, Doubiago added pointedly, "and that is why . . . unlike in any other country, the critic here is more powerful than the artist." It is disheartening to realize, nearly twenty years later, that this is still the case, and that what passes as avant-garde criticism today is even more puritanical than what comes out of the academic mainstream. In my own view, *South America Mi Hija* possesses an originality (in two senses: uniqueness in theme and form, and obsessiveness about tracking origins) that may outlast more ostensibly sophisticated writing. Besides which, I find it beautiful and powerful.

There are, of course, precedents and sources for the kind of poetry I am describing here. H.D.'s "The Walls do Not Fall," Rukeyser's own "The Book of the Dead" (quoted by Rich in "Atlas") and Allen Ginsberg's "Howl" and "Wichita Vortex Sutra" are among them. Whitman stands behind all such work, both as walker in the city and as wound-dresser during the American Civil War. There are also numerous contemporary poets who are cousins, kin, to these earlier poets. I think, for example, of Susan Howe, Suzanne Gardinier, Rachel Duplessis in *Drafts,* though in these poets the sense of a cerebral or ideological distance mitigates the sense of vulnerable personal engagement I feel in Rich, Forché, and Doubiago. On the lyric side, I think of how Gerald Stern's rambunctious voice feels like a stave beating and beating away at a world-sorrow that keeps lapping at his toes, or how Cyrus Cassells's visionary compassion forms itself into a limpid mirror of particular people who have suffered and died in this century in Catalonia, Auschwitz, Argentina, Russia, Little Rock. Close by, in their serried ranks, stand poets like Olga Broumas in mourning and ecstasy, Jorie Graham anatomizing self and history, Marilyn Krysl bathing dying women in Mother Teresa's hospice, and helplessly receptive Adrian Oktenberg in *The Bosnia Elegies*:

> The messages continue to come in   daily, hourly
>   desperate messages   messages of all kinds
>   the second-to second pulses   of lives flickering out
> the messages come in   come in   come in   come in   come in
> and disappear

I am sure I could add more names and titles to this list, and that my readers can add more as well. The point here is not to canonize but to sketch a moment, a gesture. What the three volumes I have glanced at in this essay have in common is not merely the act of witness. Formally, stylistically, what they represent is a crisis that is at once global and intimate: the simultaneous impossibility of *objective* witness and of *subjective* wholeness. It is like a poetic version of Heisenberg's Uncertainty

Principle. Nobody and nothing stands outside history in these books. The poet's self is a palpable, desiring, and suffering presence, yet there is no possibility of a self free of the disasters it confronts. In all these books, imagery of the pathos and vulnerability of the physical body becomes, as it were, metonym for the nightmare of history. The books' patchwork quality becomes in part structural correlative of this vulnerability, in part serves several other significant functions. In Rich and Forché, the fragmentation is almost a parody of the way we learn "the news" from the flickering tube or the advertisement-studded paper; in Forché and Doubiago it captures the inadequacy of travel as a source of knowledge or wisdom. It stands for the little we can comprehend, the silence we must honor, the frustration of our powerlessness. Their incompleteness means, as well, that you will not be able to read any of these books with ease; you will not be able to read them at all without entering into them, struggling to untangle their meanings, to fill in what they have omitted; you will be torn, as they are, "between bitterness and hope."

These book-length works wrestle, it seems to me, for the soul of epic poetry. Individually and collectively, they are up against the weight of a tradition that begins with Homer and the Book of Joshua and extends to the latest *Rambo* movie, in which war is glorified and warriors are heroes; we must recognize that "great" poetry, "great" literature—that literature which defines a society and a nation to itself—has, throughout the centuries, affirmed war, affirmed violence and sacrifice. Is there another path to poetic greatness? Can poetry convey the betrayals of the body within the violence of human history without either endorsement or surrender? Is there a poetry in which the body's language teaches not only resistance but transformation? In which the "I" exists as a kind of bridge between hopelessness and renewed desire? Doubiago, in her essay on Forché, writes, "The tone is of great sorrow, of world weariness, but not of the resignation so typical of her contemporaries." The description applies as well to her own writing and that of Adrienne Rich. These works of postmodern witness begin, I believe, to construct such a poetry, such a poetics.

Notes

1. This essay is intended as a footnote to the title essay of my recent *Dancing at the Devil's Party: Essays on Poetry, Politics and the Erotic,* in which I discussed three sorts of formal strategy in women's political poetry since the 1960s: the exoskeletal style, Black English, and the use of the semiotic register of language in poetry of communal ritual.

Adrienne Rich

In Those Years

In those years, people will say, we lost track
of the meaning of *we,* of *you*
we found ourselves
reduced to *I*
and the whole thing became
silly, ironic, terrible:
we were trying to live a personal life
and, yes, that was the only life
we could bear witness to

But the great dark birds of history screamed and plunged
into our personal weather
They were headed somewhere else but their beaks and pinions drove
along the shore, through the rags of fog
where we stood, saying *I*

1991
from *Dark Fields of the Republic: Poems 1991–1995*

Notes on Contributors

JOAN ALESHIRE received an M.F. A. in Writing from Goddard College and has published three books of poetry: *Cloud Train* (Texas Tech), *This Far* (QRL), and *The Yellow Transparents* (Four Way Books). She has taught in the M.F.A. Program at Warren Wilson College since 1983, and lives in Cuttingsville, Vermont.

FRANK BIDART is the recipient of the 2001 Wallace Stevens Award. His poems are gathered in *In the Western Night: Collected Poems 1965–90* and *Desire,* which was a finalist for the National Book Award and the National Book Critics' Circle Award in 1997. He has recently edited Robert Lowell's *Collected Poems.* He lives in Cambridge, Massachusetts, and teaches at Wellesley College.

KIMBERLY BLAESER is the author of two poetry collections, *Trailing You,* which won the First Book Award from the Native Writers' Circle of the Americas, and *Absentee Indians,* forthcoming from Michigan State. She is also author of a critical study, *Gerald Vizenor: Writing in the Oral Tradition* and editor of a collection of Anishaabe prose, *Stories Migrating Home.* A professor of English at the University of Wisconsin-Milwaukee, she lives in the woods and wetlands of rural Lyons township in Wisconsin.

JOSEPH BRUCHAC has authored more than seventy books. Recent titles include *Sacajawea,* a novel, and *No Borders,* a collection of poems. Winner of the Lifetime Achievement Award from the Native Writers Circle of the Americas, his writing often draws on his Abenaki Indian ancestry. He lives in the Adirondack foothills town of Greenfield Center, New York, and is founder of the *Greenfield Review.*

MARILYN CHIN is the author of *Dwarf Bamboo* (Greenfield Review Press), *The Phoenix Gone, The Terrace Empty* (Milkweed), which won the PEN Josephine Miles Award for 1994, and *Rhapsody in Plain Yellow* (forthcoming from Norton in 2002). Her awards include a Stegner Fellowship and two N.E.A. fellowships, and her poems have appeared in *Best American Poetry* and *The Pushcart Prize* anthologies. She also co-translated *The Selected Poems of Ai Qing* (Indiana University Press). Born in Hong Kong, she currently lives in San Diego and teaches in the M.F.A. program at San Diego State University.

BILLY COLLINS has published six books of poetry, including *Sailing Alone Around the Room: New & Selected Poems, The Art of Drowning, Questions About Angels* and *Picnic, Lightning.* He was educated at Holy Cross College and the University of California at Riverside. He teaches at Lehman College (CUNY), is a visiting writer at Sarah Lawrence College, and was recently appointed U.S. Poet Laureate. He lives in Westchester County, New York.

STEPHEN DUNN is the author of eleven collections of poetry, including the 2001 Pulitzer Prize winner *Different Hours* (Norton). Also recently published is a new and expanded edition of his *Walking Light: Essays & Memoirs* (BOA). He lives in Port Republic, New Jersey, and teaches at Richard Stockton College.

ANNIE FINCH's books of poetry include *Eve* (Story Line); *Marie Moving* (forthcoming in 2002); *Calendars,* a recent finalist in the National Poetry Series; and a translation of the Renaissance poet Louise Labé. She has written, edited, or coedited five critical books on poetry, including *A Formal Feeling Comes* (Story Line), *The Ghost of Meter* (Michigan), and, with Kathrine Varnes, *An Exaltation of Forms* (Michigan). She teaches at Miami University of Ohio and lives in Cincinnati and in Maine.

CAROL FROST's most recent publications include *Pure, Venus and Don Juan,* and *Love and Scorn: New and Selected Poems,* all from Northwestern University Press. She lives in upstate New York where she is writer-in-residence at Hartwick College and founder and director of the Catskill Poetry Workshop.

BRENDAN GALVIN is the author of thirteen collections of poems, most recently *The Strength of a Named Thing* and *Sky and Island Light,* both from Louisiana State University Press. *Place Keepers* (LSU) will appear in 2003. His translation of Sophocles' *Women of Trachis* appeared in the Penn Greek Drama Series. He lives in Truro, Massachusetts.

PAMELA GEMIN is the author of *Vendettas, Charms, and Prayers* (New Rivers) and coeditor of *Boomer Girls: Poems by Women from the Baby Boom Generation* (University of Iowa). A recent graduate of the M.F.A. Program at Vermont College, she teaches at the University of Wisconsin-Oshkosh.

LOUISE GLÜCK was awarded the Bollingen Prize in 2001 for *Vita Nova.* She also received the Pulitzer Prize in 1993 for *The Wild Iris.* Most recent of her many other collections of poetry is *The Seven Ages.* She is also the author of *Proofs & Theories: Essays on Poetry* (Ecco), which won the PEN/Martha Albrand Award for Nonfiction. She teaches at Williams College and lives in Cambridge, Massachusetts. In 1999 she was elected a Chancellor of The Academy of American Poets.

DAVID GRAHAM's six collections of poetry, include *Stutter Monk* (Flume Press), *Second Wind* (Texas Tech), and *Magic Shows* (Cleveland State). His essays have appeared in the *Georgia Review, The American Poetry Review,* and elsewhere. Born and raised in Johnstown, New York, he has served as poetry editor of *Blue Moon Review* and been Poet in Residence at the Robert Frost Place in Franconia, New Hampshire. He lives in Ripon, Wisconsin, where he is a professor of English at Ripon College.

KIMIKO HAHN is the author of five collections of poetry: *Mosquito and Ant* (Norton); *Volatile* (Hanging Loose); *The Unbearable Heart* (Kaya), which was awarded an American Book Award; *Earshot* (Hanging Loose), which received The Theodore Roethke Memorial Poetry Prize and an Association of Asian American Studies Literature Award; and *Air Pocket* (Hanging Loose). She is a professor in the English Department at Queens College/CUNY.

JUDITH HARRIS is the author of three books of poetry: *Poppies* (Washington Writers' Publishing House), *Song of the Moon* (Orchisis Press), and most recently *Atonement* (LSU). Her book of critical essays, *Signifying Pain: Constructing and Healing the Self Through Writing*, is forthcoming from SUNY Press. She is an assistant professor of English at George Washington University.

ANDREW HUDGINS is the author of five books of poetry, all with Houghton Mifflin: *Saints and Strangers, After the Lost War, The Never-Ending, The Glass Hammer,* and most recently, *Babylon in a Jar.* He has also published a book of essays, *The Glass Anvil* (University of Michigan). He is currently Distinguished Research Professor and Professor of English at the University of Cincinnati.

COLETTE INEZ has authored eight collections of poems, including *Getting Under Way: New and Selected Poems* (Story Line), and most recently *Clemency* (Carnegie Mellon). She has received fellowships from the Guggenheim and Rockefeller Foundations, and twice from the N.E.A. Currently on the faculty of Columbia University, she lives in New York City.

YUSEF KOMUNYAKAA won the Pulitzer Prize in 1994 for *Neon Vernacular: New and Selected Poems.* Subsequent collections are *Thieves of Paradise, Talking Dirty to the Gods,* and *Pleasure Dome: New and Collected Poems.* With Sascha Feinstein, he is also coeditor of *The Jazz Poetry Anthology* and its sequel, *The Second Set.* His essays have been collected in *Blue Notes: Essays, Interviews, and Commentaries* (University of Michigan). He is a professor in the Council of Humanities and Creative Writing Program at Princeton University.

TED KOOSER is the author of eight books of poems and a number of chapbooks and special editions. His most recent collection of poems is *Winter Morning Walks: 100 Postcards to Jim Harrison* (Carnegie Mellon). He is a retired life insurance executive who lives on land near Garland, Nebraska.

SYDNEY LEA is author of ten volumes across the genres, including seven poetry collections, one of which, his new and selected poems, *To the Bone,* won the 1998 Poet's Prize. His book, *Pursuit of a Wound,* was one of three finalists for the 2001 Pulitzer Prize. Recipient of fellowships from the Guggenheim, Rockefeller and Fulbright foundations, Lea was also founder of *New England Review.* He teaches in the English department at Dartmouth College and in the Vermont College M.F.A. program and lives in Newbury, Vermont,

WILLIAM MATTHEWS taught and lectured all over the United States. His dozen collections of poetry include *After All: Last Poems, Time & Money,* and *Selected Poems and Translations, 1969–1991,* all from Houghton Mifflin. *Curiosities,* his first book of essays, appeared in 1989; a second volume of prose, edited by Stanley Plumly, will be published by The University of Michigan Press. At the time of his death in 1997 he was a professor of English and director of the writing program at the College of the City University of New York.

The author of, most recently, *Last Chance for the Tarzan Holler,* a volume of poetry, **THYLIAS MOSS** teaches at the University of Michigan, where she currently finds herself equally obsessed with what may be observed through both microscopes and telescopes. She is fortunate that any necessary tranquility may be found sharing space and time with her husband and two sons.

CAROL MUSKE-DUKES is author of six books of poems, most recently *An Octave Above Thunder: New and Selected Poems* (Penguin). She has also authored three novels, most recently *Life After Death* (Random House) as well as two collections of critical essays, *Women & Poetry* (University of Michigan) and *A Poet in Hollywood,* forthcoming from Random House. She is director of the graduate program in Creative Writing and Literature at the University of Southern California in Los Angeles.

SHARON OLDS is the author of six books of poems, most recently *Blood, Tin, Straw* (Knopf). Her awards include the San Francisco Poetry Center Award, the Lamont Poetry Selection, and the National Book Critics Circle Award. She teaches in the Graduate Creative Writing Program at New York University in New York City and was New York State Poet Laureate for 1998–2000.

ALICIA OSTRIKER is the author of nine volumes of poetry, most recently *The Little Space: Poems Selected and New,* which was a National Book Award finalist. She is also the author of *The Nakedness of the Fathers: Biblical Visions and Revisions,* a combination of midrash and autobiography, and *Dancing at the Devil's Party: Essays on Poetry, Politics, and the Erotic.* Ostriker is a professor of English at Rutgers University.

STANLEY PLUMLY's most recent volume is *Now That My Father Lies Down Beside Me: New and Selected Poems 1970–2000* (Ecco). His work has been honored with the Delmore Schwartz Memorial Award and nominations for the National Book Critics Circle Award, the William Carlos Williams Award, and The Academy of American Poets' Lenore Marshall Poetry Prize. He is currently a Distinguished University Professor and a professor of English at the University of Maryland.

CLAUDIA RANKINE is the author of three volumes of poetry: *Plot* (Grove/Atlantic), *The End of the Alphabet* (Grove/Atlantic), and *Nothing in Nature Is Private* (Cleveland State). She lives in New York City and teaches at Barnard College.

ADRIENNE RICH's most recent books of poetry include *Midnight Salvage, Dark Fields of the Republic,* and *An Atlas of the Difficult World,* all from Norton. Her many awards include a National Book Award, a MacArthur Fellowship, and the Dorothea Tanning Prize for "mastery in the art of poetry" given by The Academy of American Poets.

KATE SONTAG won the 1995 Ronald H. Bayes Poetry Prize. Her collection *Step Beautiful* has been a finalist in many national competitions, and her poems have appeared in journals and anthologies such as *Boomer Girls, In Praise of Pedagogy, The Chester H. Jones National Winners Anthology, Prairie Schooner, Green Mountains Review, Southern Poetry Review, Salt Hill Journal, Kalliope,* and elsewhere. She received an M.F.A. from the Iowa Writers' Workshop and teaches at both the University of Wisconsin-Oshkosh and at Ripon College.

ALAN WILLIAMSON is the author of four volumes of poetry, including *Love and the Soul* and most recently *Res Publica,* both from the University of Chicago. He has also authored three critical collections, most recently *Eloquence and Mere Life* (University of Michigan). He teaches at the University of California at Davis.

Acknowledgments

Kate Sontag wishes to thank her colleagues in the English Department at the University of Wisconsin-Oshkosh for their ongoing support and encouragement, especially Estella Lauter, Paul Klemp, and the Research & Publications Committee. She also wishes to thank the University's Faculty Development Board for a grant early on in this project. In addition, she is grateful to the Associated Writing Programs for sponsoring panel discussions that helped incubate the ideas in this book. Gratitude is due as well to Jill Bialosky, Harriet Levin, and Ken Sherman for their loyalty and wisdom, and to her friends and colleagues in the Ripon College community.

David Graham wishes to thank the Ripon College Board of Trustees for a sabbatical leave which greatly facilitated work on this book. In addition, he is grateful for the continuing encouragement of Ripon College colleagues too numerous to mention, but with special thanks to Bill Schang, Robin Woods, and Kate Wheeler, his colleagues in the English Department. With respect to this project, particular appreciation to Bob Wallace, Dean David Seligman, and Dean Leslie Brown for their support at key moments, and to Leslie Bessant for teaching him much about the nature of collaborative work.

Both editors wish to thank Vida Vande Slunt and Donna Marquart at Ripon College for their speedy and excellent secretarial assistance.

They also wish to thank Pamela Gemin and Paula Sergi for their friendship as well as editorial inspiration.

Finally, our deepest gratitude goes to our spouses, David Seligman and Lee Shippey.

The text of this book has been set in Adobe Garamond, drawn by Robert Slimbach, and based on type cut by Claude Garamond in the sixteenth century. This book was designed by Wendy Holdman, set in type by Stanton Publication Services, Inc., and manufactured by Friesens Corporation on acid-free paper.

Graywolf Press is a not-for-profit, independent press. The books we publish include poetry, literary fiction, essays, and cultural criticism. We are less interested in best-sellers than in talented writers who display a freshness of voice coupled with a distinct vision. We believe these are the very qualities essential to shape a vital and diverse culture.

Thankfully, many of our readers feel the same way. They have shown this through their desire to buy books by Graywolf writers; they have told us this themselves through their e-mail notes and at author events; and they have reinforced their commitment by contributing financial support, in small amounts and in large amounts, and joining the "Friends of Graywolf."

If you enjoyed this book and wish to learn more about Graywolf Press, we invite you to ask your bookseller or librarian about further Graywolf titles; or to contact us for a free catalog; or to visit our award-winning web site that features information about our forthcoming books.

We would also like to invite you to consider joining the hundreds of individuals who are already "Friends of Graywolf" by contributing to our membership program. Individual donations of any size are significant to us: they tell us that you believe that the kind of publishing we do *matters.* Our web site gives you many more details about the benefits you will enjoy as a "Friend of Graywolf"; but if you do not have online access, we urge you to contact us for a copy of our membership brochure.

www.graywolfpress.org

Graywolf Press
2402 University Avenue, Suite 203
Saint Paul, MN 55114
Phone: (651) 641-0077
Fax: (651) 641-0036
E-mail: wolves@graywolfpress.org

Other Graywolf titles you might enjoy are:

By Herself: Women Reclaim Poetry,
 edited by Molly McQuade

De/Compositions: 101 Good Poems Gone Wrong
 by W. D. Snodgrass

Burning Down the House
 by Charles Baxter

Feeling as a Foreign Language: The Good Strangeness of Poetry
 by Alice Fulton

If You Want to Write
 by Brenda Ueland

Readings
 by Sven Birkerts